Astrology Revealed

A Simple Guide
to Unlocking the
Secrets of Astrology

Paul Fenton-Smith

SIMON & SCHUSTER

AUSTRALIA

This book is dedicated to Alexander
who taught me the meaning of the phrase
'The boy is father to the man'.
He taught me well.

With thanks to Cathy and Brigitta,
two of the most tactful editors
a writer could have.

Thanks also to Victor for his inspiration
and to Margaret for the illustrations.

ASTROLOGY REVEALED

First published in Australasia in 1997 by
Simon & Schuster Australia
20 Barcoo Street, East Roseville NSW 2069

A Viacom Company
Sydney New York London Toronto Tokyo Singapore

National Library of Australia
Cataloguing-in-Publication data

Fenton-Smith, Paul.

   Astrology revealed: a simple guide to unlocking the
   secrets of astrology.

   Bibliography.
   Includes index.
   ISBN 0 7318 0672 7.

   1. Astrology. I. Title.

133.5

Design by Anna Soo
Diagrams by Margaret Hastie
Printed in Australia by Australian Print Group

B

Astrology Revealed

Contents

Part 1: Introduction   7
What is astrology?   8
The history of astrology   8
The purpose of astrology   10

Part 2: The Basics   11
The signs of the zodiac   12
The houses   54
The solar chart   58
The Moon   59
The phases of the Moon   71

Part 3: The Planets   73
Mercury   76
Venus   85
Mars   93
Jupiter   101
Saturn   109
Uranus   117
Neptune   126
Pluto   135

Part 4: A Deeper Awareness   145
Many happy returns   146
The Moon's nodes   147
The Ascendant   162
Progressions   164
Planetary aspects   165
Chart-reading procedure   186
Relationships   191
Health and the Sun signs   194
Practice charts   196
Gaining practical experience   197

Bibliography   198

Index   199

Part 1

Introduction

WHAT IS ASTROLOGY?

Astrology is the study of the effect the planets have upon one another, the universe and upon human beings. The study of astrology is the study of life's big picture. It is easy to become bogged down in the day-to-day responsibilities of life and to lose sight of the external forces that contribute to our welfare. Keeping the bigger picture in mind helps us to accept life's restrictions and plan for life's opportunities. A good gardener plans according to the seasons, the soil and the desired outcome: the crop. Astrology helps us to better understand ourselves, life and those around us. With this under-standing we can plan and prepare for a life which will most benefit us.

Knowing who we are and being aware of our strengths and weaknesses can assist us in deciding how best to approach life and when to move in order to achieve our goals.

Astrology is much more than simply knowing what sign you are, for everyone knows somebody who doesn't fit the standard type. *Astrology Revealed* is designed to introduce you to astrology in a simple step-by-step manner, to demystify this ancient method of classification. Included are numerous real-life examples to illustrate each point — past experience has shown me that students love stories, as it helps them to remember the types.

The real test of astrology, of course, is with strangers. After you have examined your own chart and the charts of your close friends and family, you can then move on to friends of your friends, whom you will probably know little about. In time, and with practice, you may be able to pick a person's Sun sign or Ascendant by careful observation. This is where astrology can help you in everyday living, for in understanding other people we can learn better ways of relating to them.

THE HISTORY OF ASTROLOGY

Astrology was employed by many of the ancient civilisations, including the Chinese, the Mayas, the Aztecs, Incas, Indians and the Chaldeans, where it is traceable back as far as 3000 BC. Astrology was brought to Greece by the Arabs, where it rapidly established itself in the culture. From Greece it spread throughout Europe and it can be found in all the more recent cultures of Europe and the Western world.

Moon cycles were carefully charted by the Aztecs and the ancient Chinese, who used these cycles as a guide for planting and harvesting. They discovered that seeds planted on the waning or shrinking phase of the Moon did not grow as well as the seeds planted soon after the new Moon, when the Moon is waxing or growing in its cycle.

When you consider that Aries, the first sign of the zodiac, starts on the first day of spring in the northern hemisphere, it is readily apparent that the seasons and cycles of life were carefully charted and observed in ancient times.

Later, particularly in Europe, the church renamed some of the ancient festival ce-lebration days to establish itself in the yearly calender. Easter, for example, usually falls on the first weekend after the full moon in Aries, which was traditionally the planting festival. This was a time to celebrate spring and the return of growth in expectation of the harvest. The festivities included the ritual planting of seeds and observing the sprouting of the first growth three days later. The Christians later renamed this festival Easter.

Another example is Christmas, which falls on December 25 each year. In the northern hemisphere the days are growing shorter in December, up to the shortest day, the winter equinox, around December 22. In ancient times, some civilisations who worshipped the Sun as God believed that their God was deserting them, and that by making sacrifices, they could reverse their God's decision to abandon them. These sacrificial ceremonies usually occurred on or around December 22, and three days later on December 25, the Sun began its return, as the northern hemisphere began to draw closer to the spring equinox, and the days began to lengthen (ever so slightly) again. Celebrations resulted when, on or around December 25, it was realised that the Sun had stopped 'going away' from them. The Christians renamed this date Christ's birthday.

The Egyptians used astrology as a tool to aid their understanding of the cycles of the year and of life. Our current solar calendar of the 365-day year is based upon the solar calendar used by the ancient Egyptians and adapted by Julius Caesar around 50 BC. The Egyptians used the 365-day year, although they were aware that each year contained an extra quarter of a day as they noted through keeping a close eye upon the night sky that every four years Sirius rose one day later. It was Julius Caesar who determined that the start of the year was to be January 1. Before this time it started at the spring equinox or the first day the Sun entered the sign of Aries.

With a little refinement the current calendar was pressed into use and this explains why the signs of the zodiac seem to start at odd times throughout the year. To add a little more confusion, the starting date for each sign can vary by one day according to the year. An example of this is that the Sun entered the sign of Aries on March 22, 1933, 1934 and 1935, yet it entered Aries on March 21 in 1944, 1948 and 1949. Our calendar is the best system we have for measuring the days and years, but it is not perfect. In most cases a leap year is the cause

of the delay in the starting date of the signs and sometimes it takes two years for the starting dates to return to normal.

Astrology continued in a quieter fashion through the Dark Ages, and it resurfaced in Europe in the 16th century when astronomers studied astrology as part of their discipline. Nicholas Copernicus (1473–1543), a cleric and physician, wrote a book which carefully detailed an argument that if the earth and the other planets were rotating, then they were rotating around the Sun, and that the Earth was not in fact the centre of the universe as had been believed for centuries. It caused trouble with the church and several eminent astrologers who furthered his arguments in the 16th and 17th centuries were excommunicated, persecuted or burned at the stake for their beliefs, which we now know were accurate.

In the late 19th and early 20th centuries, W.F. Allen (who worked under the name of Alan Leo) and W.R. Old (who used the pseudonym 'Seraphial') presented astrology in a new light, with more clarity and in a more accessible manner.

Modern writers have used psychological and social styles, whereas Galileo used the mathematical approach. Personally, I tend to see patterns in behaviour, in circumstance and in life, so my approach is more one of observing human nature. Astrology is perfectly suited to all the above approaches as it encompasses all of life and it is a system of classification which is still developing.

An example of more recent developments in astrology is the discovery of Neptune in 1846 and Pluto in 1930. These sightings came about after observations of irregularities in the natural orbit of other planets.

In 1977 Chiron was discovered, partly due to modern technology enabling an improved vision of the universe. It is inevitable that more and more planets, asteroids, comets and even solar systems will be discovered as technology improves our vision of the universe.

THE PURPOSE OF ASTROLOGY

To know where we fit in this world is to know the path to peace and fulfilment. The purpose of astrology is to know ourselves better, so that we might better fulfil our purpose here on Earth. To unlock the door that leads to the truth about life and the universe we must have a key. There are many keys to this door; astrology is one of them.

In previous books I have detailed the keys of palmistry and the tarot, which also unlock this door to universal knowledge, and although each approach has its strengths, each also has limitations. If you have a palmistry reading and an astrology chart compiled, there are clear similarities in these that go far beyond coincidence. From character traits to major turning points in your life, each method illuminates your life.

The purpose of studying astrology is not to let us blame our failures upon some unseen planet or constellation in the night sky, but rather it allows us an opportunity to know when is the best time to strive for our greatest success and when is the time to rest and to reflect. The day when a court of law would allow as acceptable evidence the plea that 'My Mars in opposition to my Moon made me do it, your Honour,' is unlikely. We each have free will, and what we do with our lives is up to us. However, as actions have consequences, astrology is a reminder that sometimes our desire to act is itself a consequence of outside forces acting upon us.

Children offer us clear examples of how each astrological sign approaches life, for their unselfconscious expression of themselves is not complicated by the adult qualities of reason and justification.

Knowledge of astrology is useful when dealing with your children, your partner, family members or work colleagues. Realising that most Taureans don't like change or that sulking quietly is likely to drive your Gemini partner crazy can help you to improve your relationships and your life.

Selecting a suitable vocation can be made easier with a working knowledge of astrology. Or perhaps more importantly, selecting a suitable career for yourself can be simplified with an understanding of the planets and their influences upon us.

Part 2

The Basics

THE SIGNS OF THE ZODIAC

In the course of a calender year, the Sun passes through each of the 12 signs of the zodiac. When people ask 'What sign are you?', they are in fact asking you where the Sun was on the day you were born. If you reply 'I'm a Gemini', you are stating that the Sun was in Gemini when you were born. That is why the zodiac signs are called Sun signs. The names of each Sun sign and the approximate dates are as follows:

Aries:	March 21 – April 20
Taurus:	April 21 – May 21
Gemini:	May 22 – June 22
Cancer:	June 23 – July 23
Leo:	July 24 – August 23
Virgo:	August 24 – September 23
Libra:	September 24 – October 23
Scorpio:	October 24 – November 22
Sagittarius:	November 23 – December 21
Capricorn:	December 22 – January 20
Aquarius:	January 21 – February 20
Pisces:	February 21 – March 20

Note: If you were born on a cusp (that is, a point where two signs meet, such as January 20 or October 23), you will need to check an *ephemeris* (a book charting all planetary positions in a calendar format) to find out your correct sign, because the dates can vary by one day each year.

The 12 signs are grouped according to the four elements — fire, earth, air, water — which represent four basic approaches to life. This classification is called *triplicities*, as each group consists of three signs.

Fire approaches life enthusiastically, seeing it as a challenge. Fire types look forward to opportunities to achieve goals. The fire signs are Aries, Leo and Sagittarius.

Earth approaches life in a realistic manner, and is essentially conservative and pragmatic in its approach. Earth types are usually prepared to work hard to make their dreams a reality. They prefer to live in the present. The earth signs are Taurus, Virgo and Capricorn.

Air approaches life through thought, preferring to understand the who, what, when, where and why of life. Air types seek to understand life by observing patterns of behaviour. They question things in life that the other types often take for granted. The air signs are Gemini, Libra and Aquarius.

Water approaches life through feelings and creativity. Water types need to feel sure of something before they proceed. The water signs are Cancer, Scorpio and Pisces.

The 12 signs are further divided into *quadruplicities*, or three groups of four signs: cardinal, fixed and mutable.

Cardinal signs (Aries, Cancer, Libra and Capricorn) are active or changeable in nature. Fixed signs (Taurus, Leo, Scorpio and Aquarius) are unchanging in nature. Mutable signs (Gemini, Virgo, Sagittarius and Pisces) are ever-changing in nature.

This brief overview may seem confusing at first, but most questions will be answered as we examine the signs in detail.

Each Sun sign is described in general first, then broken down into relationships, health and the negative type. The Sun signs have positive and negative characteristics, and it is necessary to understand both sides to form a complete picture.

Each sign also has a lesson to be mastered in this lifetime and they are included here so that you can understand the challenges people face according to their sign.

Aries

Aries:	March 21 – April 20
Planetary symbol:	The Ram
Glyph:	♈
Element:	Fire
Type:	Cardinal
Ruler:	Mars

Aries is ruled by the planet Mars, which radiates the Aries colour: red. Being a fire sign, Arians are motivated by goals and challenges, but because they are also a cardinal type, they tend to lose interest or run out of energy before the goal is reached or the project completed. In general terms, the fire signs are not the most diplomatic types in the zodiac, preferring to be honest rather than tactful. They are best suited to situations where energy and enthusiasm are required, as they have these qualities in abundance.

Arians are usually courageous, independent and forthright — what you see is what you get. In mythology, Mars (or Ares) was the god of war, and Arians can display some of the Mars war-like qualities when the need arises.

Arians enjoy the outdoors and walking in particular, which seems to relieve stress and clear their minds of worries. I have noticed that when an Arian has a problem they seem unable to solve, despite a few days spent indoors pondering the issue, they can usually sort things out with a brisk 30-minute walk. It is as if the physical act of walking helps them to *think* towards a destination or solution.

As children, Arians prefer to be outdoors exploring and, because this is a masculine sign, Arian girls often prefer exploring to dolls or more passive pursuits.

Often original and easily inspired to action, Arians are quick to start new projects, but can become impatient if the planning stage takes too long. They need to develop patience with those who prefer a steadier, more moderate approach, for their enthusiasm can be interpreted as bossiness by some of the less hasty signs.

Having a worthy goal is essential for the typical Arian, and Fiona was characteristic of the type. A salesperson at an exclusive interior design store in England, Fiona won the salesperson-of-the-month award so many times that the company was running out of ideas for her next reward. She proudly told me of her prizes, which included a car stereo, homewares and weekend trips to most cities in Europe. Fiona was well suited to her work, as she was clear-thinking, forthright and enthusiastic. When she asked me to suggest the prize for her next award, I teasingly proposed a month-long meditation retreat. 'Get out of here,' came the reply. 'I'll sleep when I'm dead!'

Arians are usually impulsive and bold in their approach to life. When opposed in their plans, they are liable to counter with force, either physical or verbal, to overcome obstacles and achieve their goals.

When emotionally mature, Arians are able to take into account the wants and needs of others, making them efficient and inspiring leaders. An Arian leader will not usually ask a subordinate to do anything that they are not prepared to do themselves. They lead by example and are happy with a hands-on approach.

Arians are suited to goal-oriented careers such as professional sportspeople and salespeople, and outdoor careers such as farmers, travel guides and explorers. They respond positively to challenges in the workplace and thrive on competition. The military, surgical medicine, demolition (building industry) and butchery are also Arian careers.

Relationships

Since Arians thrive on challenge, they enjoy the thrill of the chase, sometimes even more than the relationship itself. Their authoritative natures can cause friction if they ignore the opinions and needs of their partners.

Independence is another Arian trait and they need plenty of room to pursue their own projects and goals. If these goals relate to their careers, they may neglect their partners for long periods as they throw themselves into the task at hand.

Although Arians are passionate about their own independence, they do not appreciate independence in their partners. The typical Arian needs to learn to cooperate more and to lead less.

When out of temper, their outbursts are usually noisy and short-lived — short-lived, that is, for them. By the time they have released their frustration and have calmed down, their partners are likely to be feeling pretty wound up as a result.

Health

Arians tend to suffer from headaches or from bumps to the head. As they usually love the outdoors and exercise, they often enjoy good blood circulation.

If they have an accident, it usually affects the head area and a close examination will often reveal many small scars from past mishaps. They are also prone to fevers.

Negative Aries

When negative, Arians can be self-centred, loud, forceful and aggressive. They can become so passionate about an idea or goal that they will trample over others in order to fulfil their desires. The innate arrogance of negative Arians hampers the smooth running of any relationship or business partnership, because they refuse to listen to others or acknowledge that there might be a different way to do things.

Negative Arians have a tendency to dismiss the ideas or opinions of others, or to become rude and impatient when other people fail to share their enthusiasm for a particular goal. Impatient for results, they will force others to adopt their views, regardless of the consequences. They seem unable to delay gratification, so when a project slows down or becomes complicated, they are apt to discard it in favour of something new. The typical Arian, whether positive or negative, is often better at starting a project than completing it.

In the negative type, the Mars qualities are evident, and the negative Arian is constantly at war with those around them. They are bullies who fight with coworkers, harass the next-door neighbours and make life hell for their partners or children.

Jason was a typical example of the negative type. Preferring his independence, he maintained the life of a single man, despite the fact he was married with four children. After countless arguments with his wife, he left and pursued his own goals.

Instead of grief and loss, his family breathed a collective sigh of relief. The constant arguing, persistent bullying and furious outbursts were no longer a part of their lives, although word filtered back from time to time that Jason was still at war wherever he went, especially with those who became close to him.

Aries lesson

The lesson for Aries is one of *self-discipline*. Self-discipline sounds easy enough to master, but when paired with the enthusiasm and impatience of the typical Arian, it can prove elusive.

When Arians master self-discipline, they are able to pace themselves better, successfully completing more of the projects they begin. Having learned their lesson, Arians soon build a reputation for keeping their promises and 'delivering the goods'.

Taurus

Taurus:	April 21 – May 21
Planetary symbol:	The Bull
Glyph:	♉
Element:	Earth
Type:	Fixed
Ruler:	Venus

Taureans are placid, level-headed, reliable people who resist change and enjoy their physical comforts. Being an earth sign, Taureans are practical and determined by nature. They move slowly but resolutely towards a goal, usually achieving what they set out to achieve. Taureans are good to have around in times of crisis, as they lend an air of stability and security.

Taureans are trustworthy and loyal, and they prefer their friends to be faithful and reliable. They favour routine over change and usually have a favourite chair in the living room and particular habits or routines by which you could set a clock.

Adrian was a typical Taurean, precise and exact. Each morning before driving to work he would walk around his van, checking the tyres and the van's general condition. In an effort to determine the life extpectancy of his gearbox, he once counted each and every gear change he made in the course of the day.

The planet Venus rules Taurus, hence Taureans appreciate beauty, particularly in music. It is often possible to pick a Taurean man by the size or quality of his home music system. A little background noise is not for them, and they are often prepared to go to great lengths to own a stereo system capable of producing good, clean sounds. Daniel, a Taurean friend, spent a rainy Saturday afternoon with a pen, pad and calculator, designing his perfect speaker enclosure, which he then constructed in his spare time.

In their later years, many Taureans enjoy gardening and often produce healthy herb or vegetable gardens.

When out of temper, soothing music or a favourite food usually calms Taureans down.

The typical Taurean enjoys food and has a tendency to go through phases with preferred foods. One month it may be a desire for shavings of soft cheese inside a warm roll, the next month it may be ice-cream.

When a Taurean assists you in some way, consider it a trade, as they will doubtless expect assistance in return at some stage. This is not to suggest that Taureans are calculating, but that fairness is important to them.

The nature of the Taurean is one of accumulation. Whether it's money, possessions, houses, musical instruments or simply stockpiling food, they work hard to get what they want and derive great fulfilment from ownership.

The innate Taurean acquisitiveness was shown to me when three-year-old Lisa came to visit. I heard that she collected coins, so I searched out a few old foreign coins to add to her collection. A pair of wide blue eyes stared solemnly as her outstretched hand accepted the three Thai coins I offered her. She placed them carefully on the piano stool and, producing her pink purse, emptied the contents onto the stool alongside the silver coins.

I watched this child sort carefully through her coins to assure herself that I was not simply returning her own coins. Satisfied that the Thai coins were new to her collection, she looked up at me again and her eyes softened into a smile. 'It's my money,' she said at last, and hastily crammed all the coins into her well-worn purse.

This little Taurean is true to type, and knows that money is important, even if she is too young to count it. When I mentioned this incident to her mother, she chuckled quietly. 'You should see the tantrums if we leave home for the day and Lisa discovers that she's left her purse behind. You'd swear it contained the family jewels.'

When Taureans want to purchase something they search hard for a bargain. They want good quality, but it need not be fancy. They expect their possessions to last a very long time, which they usually do because Taureans look after their possessions carefully.

Taureans need to guard against valuing things above people, for their pursuit of material possessions can sometimes come between them and their partners or families.

As parents, Taureans are patient and compassionate. They rarely lose their tempers and will put up with a great deal before they become angry. However, they can be very stubborn and it is difficult to move a bull when it digs in its heels.

Singers and musicians often have strong Taurean influences in their charts, as Taurus rules the neck and throat, enhancing self-expression through the voice. They are suited to careers in music or selling and maintaining musical instruments. They prefer a steady, stable work environment and resent being rushed to complete a project. Being essentially methodical and practical, they are suited to work where patience and steady application are required. This includes engineering, accounting and real estate.

Relationships

Taureans are generally affectionate and sensual, typical earth sign characteristics. However, they can be possessive and are happiest in a relationship which is based around routine, as this increases their feelings of security.

Essentially realistic, Taureans are prepared to work hard to win the one they love and to build a relationship and a lifestyle which centres around all the creature comforts. The way to a Taurean's heart is through their stomach.

Because they are slow to change patterns, Taureans like plenty of time to think things through, in order to get used to the idea of a new behaviour before they have to embrace it. This is why Taureans plan relationship changes carefully. When a Taurean spontaneously tells you about a change they are going to make, you can be sure that they have thought it through very carefully. They like to appear to be spontaneous, while enjoying life's routines.

Health

Taureans often experience tension in the neck and throat when stressed and, because of their sensual nature, they respond well to massage to relieve the tension.

The thyroid gland, located in the neck, regulates the rate of metabolism and, consequently, body growth. This is another area of concern for Taureans when they are placed under great stress.

Earth signs value their physical health, and Taureans usually exercise regularly and maintain a balanced diet as part of their routine, thereby ensuring continued good health. If they do not exercise regularly, excess weight can become a health issue in later years.

Negative Taurus

Negative Taureans can be lazy, jealous, stubborn, self-centred and extravagant. The usual Taurean sense of fairness and loyalty are missing in this type, and they will often insist that their relationship partner changes to suit them. They can be unfaithful in love and greedy, both in their physical and sensual appetites. Sometimes, as a result of a great loss, the negative Taurean can become detached from everyone and everything, using relationship partners only for sensual fulfilment and then discarding them. This type often fails to value material possessions, which they routinely lose or destroy.

Some negative Taureans, however, value material things above people and spend their lives in pursuit of material possessions. One of my clients, Tracy, came to see me about her new partner Tom, a negative Taurean. Tom is wealthy and showered Tracy with jewellery, including several gold bracelets, an expensive watch and two diamond rings. However, every time they had a disagreement, Tom would turn into a tyrant, arguing fiercely before demanding that all his 'gifts' be returned. Tracy would then remove the jewellery and hand it back to him. He usually calmed down the following day and gave the jewellery back to her. In Tom's mind, the jewellery was a sign of his love for Tracy.

On one occasion, Tracy refused to accept the jewellery back, which unnerved Tom so much that he went out and bought her a sports car. 'It's only on loan to you I suspect,' I ventured. Tracy nodded in agreement.

Taurean lesson

The most important lesson for Taureans is to *decide what is valuable in life*. As earth signs enjoy the material world, there is a tendency for Taureans to place a greater emphasis on possessions rather than people and learning. Also, because Taureans prefer stability to change, they need to be aware that theirs is not the only way to do things, not the only way to live a life, earn an income, raise a family and so on.

Taureans need to guard against single-mindedness as this can lead to a narrow view of life. When Taureans learn detachment, they can see there is more to life than possessions. Once this lesson is learned, true peace and contentment awaits.

Gemini

Gemini:	May 22 – June 22
Planetary symbol:	The Twins
Glyph:	♊
Element:	Air
Type:	Mutable
Ruler:	Mercury

The typical Gemini has an active mind and body, loves a good conversation and is capable of seeing both sides of an argument at once. Like mercury, the silver-white metal remarkable for its fluidity at ordinary temperatures, Geminis are remarkable for their fluidity of mind. They can switch from one thing to another in an instant.

Mercury, Gemini's ruling planet, is named after the Roman messenger of the gods, who was renowned for his business acumen, his eloquence and his physical dexterity. This sums up the Gemini type in a nutshell.

Geminis are drawn towards businesses where their communication skills are an asset. Geminis are not afraid to speak out and are rarely at a loss for words. Such was the case with Renee.

One hot summer's night, Renee dozed off to sleep with all the windows of her townhouse wide open. Her bedroom window opened directly into a busy inner-city street, and it proved too much of a temptation for the man who decided to climb in. Renee awoke the moment the intruder entered her room and, not knowing what else to do, she spoke up. 'Get back out that window!' she ordered, and the dark figure at her bedside promptly responded, disappearing over the window ledge. 'And don't come back,' she followed. Wide awake now, she locked all the windows and spent the next two hours on the phone with friends, telling them what had happened.

If you want to hire someone with contacts, hire a Gemini. If they don't know who can help you, they'll know someone who knows someone.

Geminis often have amazing memories for numbers and quirky data. Telephone numbers and birth dates are stored away for retrieval at a moment's notice. Carl's mother possessed a typical Gemini memory. Over dinner one evening, I gave her the birth dates of six members of my family; a year later she rattled off all six names and birth dates in perfect order.

The Gemini memory can work to their disadvantage, however, when they need to decide between several alternatives. Typically, Geminis will scan their memories in search of relevant information, sometimes becoming overwhelmed with information in the process.

As an air sign, Geminis often display an adaptable intellect, adaptability also being a common characteristic of the mutable signs of the zodiac. They have a thirst for information, so television, newspapers and books are highly valued. It is not unusual for Geminis to be halfway through five or six books at one time.

Naturally perceptive, Geminis are also eloquently witty in their appraisal of others. An example of this is Clare, who, tiring of her partner Roger's continual double standards in their relationship, commissioned the perfect birthday present: a double-standard lamp.

Their ability to see both sides of an issue can make it difficult for Geminis to make decisions, not because they want to be sure they select the *best* option, but because they want *every* option. Watching a Gemini trying to make a decision can prove exhausting. They will often discuss the choices with everyone who happens to walk by or with whoever answers the phone, just to make sure there is not a point of view they have overlooked.

Gifted communicators, Geminis are well suited to careers in fashion, teaching, advertising, writing, editing, sales, journalism, medicine and natural therapies, the diplomatic corps and the law. In legal battles, Geminis are able to turn the tide of an argument by seizing the moment and speaking convincingly and clearly, using their extensive memories to support their views.

The next time you have a conversation with a Gemini, take note of the way they seem to receive more information than they give. Geminis prefer to ask the questions; when questioned about themselves they will quickly steer the conversation to another topic, or will clam up tight.

Sport appeals to Geminis, especially those disciplines which call for physical dexterity, such as gymnastics, high-jumping, dancing and so on. As Geminis tend to want to try everything possible and often several things at once, they are not the most reliable sign of the zodiac. They also have a strong natural curiosity, so if privacy is an issue, beware the prying eyes of a Gemini.

Relationships

Preferring reason and logic to emotions, Geminis often fall in love with someone for the way their mind works or for their conversation. Instead of the Taurean sensuality, Geminis flirt with words. Long phone conversations that cover every topic imaginable are a natural part of the typical Gemini courtship, as the telephone enables them to be intimate yet physically distant.

Emotionally, Geminis can be somewhat inconstant, and you cannot expect them to be feeling the same way about you this afternoon as they were this morning. After all, hours may have passed since your last communication and, in that time, many conversations, thoughts, decisions and actions have taken place. As a mutable air sign, Geminis can be like a wind which blows hot and cold.

When frustrated in a relationship, Geminis can become critical, their tongue every bit as sharp as a razor. Sometimes it is deliberate; at others, they fail to realise the power of words.

Trevor, a Gemini, was feeling trapped in his relationship with Cassandra and arguments erupted over the smallest things. One morning he awoke and, in his most well-mannered tone, described his dream to Cassandra.

'It was your typical nightmare, really. I dreamed that I was 30 years old and still living with you.'

'But you'll be 30 next week.'

'Yes, only this time I'm awake.'

If you are in a relationship with a Gemini and experiencing communication difficulties, it may be worth your while to venture outside with your mobile phone or find a telephone booth and call them. A conversation which isn't face to face can sometimes allow Geminis to open up more easily.

Geminis prefer plenty of freedom in relationships to explore life and its myriad possibilities. When feeling trapped or unable to leave a situation because of their commitments, Geminis will often escape via the telephone, enjoying conversations with people who are removed from their present situation.

Health

The nervous system is a weak area for Geminis, and if they exhaust themselves on a daily basis, you can often see a tremor in their hands. Asthma and bronchial trouble need to be guarded against, because Geminis have a tendency to develop problems with the chest and lungs. All these areas need extra attention when Geminis are feeling stressed.

Negative Gemini

The sharp wit and quick mind of the Gemini can make this type caustic when negative, and somewhat two-faced. As they tend to agree with whoever is standing close to them at the time, it is easy to change the mind of a negative Gemini.

Negative Geminis can find it difficult to make a commitment to one partner at a time and can end up juggling several part-time lovers. They are usually able to justify their actions, no matter how inconsistent they may be, often believing that rules are for other people. Such was the case with Richard. He consulted me because his wife demanded that he seek help for his continual extramarital affairs. He spent the first 30 minutes attempting to enlist my help in explaining to his wife that she was being unreasonable, that he actually *needed* more than one sexual relationship at a time. I wasn't accepting any of it, so when he tried the old line 'My wife doesn't understand me', I ventured, 'Perhaps your wife understands you all too well'.

Often restless, critical and impatient, negative Geminis are quick to tell you that they can do your job better and more accurately than you, but in reality they have no intention of doing so, as action requires more effort than words. Their powers of observation are brought to bear upon those close to them, and they know how to inflict the deepest wound with the minimum number of words.

In the negative type, paranoia is often evident and, because they know the power of information, they are reluctant to give out any information about themselves. Sometimes the negative Gemini can leave you feeling like you have just been interviewed by an investigative journalist.

Negative Geminis can be sceptical and are quick to ridicule any ideas or beliefs you hold with a savage comment or an off-hand verbal slap. They can become chronic complainers who criticise everyone and everything around them.

As forgers or counterfeiters, negative Geminis excel, for lying comes as naturally to them as speaking. In sales positions, they have no conscience. They'll rent you a room in a hotel that hasn't yet been built or sell you a car that isn't theirs to sell and throw in a case-load of your own clothes at 'half the usual price'.

Gemini lesson

The lesson for Geminis is to *learn to decide*. This sounds easy, but in deciding between several alternatives, it is necessary to choose one and eliminate the others. Geminis have difficulty accepting this, because they don't want to exclude any of the other options.

Making a decision can be difficult when you only have your mind to guide you. Geminis need to apply their mind, heart *and* feelings to decide the best path in a given situation.

Mental discipline is another part of the lesson for Gemini. When the mind is disciplined, the heart can be heard, which is especially important when making significant life choices.

A Gemini friend of mine once suggested that all problems in life are in fact decisions, and that when we make a decision, we take a step towards resolving the problem. He went further, suggesting that even problems over which we have no control leave us with a decision: to accept or to deny our circumstances.

Cancer

Cancer:	June 23 – July 23
Planetary symbol:	The Crab
Glyph:	♋
Element:	Water
Type:	Cardinal
Ruler:	The Moon

Cancerians have a strong nurturing instinct. The glyph for Cancer depicts a mother's breasts, because the first nurturing a child receives after birth is usually suckling at their mother's breast. The crab is also an apt symbol for this sign because, like the crab, Cancerians have a hard outer shell and a soft centre. They rarely move forwards to achieve a goal, preferring to approach it sideways, as if sidling up to their opportunities. Being a cardinal type, they are ambitious and will initiate action to achieve their desired goals.

Cancerians understand life through feelings, a characteristic of the water signs, and it can be difficult for them to understand something they cannot feel. They are naturally intuitive, able to sense the emotions of a group of people rapidly and adjust their response accordingly.

Cancer is ruled by the Moon, which has a noticeable effect on Cancerians. When it is a Full Moon, they are often more energetic or restless than usual, and around the New Moon, more sluggish. They prefer the evening to the early morning, and their vivid imaginations make them valuable writers, painters and storytellers. Many Cancerians have slow lymphatic systems and are consequently somewhat slow physically, which heightens their imaginative tendencies.

When Carl, a Cancerian, was a teenager, he entertained his younger sister (also a Cancerian) with his vivid bedtime stories. The stories were always variations on a theme, and the theme was The Three Bears. Being a teenager, he was not content with a tame version of The Three Bears, so into the story came the bootleggers, in their 1920s cars with machine-guns blazing. Two tiny hands would grip the sheet tighter and tighter as the story built to its climax. His sister's furrowed brow told Carl when it was time to draw the story to a pleasant conclusion. The little bear would awaken from his bad dream to the smell of fresh porridge and the sight of the first daffodils of spring. The sun would be out and a gentle breeze would coax the bear out of bed and into the kitchen, where fresh bread was baking and a warm fruit bun awaited him. By this point Carl's sister would be fast asleep, dreaming of porridge and fruit buns.

Cancerians are patient, sympathetic and protective people. They are suited to careers that involve caring and compassion, such as child care, infant or primary school teaching, or managing a bed and breakfast or private hotel. They have a subtle sense of colour, which suits them to interior design and interior decorating. They can enjoy working in the hospitality industry and when grounded by financial fears and insecurities, they often seek clerical or accounting work as it is secure.

A Cancerian was the perfect person for Leonard, whose parents died when he was very young and who decided to hire a mother figure to visit him once a week and prepare meals in his kitchen. Not just for the food, but for the clattering of pots and pans in the kitchen, the sounds of a mother he never had as a child. Diana was the perfect choice, a chatty woman in her fifties, who loved nothing more than the thought that someone appreciated her cooking. In her typical Cancerian way, Diana arrived the first day with a bunch of flowers from her garden, and soon the smells of homemade pastry permeated the whole house. Cups of tea arrived regularly and since that first day, Leonard has grown and blossomed, both within himself and in his business.

Cancerians enjoy the sea, rivers and lakes, but prefer appreciating the beauty of these things to getting wet. Work involving boats or liquids (including alcohol) appeals to them.

Natural hoarders, Cancerians collect mementos of every event or phase in their lives. Once in a while they will gather together their photographs, books, records and CDs and wallow in nostalgia. They can be quite acquisitive, and again the crab is symbolic of their nature, its strongest parts being its claws. They are apt to want to live in the past, so a Cancerian or someone with strong Cancer qualities would be the person to consult for historical details if you were putting together a family tree.

Cancerians often possess deep memories, especially for emotional hurts, and it is not unusual for them to recount an incident from 10 years ago in great detail if it has upset them in some way.

Home and family are important to Cancerians, and a characteristic of their homes can be that every ledge and flat surface is crowded with books, cards, trinkets and collectables. They love cooking, and usually prepare more food than necessary. Cancerian Rachael usually cooked for six when there were only four for dinner, because she always expected people to turn up at the last minute and worried that they would be hungry. Word soon spread about her cooking and, sure enough, four people to dinner meant six or seven.

Cancerians are inclined to be emotionally possessive of their loved ones and need to curb their tendency to worry about family and friends. As parents, they can find it difficult to let go of their children when they want to leave home or assert their independence. With smaller children, however, Cancerians excel. They are patient and doting, and, because of their vivid imaginations, are excellent storytellers.

Essentially romantic, Cancerians enjoy travel and learn languages easily by absorbing the sounds around them and committing them to memory. They are much better at learning a language when immersed in the culture than in a school-type environment.

Cancerians are often highly intuitive, particularly through their dreams at night, and keeping a dream journal can be a very rewarding process for them. With a little training, the average Cancerian can program their dreams to give them solutions to problems in their daily life. Sometimes, when life's problems overwhelm them, Cancerians can retreat into their dreams and their rich fantasy life.

Cancerians can be moody, especially when they feel insecure, and logic doesn't help them feel any better. Emotional reassurance is necessary and they respond well to hugs. Being such good nurturers, they also respond well to a little nurturing in return. When a Cancerian feels unappreciated, they tend to moan, nag and criticise, dampening the mood of all those around them.

Relationships

With their active imaginations and vivid memories, Cancerians delight in romance. When separated from the one they love, they like to know they are remembered, so sending cards, letters, flowers or small gifts to a Cancerian partner goes a long way towards winning their heart. All these gifts or letters are carefully tucked away for later review, to be savoured hundreds of times at leisure. In return, Cancerians love to send cards and letters, and will spend hours dreaming of how their partner felt when they received them.

Cancerians are very nurturing and are usually gentle in their displays of affection. Fond of family life and domestic harmony, the Cancerian enjoys a homely abode which is often cluttered with family photos and collectables.

Being a water sign, the Cancerian is usually in tune with their partner's feelings, even when they are apart from one other. These people tend to worry about their financial security, their loved ones and the state of the world generally, so emotional turbulence in a relationship can be very debilitating for them.

Owing to their romantic nature, Cancerians sometimes love their partner more intensely when that person has left them or is unavailable. 'Absence makes the heart grow fonder' aptly describes the Cancerian approach to relationships.

Health

The sign of Cancer rules the stomach, the digestive system, the breasts and the lymph glands. A slow lymphatic system is characteristic of Cancerians.

The Cancerian imagination is usually well developed, and it is important for these people to recognise that their minds can direct their imaginations towards creative things or towards fearful things. When directed towards fearful events, Cancerians worry incessantly, stressing their already delicate stomachs and digestive systems, which can result in ulcers.

Negative Cancer

Negative Cancerians are worriers. Often crippled by fear of disastrous consequences, they fail to seize the moment and succeed with their plans. Their vivid memories are cluttered with past hurts, both real and imagined, preventing them from forgiving and living in the present. They tend to be martyrs who moan loud and long about life's injustice. They can be quite selfish, stingy and loath to spend money.

When negative, Cancerians are unable to give or receive nurturing, and they often retreat into dreams when presented with problems. This hardening of their soft natures can be as a result of difficulties in childhood, which seem to affect Cancerian types more than any of the other signs. In many cases, they hold a grudge against their mother, blaming her for ruining their life. Their lymphatic disposition means they retain wastes in their physical bodies; in turn, they can experience emotional retention and an inability to forget or release past hurts. They are moody, often retreating into themselves without warning and proving unreachable to those around them.

Being a water sign, the negative Cancerian can be an emotional and psychic sponge, draining those around them and casting a gloomy shadow over everything. Slovenly in habit, they invariably choose the path of least resistance while expecting the greatest success.

Fearful of emotional and financial bankruptcy, negative Cancerians hoard all that they can, both physically and emotionally. These people are usually unsuccessful in their own business, as they worry too much. Negative Cancerians can also seem emotionally unavailable in relationships, as they are still emotionally attached to some past partner. The Cancerian tendency to love someone more once the relationship is over is stronger in the negative Cancerian. I have even seen a negative type cling to the dream of fulfilment with a past lover for over 20 years.

Decisions prove very difficult to make for the negative type, as their sense of loss can be overwhelming. When helping a Cancerian with a relationship choice recently, I asked her the following question: 'Which of these two partners would you miss less, if you chose the other partner?' She burst into tears, anticipating the loss ahead of her, aware that she would spend many hours looking back and wondering about possible fulfillment with the partner she had not chosen. I explained to her that making the right choice could limit her feelings of loss.

Whereas fire signs look forward to opportunities with anticipation, water signs (especially Cancerians) often look back to past opportunities not taken, particularly when they are in need of an escape route from their current circumstances.

Cancerian lesson

The lesson for Cancerians is to *decide through a combination of feeling and thought, and then to fulfil their plans despite fears and obstacles.*

While Geminis attempt to decide using only thought, Cancerians can become overwhelmed by feelings and lose sight of the rational approach.

When deciding, Cancerians often consider the effects any choice they make might have on those around them, as their sense of community is well developed. This means that they can take quite a long time to make decisions and they can feel the need to make sacrifices to ensure the happiness of those they love.

Leo

Leo:	July 24 – August 23
Planetary symbol:	The Lion
Glyph:	♌
Element:	Fire
Type:	Fixed
Ruler:	The Sun

Leos think of life as a great adventure, with risks to be taken and glory to be won. They are naturally enthusiastic, energetic, flamboyant and, at times, tactless — all typical characteristics of a fire sign. As a fixed type, Leos are determined and persistent, but they also possess the qualities of positivity and optimism.

Leos are ambitious people, yet they are rarely ruthless or cunning in their pursuit of a goal. They think in grand terms, with a disregard for the tiny details. Gavin is a typical example of this: in one phone call he raised $15,000 for a new kitchen, only minutes after admitting he had no money to pay the man who mowed his lawns.

Leos have a tendency to organise the lives of others, which can lead to arguments and disagreements. It is often out of genuine caring for others that Leos offer solutions, but they sometimes fail to realise that their help is neither sought nor needed.

When angered, Leos are inclined to put their noses in the air and treat the offender with condescension. They can be outspoken when out of temper, revealing an arrogant side that is both abrasive and intolerant. However, their anger usually does not last long and their positivity and good humour returns swiftly. Leos quickly forget past arguments, but those they were arguing with may not be so quick to forget, especially after some of the things the Leo has said.

Where money is concerned, it is as though Leos possess a diploma in spending. They seem to believe that there is 'plenty more where that came from', and spend it as they please. They believe that tomorrow will provide for today's purchases, so happily live on credit. Leos have bold plans and dreams, and take risks which lead either to riches or to poverty. They can often find others who will fund or support their dreams, enabling their dreams to become a reality.

Leos believe that quality lasts long after price has been forgotten. Even poverty-stricken Leos have one good outfit or possession. For Bradley it was a gold watch. Not any gold watch, though: the one he had decided to buy cost more than $700. That might not seem too much to pay for a watch, but Bradley was still at school and it took him 20 months of hard work to save the money.

When financial problems loom, Leos are more likely to increase their incomes than decrease their expenses. Essentially spontaneous, they will risk overextending themselves financially from time to time.

Leos can be very generous, but sometimes their generosity is simply a show to attract the admiration of others. They tend to see themselves in terms of how they want to be seen by others, and this can lead to self-compromise.

With their natural flair for socialising, Leos are a boon to almost any gathering, and are unafraid of being the centre of attention. Even shy Leos are happy to be in the limelight when it suits them. Leos thrive on attention, praise and recognition from others, and these things are likely to motivate the typical Leo to work tirelessly towards a goal. They respond well to praise and even an occasional positive comment can rekindle their commitment and enthusiasm.

Leos are loyal and courageous, and, in

their later years, when their outer pride has softened, they often reveal themselves to be big-hearted, soft-centred people, with a sense of playfulness and fairness. They enjoy strong leadership abilities and a natural creativity. When these skills are harnessed, Leos can achieve great success, especially as they also possess an inborn vitality and a confidence in their own abilities.

Leos may stubbornly resist change when shown a new idea or method but, given time to think it over privately, they are able to appreciate the other viewpoints. However, if pressed to change their beliefs or accept a new concept, they will often be loud in their condemnation, as they would rather dismiss something outright than admit they lack knowledge.

Leos make wonderful teachers as they are enthusiastic and can easily inspire their students. They love to talk and thrive on an audience, which suits them for sales and leadership positions. Their innate need to express themselves suits them to creative careers, provided they can find the inner strength to pursue their goals.

Relationships

In love, Leos are incredibly romantic, but sometimes they are more in love with the idea of being in love than with the person they are courting. Fabian is such a man. Soon after he met Sandra, he sent her flowers every day for four weeks. First there were yellow roses with notes of friendship. These were followed by pink roses with words reflecting his deepening feelings. Next, he sent red roses with accompanying poems and letters of love which were cut into pieces like a jigsaw puzzle. Then came invitations to the theatre.

What finally won Sandra's heart was the ice-cold bottle of champagne delivered on a silver tray with a mobile phone. Soon after they were delivered, the phone rang and Fabian invited Sandra to dinner. When she asked him where they would be eating, he asked her to look outside. On the front lawn, Fabian sat at a linen covered table which had

been set for two. A waiter was tossing a salad as Fabian beckoned her to join him.

Sometimes Leos can irritate their partners by forgetting that their partners are not merely an extension of themselves. A Leo's partner may find it necessary to assert themselves from time to time, especially when the Leo orders dinner for them, tells them what to wear or offers advice which is uninvited.

Generally, Leos are loyal in relationships and although they may seek the attention of others to feed their egos, they prefer one partner at a time.

Health

The heart is a main area of concern to the Leo, as is the spine. As their bodies are quite flexible, they can sometimes suffer from back problems.

When under emotional stress, Leos can experience occasional muscle cramps or spasms. When depleted of energy, fevers can be a common complaint, but generally Leos have good recuperative powers.

Negative Leo

Negative Leos are usually vain, ego-driven, intolerant and given to wearing ostentatious clothing.

By nature domineering, negative Leos bully their friends and dominate conversations, believing what they are saying is most important. They seek recognition shamelessly and sulk if they cannot win at everything they attempt. Competitive and dismissive of the success of others, negative Leos arrogantly claim to able to do better and are usually conceited enough to believe their own empty posturing. Cruelty can replace the usual Leo big-heartedness, resulting in the negative Leo being alone and bitter in old age.

As parents, these people can abuse their authority with an aggression which saps the child's confidence. Henry was one such Leo parent. He insisted that his 10-year-old son Mark learn tennis, then he beat the boy in every game for four and a half years on a weekly basis. When Mark eventually won a match, Henry stormed off and refused to play again.

Another type of negative Leo exists, and this is the shy, nervous Leo. This person wants to please others and will say or do whatever it takes to win approval. Once they have this approval, however, they are likely to be resentful of others having control over them. What this type of Leo fails to understand is that they chose to surrender themselves to others for approval, and that at any time they can also choose to disagree with that point of view. They need to become aware that they *can* hold different opinions from others and still be on good terms with them.

When negative, the Leo partner can be demanding and intolerant. They are stubborn and self-absorbed, preferring to be the ruler rather than an equal partner. The negative Leo partner often seeks drama to give them a sense of 'aliveness', favouring passion over love.

Leo lesson

The lesson for those born in the sign of Leo is to *find their inner strength*. This lies beyond the ego and its quest for recognition, and is found in humility and open-heartedness, which involves the expression of the creativity that is unique to each of us.

Finding the strength to reinforce ego boundaries is necessary for Leos, as they can lack an awareness of where they end and others begin, physically, emotionally and mentally. This lack of awareness can result in them traversing physical boundaries (for example, borrowing other people's possessions without asking), emotional boundaries (for example, not knowing when to give their partners emotional space) and mental boundaries (for example, assuming ownership of ideas which other people originated).

Once they have found their true strength, the lesson for Leos involves *expressing their individuality through some creative means*. More than any other sign, Leos have an innate need to express themselves. They can find it difficult containing themselves at times, as their enthusiasm is overwhelming.

Virgo

Virgo:	August 24 – September 23
Planetary symbol:	The Virgin
Glyph:	♍
Element:	Earth
Type:	Mutable
Ruler:	Mercury

Being a mutable earth sign, Virgo shows the adaptable side of the practical element of earth. The glyph for Virgo represents the female sexual organs and the planetary symbol is that of a young woman; a virgin.

The typical Virgoan is analytical and exacting, with a mind that prefers to reduce things to their purest form in order to understand them. Virgoans are usually industrious and reliable. When a delicate job needs to be completed in a precise and thorough manner, a Virgoan is the person to do it.

Unlike the sometimes ostentatious Leos, Virgoans prefer to be understated in dress and in their surroundings. If the atmosphere becomes too noisy or flamboyant, Virgoans are easily spotted because they will be observing rather than participating.

These people are conservative by nature, and can be effective organisers who manage to remain in the background. As business managers they excel, for the Virgoan ability to judge a person's nature and select the right person for the job helps everything run smoothly. Virgoans dislike drama, so any business venture has to run with a minimum of fuss for the Virgoan to be content.

Virgoans are systematic, especially where numbers are concerned, and their precision suits them to accountancy, medicine, small business, chemistry and natural therapies. They possess an innate love of order and symmetry, so can often be found as craftspeople. Whatever they do for a living, Virgoans do it with a desire to be perfect.

With their gift for detailed work, Virgoans will continue to work on a project long after others are satisfied, until they have satisfied themselves. Their excess of nervous energy means they are often restless and their minds are usually more active than their bodies.

Virgoans love puzzles, problems which require careful reasoning to arrive at a solution and the opportunity to test their mental powers. These people usually have good, clear memories, which increases their problem-solving skills.

As they push themselves towards perfection, Virgoans can be hard on themselves, expecting more of themselves than others expect of them. This can be extended to friends and family, and they can become critical of those close to them when they feel that better results could have been achieved.

Being an earth sign, Virgoans look after their health and their physical bodies, and are careful about diet, exercise and rest. They can become obsessed with their physical health to the point where they are fanatical about what they eat and tend towards hypochondria.

Virgoans prefer to go about things quietly, without drawing any attention to themselves. They are suited to positions involving service to others. Whereas the Leo usually wants to be the king, the typical Virgoan is content to take second place. Their reward is not the praise they receive from others, but the inner satisfaction they derive from a job well done.

Virgo children are serious students, who work hard and enjoy routine and discipline as it gives them a sense of security. Even when young, these people are neat and tidy. I have seen Virgo toddlers step around a puddle to avoid getting wet or dirty, something that could rarely be said of Arians or Sagittarians.

Virgoans like to surround themselves with subtle colours and simple lines in furnishings. Subtle, earthy tones suit them, as these allow the Virgo mind to ponder without distraction.

Virgoans can appear to be aloof when you first meet them, but chances are that they are observing you, deciding who you are before they commit themselves in any way. They choose their words carefully, meaning exactly what they say. Unlike the Gemini who is happy to talk, the Virgoan prefers to speak economically. Theirs is a serious expression, but the Virgo sense of humour is subtle and quick. Comments are often offered quietly and with a straight face; if you are not alert, you can miss the humour entirely. In the film *Being There*, Peter Sellers (a Virgoan) demonstrates the typical subtlety of the sign with brilliant understatement.

At any age, Virgoans benefit from a quiet period each day to rest and to reflect. Although their bodies relax, their minds are usually active, and they resolve problems while they work. Idle hands are not usually Virgo hands and Giselle is a typical example.

Whenever Giselle has a problem to sort out, she cleans the house from top to bottom. Every window, all the light switches, the oven, the floor underneath the refrigerator and the light fittings are systematically cleaned before she sets about rearranging the contents of all the cupboards. If she has not resolved the problem by this point, she does the ironing and cleans the glass in all the photo frames on the mantlepiece and all the pictures on the walls. It is exhausting simply watching her. The harder she thinks, the harder she works.

Relationships

In love, the typical Virgoan is an example of emotional restraint. In place of splashy demonstrations of affection, the Virgoan helps their partner's life to run more smoothly. An example of this is Patricia, who finds the time to write all the cheques and balance her husband's ledgers every month, even though she has eight children to care for and a full-time job.

Happiness for a Virgo lies in the smooth running of day-to-day living, and the Virgoan is able to ensure that most things run according to plan.

Sometimes Virgoans are not as quick to praise their partners as to criticise, but when they do offer praise, it is deserved. To the typical Virgoan, the very fact that they have chosen you as their partner is enough to ensure that you are not like the rest of humanity. These people are extremely discerning and they usually choose their partners carefully, knowing that a wrong choice can result in chaos and pain.

Virgoans are reliable and loyal partners. It takes time for a Virgoan to open up to their partner, so patience is necessary. When hurt in love, the Virgoan can retreat into themselves and become critical of others and of life. In particular, they can be critical of themselves for not anticipating the turn of events.

Virgoans usually work hard for their families, finding service to others a worthwhile expression of love.

Health

Virgoans tend to be overly conscious of their health, often needlessly. Areas which can be of concern include the hands, the intestines and the pancreas.

As the pancreas helps regulate sugar levels in the blood, Virgoans need to limit their intake of sugary foods. Virgoans tend to prefer savoury rather than sweet foods and they are usually moderate in food, drink and exercise.

Regular physical exercise to offset the mental exercise helps to keep Viroans balanced. In the negative type, Virgo people can become health obsessed. Julianne spent an entire year with a range of puzzling symptoms after carefully reading a medical text from cover to cover. She confounded doctors, natural therapists and her friends with symptoms which appeared sporadically and disappeared before an accurate diagnosis could be made. Every time Julianne heard or read about a new and exciting disease, she developed the symptoms. I have never witnessed such an array of skin rashes, blotches, lumps, dizzy spells and inflammations as Julianne displayed.

Inflammation of the intestines is another area of concern for Virgoans, and this can sometimes be avoided by following a high-fibre diet.

Negative Virgo

When negative, Virgoans possess a great deal of scepticism. In their search for the purest form of any thing, belief or quality, they risk eliminating many acceptable alternatives. Highly critical, the negative Virgoan often considers the opinions of others worthless and they are quick to reveal the flaws in any argument.

Negative Virgoans can be aloof and self-centred. Those who are not fully conversant with their current interests are considered fools. The Virgoan powers of observation allow these people to inflict the greatest pain with the minimum effort. They can be condescending and scathing with their dismissive remarks. I overheard a Virgo man dismiss a woman at a party saying, 'You know darling, I think you'll make someone a perfect ex-wife one day'.

Extremely exacting and neat, these people bring a sense of fanaticism to the word 'orderliness'. They sometimes see only the cracks in the china, the hair out of place, the tiny piece of food on the chin of the small child or that someone has moved the sofa 4 centimetres to the left.

Life can be miserable for the negative Virgoan, because no amount of effort seems to rectify the imperfections they see around them. Their friends and family suffer too, because they bear the brunt of this quest for perfection, and are constantly criticised, compared and examined for faults.

The fear of making mistakes can sometimes prevent any action at all, and the negative Virgoan fears criticism for not getting it right the first time. They don't seem to realise that nobody is as critical of their achievements as they are themselves, and until they see this, they fear new things, in case they appear foolish.

Time spent with Arians or Sagittarians helps the negative Virgoan to relax a little, as these other signs are usually prepared to try everything once, and often laugh off any mistakes.

Virgo lesson

In learning, there are often three distinct stages. The first is desire or planning; the second, action; the third, reflection. First you desire, then you act upon your desires, and lastly you think about which actions were useful and which were wasted. While Arians are eager for the action part of learning, Virgoans prefer the reflection.

In observing and reflecting upon the actions of others, Virgoans can often learn without having to make their own mistakes. This appeals to the Virgoan, as they detest mistakes. However, this approach stifles experimentation and can limit invention, which is unfortunate because mistakes have lead to some of the greatest inventions in history.

The lesson for Virgo is to *learn to analyse*. It involves scrutinising life and sorting each component according to its use and purpose. To do this, Virgoans need to step back from life, in order to observe it clearly. In learning their lesson, Virgoans need to be aware not to stay too long observing, for it can limit the true understanding which comes from doing and being.

Libra

Libra:	September 24 – October 23
Planetary symbol:	The Scales
Glyph:	♎
Element:	Air
Type:	Cardinal
Ruler:	Venus

The sign of Libra is represented by the scales and Librans tend to weigh things up carefully before making any decisions. Balancing scales can be a difficult task, and keeping them balanced requires a different kind of effort.

Whereas Geminis cannot decide between two alternatives because they want both of them, Librans take time to make decisions because they are more aware of the consequences of actions. Librans also like to please those around them and include the needs of others in their decision-making. This can make deciding a difficult and drawn-out process for Librans, but, when they do decide, they are usually sure of themselves, having weighed up the consequences carefully.

New ideas, conversations and perspectives appeal to Librans because, as an air sign, they usually have active minds. The sign of Libra is also a cardinal sign, meaning that these people are ambitious and eager to start new things.

Librans often possess a strongly developed sense of fairness and will vigorously defend the rights of others, sometimes before defending their own rights. Librans are usually diplomatic, tactful and aware of the needs and feelings of others. Being naturally cooperative and sociable, Librans enjoy group participation and often work at securing group consensus and harmony. Essentially idealistic and helpful, Librans excel where negotiation is required and they work hard for the benefit of a group rather than for personal gain.

These people are typically generous, especially in giving up their own time to help others or in sharing whatever resources they have, even if they are in short supply.

Keenly sensitive to balance in their environment, Librans need pleasant and harmonious surroundings to feel a sense of inner harmony. When their surroundings are disharmonious, Librans are often unable to function well or maintain an inner sense of balance.

Ruled by Venus, the planet of love, Librans prefer the company of others to being alone. In some cases they will go to great lengths to ensure that they are not alone, even when it means being in company that does not suit them. They can display a tendency to want peace at any price and will compromise themselves for the sake of outward harmony. This can lead to inward disharmony and to stress and health imbalances.

Librans are subtle organisers and can have others around them hard at work on a project without the workers realising that they are fulfilling the Libran's plans. Being tactful and diplomatic, Librans are able to motivate others and oversee a project without treading on the toes of those involved.

Librans are able to present criticism in a way that is palatable to almost anyone. They are suited to careers where handling delicate matters or difficult people is part of the job, such as telemarketing, the law or any job which involves mediating between two parties. An example is Annette, who has the unenviable job of being the go-between for musical promoters and musicians on tour. When tension rises and arguments erupt, she needs to be able to see both points of view and offer solutions which leave both parties feeling like they have been heard and that their needs are being met. When you add huge egos, exhaustion and frayed tempers to the mix, things can get out of hand very quickly. Annette has had to find solutions while one party holds the other at knife-point, a real test of her Libran diplomacy and negotiation skills.

Librans are also attracted to working in art or craft galleries, as their Venusian rulership suits them to working with anything that is aesthetically pleasing. The hospitality industry appeals to Librans because they thrive on social contact.

Relationships

Relationships are never far from the minds of most Librans, and they seem happiest when in the company of their partners. These people tend to think in terms of 'we' rather than 'I' and will often go to great lengths to ensure that they are not alone.

Their need for company can sometimes prevent Librans from leaving a destructive relationship and their need for peace at any price can allow a partner to take advantage of them. They need to guard against co-dependence in a relationship as this stifles their growth and keeps the Libran scales out of balance. Generally, Librans are happy when those close to them are content, and to this end they will make great sacrifices.

When Librans are in a happy relationship, all is right with the world as far as they are concerned. They can live without many of life's basics if they have love.

Health

The primary area for concern with Librans is the kidneys. With Venus ruling Libra there is tendency to prefer sweet foods, which can increase the stress placed upon the pancreas as it tries to re-balance the blood sugar levels. When stressed, Librans can experience hormone imbalances.

Generally Librans enjoy good health and this contributes to their optimistic outlook on life. However, if they overindulge in food

and drink, they are prone to skin problems such as acne and blotchy skin.

When negative, Librans can reach for food as a substitute for love, putting sweetness into their mouths instead of their hearts. Prolonged habits of this sort can lead to obesity.

Negative Libra

When negative, Librans need constant reassurance that they are attractive, as they cannot see this for themselves. This can lead to more than one relationship at a time, or a collection of admirers who serve to remind the Libran that they are indeed attractive to others.

The Libran need for peace and harmony can lead this type to put up with an unfair or imbalanced relationship rather than resolve a problem, for they can fear conflict. But there is another type of negative Libran: the war-maker. This type looks for an argument and sets up conflict between people who would otherwise be friends. It is still similar to the peacemaker, however, for this negative Libran gains a sense of being worthwhile when they step in to make peace. Those who are involved in the conflict are usually too focused upon their own issues to notice that the person making peace is the same one who created the conflict in the first place.

In love, the negative Libran likes to play one suitor off against another to increase their sense of being wanted or valued. The negative Libran longs to be loved and valued more than anything else, but they are unable to receive love, so they sabotage relationships. It seems that the dream of ideal love is more rewarding than real love for negative Librans. This is because the planet Venus is associated with learning to value self and others. When a person does not value themselves, it is unlikely that they will actually value the love that someone else is offering them, for they experience difficulty receiving what they do not believe they deserve.

Negative Librans can be lazy and self-indulgent. Unlike the Virgoan, who does their best thinking when they are busy, the negative Libran will do nothing for long periods of time if they have a problem or a decision to make. They are often indecisive and can depend upon others to make decisions for them or to do the hard work necessary for the Libran to achieve their desires.

Being natural organisers, the negative Libran can have everyone around them working industriously while they find a comfortable chair to sit in and a magazine to read.

Negative Librans are likely to say whatever is required to keep the peace and to avoid putting in too much effort, despite what they really believe.

Libra lesson

The lesson for the sign of Libra is to *learn to transform their ideal of a loving relationship into physical reality.*

It sounds easy, but Librans are idealistic where love is concerned and translating the dream into a physical reality requires a great deal of communication, cooperation, negotiation and effort.

In each day there are a hundred opportunities to demonstrate love for someone close in real and physical ways. The Libran's lesson involves deciding which opportunities to pursue in order to ensure a close, loving relationship. A healthy relationship requires effort for rewards, such as making their partner a cup of tea in the morning, and sharing food and conversation.

Librans tend to form a mental picture of what constitutes the perfect relationship, which they update according to what they read, hear about or observe in others' relationships. This can result in thoughts and plans that remain untested in the physical world.

Unlike the negative Cancerian, who will often love someone more when the relationship is over, the Libran has to decide whether to pursue the current opportunity or to wait for something more suitable.

Scorpio

Scorpio:	October 24 – November 22
Planetary symbol:	The Scorpion
Glyph:	♏
Element:	Water
Type:	Fixed
Ruler:	Pluto

The glyph for Scorpio represents the male sexual organ, which is indicative of the Scorpio fascination with sex. The sign of Scorpio is usually represented by the scorpion, although it is sometimes pictured as an eagle. When cornered, a scorpion will sting you or, if unable to do so, will sting itself. This tells us a little about the pride of those born in Scorpio. However, the eagle can rise above past hurts, maintaining its inner peace and achieving great heights of spiritual and emotional development. The eagle is representative of a Scorpio who has reached emotional maturity.

Scorpio is a water sign, so these people feel what is right for them intuitively. As a fixed sign, they can be stubborn and firm of purpose. Try dissuading a Scorpio from some plan or purpose and you'll soon understand what fixed signs are like.

As water is not suited to be fixed in nature, Scorpios can experience inner distress from time to time. Water flows, evaporates and falls, but rarely does it sit still for too long. One way to keep water fixed is to freeze it, and when applying this to emotions, it suggests periods of emotional coldness or stagnation due to unreleased emotional pain. When the heart is warmed and the ice melts, tears follow as the emotions flow once again. After the tears, Scorpios are usually open to understanding and emotional healing.

Scorpios often experience life as distinct chapters, and people and situations belonging to one chapter disappear from their lives when the chapter closes. This is due to the ruling planet for Scorpio: Pluto.

Pluto is the bringer of change, and sometimes finds it necessary to destroy the old to make way for the new. As a result, Scorpios often have only a few close friends who travel through life with them; the rest are acquaintances who pass out of their life with the closing of a chapter.

Most Scorpios have a strong intuition which usually emerges as a 'gut feeling' when they meet someone new. The typical Scorpio will size someone up in a matter of seconds and once they have made up their mind about them, they rarely change their opinions. To be fair, they are often right first time when deciding about people. They may not know a great deal about those they meet, but they know whether they can trust them.

This Scorpio intuition is strong in Janine, a Scorpio friend. Janine was visiting her friend Shelley one evening when Shelly's flatmate Damian arrived home in a state of excitement, having secured a ticket to a concert.

'He's interesting,' mused Janine after Damian had left.

'Don't bother, honey — he's gay,' replied Shelley.

'You know, I don't think so,' said Janine, who had a distinct impression that she would have a relationship with Damian one day.

Four months later, Damian awoke one morning to find a small, shaggy dog at his bedroom door. It belonged to a visitor who had stayed the night. Over breakfast, he fed the dog and was impressed by its impeccable manners. In fact, he was so impressed that he wanted to meet the dog's owner, whom he reasoned would also be well mannered.

He found her asleep on the sofa in the

sunroom. It was Janine, and he prepared her a small breakfast as they talked. Several weeks later they began a love relationship which lasted four years.

Scorpios do not make friends easily, but they are loyal to those friends they have, and defend their friends vigorously should the need arise. They are strong, silent types, who lend weight to the saying 'still waters run deep'. Naturally secretive, they can be relied upon to keep a secret, unless they have strong air sign aspect (Gemini, Libra, Aquarius) in their chart.

Scorpio people tend to test their friends and their partners, in order to discover their limitations. Although they lose some friends and partners as a result of this process, it does not seem to dissuade them.

Scorpios have the ability to penetrate to the core of a matter, and this predisposes them to investigative work. Police detectives, insurance investigators, private detectives, psychiatrists, psychologists and clairvoyants all utilise the penetrative qualities which Scorpio people possess.

Owing to their investigative nature, it can be very difficult keeping a secret from a Scorpio. Their intuition tells them that something is amiss and this activates their investigative skills, prompting them to scour their surroundings for evidence to support their feelings.

Those who attempt to deceive a Scorpio are usually unsuccessful and it is unlikely that they will be forgiven for their transgression. However, although strangers usually only get one chance to cross a Scorpio, friends are excused from time to time. It's that Scorpio loyalty again. They may forgive you, but don't delude yourself that you won't have to pay for hurting the Scorpio. You'll have to pay; probably with interest for the time they have spent waiting to even the score.

Scorpios love the sea and prefer stormy or turbulent seas to tranquil waters. Standing at the edge of a cliff overlooking turbulent seas seems to refresh them, and they are usually fearless where danger is concerned.

Relationships

Scorpios prefer strong partners. Emotional strength is tested thoroughly before a Scorpio trusts deeply. Upon meeting a partner for the first time, a Scorpio person often knows how strong they are emotionally, yet despite this they still feel the need to test their partners before they let their guards down.

Deeply passionate people, Scorpios are not ideal partners for those who desire a comfortable, peaceful relationship. Disliking any type of weakness in others, Scorpios are likely to push their partners to overcome their weaknesses, which can be an obstacle to intimacy. However, pursuing a relationship with a Scorpio is usually worth the effort.

Sex for Scorpios is about a meeting of souls, and this deep intimacy can show their partners levels of themselves they had not previously realised. For those who approach sex as a sensual act, a Scorpio partner could prove intimidating, however.

Having a relationship with a Scorpio can be like taking the fastest, most challenging ride at the fairground. It is a challenge worth pursuing.

The typical Scorpio is jealous, although they may not show it in any obvious way. Loyalty is very important to them and once they are confidant that they have someone's loyalty, they tend to relax the rules a little. It is inadvisable to cheat on a Scorpio partner, as these people have a way of instantly knowing when something is wrong. They usually find out about an affair and they are apt to get even, as in the case of Blair and Anita.

Anita met another man at an afternoon gathering and although Blair was working at home at the time, he sensed that something was wrong. Blair arrived home a few days later to see Anita hang up the phone in a nervous manner. He said nothing, but stored the number she had dialled into the phone memory with the press of a few buttons.

At the first opportunity, he dialled the number and a man answered. His suspicions were growing. When he arrived home the following day to see a note from Anita explaining her absence, he dialled the number again and asked for her. The man who answered replied that no one of that name lived there.

Blair didn't actually expect to speak with Anita. He merely wanted to let her know that he knew. He wanted to turn up the heat a little until she told him everything. A week later he bought a telephone answering machine which included a facility for listening in to the house. He could now phone home whenever he wanted and listen to what was happening there.

Anita had not confessed anything a week later, so he increased the pressure. He invented a dream and insisted that she help him make sense of it.

'It was strange really. I dreamed that you arrived home from the doctors to tell me that you had contracted a sexually transmitted disease, and we fought for a whole afternoon before you packed a bag and left,' he explained.

Anita broke down and told him everything, at which point he moved into the second phase: withdrawal and punishment. Rather than taking responsibility for his part in the breakdown of their relationship, Blair felt justified in punishing Anita in a hundred little ways.

Health

Scorpios are prone to problems with the nose, the adenoids, the sex organs, the bladder and the bowel.

In their later years, Scorpio women may need surgery owing to problems with their reproductive organs.

Negative Scorpio

When negative, Scorpios can turn their stings out towards others or in on themselves.

When they turn inwards, any anger or resentment is suppressed, leading to depression or passive-aggressive behaviour. When turned outwards, the Scorpio sting can be lethal. This is summed up neatly by

the saying 'Revenge is a dish best served cold'.

The negative Scorpio can display an unusually well-developed appetite for sex, drugs and alcohol. These people are magnets for conflict and make excellent spies, private investigators and contract killers.

Private investigators utilise some of the Plutonian qualities of investigation and the search for truth, and I was made aware of this when assisting a friend of mine, Gordon, with a case. Gordon was hired to locate a woman who had left her husband and taken his car. It seemed straightforward enough until we learned that she had run away from him because he was beating her, and that hiring a private investigator was his way of intimidating her into submission, making her believe that wherever she ran, he would find her.

It was then that it occurred to me that it is usually men who hire private investigators, often in pursuit of 'their' woman. After that one incident I refused to help Gordon again. I couldn't see how it was any different to being an assassin. By sending her back to her husband, we were sentencing her to a life of misery.

The negative Scorpio has a great deal of difficulty trusting their relationship partner, because they know how easy it is to cheat on someone. They cannot believe that their partners choose to be faithful to them.

Negative Scorpios are secretive, mistrustful and seek control over everyone and everything they come across. They clearly remember the times when they have been powerless and seek to redress these memories by gaining as much power as possible.

The negative Scorpio needs to learn how to forgive and release the past, in order to live more fully in the present.

Scorpio lesson

The planet Pluto rules Scorpio and Pluto brings change, often by destroying or removing the present structure. The lesson for those born in the sign of Scorpio is to *learn that there can be strength in surrender.* Sometimes, the most appropriate thing to do in a situation is to surrender to a force greater than yourself. The pride, tenacity, stubbornness and determination of the typical Scorpio makes it almost impossible for them to surrender.

Scorpios have no time for emotional weakness, so before they can surrender to a force that is greater than themselves, they need to understand that they are not being weak.

Knowing when to give up and when to hold on is a part of the lesson for Scorpio, and this can be simplified with the use of their intuition.

Sagittarius

Sagittarius:	November 23 – December 21
Planetary symbol:	The Archer
Glyph:	♐
Element:	Fire
Type:	Mutable
Ruler:	Jupiter

The glyph for Sagittarius represents the archer's bow and arrow. Traditionally, Sagittarius has been represented by a centaur — an animal whose upper torso is that of a man and whose lower torso is that of a horse. Part of the lesson for Sagittarius is to learn to balance the needs of the man and the animal within.

Sagittarians are enthusiastic, energetic and keen to learn new things, but they can become bored soon after they have mastered what they are learning. Owing to their need to learn and to understand new things constantly, Sagittarians are natural teachers, as they are able to simplify a technique or subject without losing its essential qualities.

Being a mutable sign, Sagittarians are adaptable and flexible. They are usually straightforward, honest and optimistic. They love to travel and even a walk outdoors can give them a much-needed sense of freedom and space. They enjoy their most productive thinking when they are out walking.

Although Leos have the reputation for enjoying the limelight, it is in fact Sagittarians who really thrive on the stage. Whether it be upon life's stage, through politics, business or higher learning institutions, or in films and in the theatre, Sagittarians flourish when given the attention of others.

Sagittarians prefer freedom to commitment, for freedom allows them to explore life's possibilities, enabling them to seize suitable opportunities.

Sagittarians are ambitious, forthright and honest, and they make friends easily. They consider themselves to be independent, yet need to guard against expecting others to assist them in their endeavours. This in itself is not a problem, but it is also not independence. Richard, a Sagittarian, is quick to tell others how independent he is because he studies at university in England, while his family lives in Australia. What he doesn't tell people, however, is that while his fellow students support themselves with part-time jobs, he strolls down to the local bank to withdraw money from his father's credit card.

Sagittarians are usually optimistic and friendly. They are keen travellers, preferring the back roads to the well-trodden path, and are likely to take the most direct route possible when endeavouring to reach a destination. These people usually have a well-developed sense of direction and if they travel the same route every day, they are likely to experiment, finding as many variations as possible.

Although Sagittarians can be clumsy physically and verbally, it is easy to forgive them for they usually mean no harm. When they are physically clumsy, they usually follow the incident with a bout of laughter, as it eases the tension for them. Of course, it can increase the tension for others, as demonstrated in the following example.

Gerry (a Sagittarian) and I were collecting Pete, the guitarist in our band, and I had instructed Gerry to be on his best behaviour in front of Pete's parents. A big mistake now that I think about it, as this only made Gerry nervous and, in turn, clumsy.

Gerry trod about a kilogram of garden soil into the entrance hall and onto the bone-coloured carpet and, noticing what he had done, he quickly sat down to examine his shoes. He sat down on the sleeping 12-year-old cat, which squealed and shot off into the garden. Out of nervousness Gerry laughed, just as Pete's mother appeared. She stared, incredulous. The mud, the cat and the laughter confirmed in her mind that her innocent son was playing guitar with a bunch of barbarians. As we departed, the door handle came off in Gerry's hand and he gave it to Pete's mother with another laugh.

The Sagittarian's verbal clumsiness is also unintended, but can be every bit as damaging if you don't know that they are a Sagittarian. An example of this is Roger.

Five of us had ventured out into the local park to play a little soccer on a late summer's evening. As we kicked the ball around in the 35-degree heat, I watched an old man stroll out of a neighbouring block of units with a bottle of beer and a glass. He looked the picture of bliss as he sipped from the glass to cool down.

The ball rolled over to his feet and Roger retrieved it. Standing about 2 metres from the man on the bench, he called out to us: 'Hey, careful you guys! Not so close to the wino next time.'

The old man carefully collected his bottle and glass and, without a word, returned from whence he came.

Philosophy appeals to the mature Sagittarians, as does gambling in all its guises. Their gambling can take the form of betting on the horses, or simply leaving town in order to live elsewhere, without any job or home awaiting them when they arrive. Things usually fall into place for Sagittarians, as they are enthusiastic and full of optimism.

Sagittarians enjoy sports and healthy competition, and they make good sports coaches or team managers. They are goal-oriented, seeking new challenges to stimulate and teach them. They are suited to careers in teaching (either in universities or places of adult learning), acting, singing and sales, especially when the sales position requires them to travel from place to place.

The most effective way to get a Sagittarian

to do something is to forbid them to do it or to dare them to do it.

A Sagittarian friend of mine once managed to talk her way into her ideal job. She was to start in two weeks. Those two week were hell for both of us, as she doubted her ability to fulfil her job description effectively. I listened to her, encouraged her, pointed out that her employer had faith in her and told her that she would be given time to learn the job. Yet she remained self-critical and unconvinced of her worth. Finally, I snapped.

'Oh, you're probably right,' I stated curtly. 'Perhaps they should have hired a man after all. Why send a girl to do a man's job?'

'Who are you calling a girl?' she snapped. 'I can do this job better than any man can.'

'I wonder about that,' I mused aloud.

'I most certainly can and, what's more, I'll prove it to you,' she stated, glaring at me.

My challenge worked. My friend mastered the job, improved the existing systems and moved on when she had learned all she could from it.

Relationships

Sagittarians often derive more pleasure from anticipating the conquest of a lover than the conquest itself. Loving freedom as they do, they are apt to want to pursue more than one relationship at a time.

It is important to remember that Sagittarians are half human and half horse. They can display the appetite of a horse in more things than food. Such was the case with Bridget's boyfriend, Claude.

Bridget sat opposite me, miserable, as she attempted to rationalise the actions of her boyfriend. Claude was having an affair, which he had told Bridget about as it was his policy to be honest.

'Are you happy to have a relationship like this?' I asked her.

She burst into tears. 'But we've talked about it. He explained to me that he needs more sex than I do, so it's not another relationship as such. It's just for the sex.'

'Bridget! The man is 33 years old and

you're buying this spiel about his overactive sexual appetite.'

'Oh no, Paul. I'm sure he'll get over it soon.'

'Bridget, have you ever tried to catch a wild horse with your bare hands? Catching this man won't be any easier.'

Sagittarians prefer plenty of space in a relationship, which allows for varied interests and friendships. They are usually forthright in their approach to love, as was the case with Julian's partner, Karen.

During lunch one afternoon, Julian told me about Karen, whom he'd met a few days earlier, and he was obviously a man entranced. The phone rang and it was Karen. After a brief conversation, he returned to the table a little shocked and in need of a drink.

'What happened?' I asked.

'She's … well, she's rather straightforward. She's just asked me when I plan to consummate this relationship.'

'Karen wouldn't be a Sagittarian by any chance?' I inquired gingerly.

In love, the Sagittarian is ambitious for their partner, and plans, organises and helps them to achieve their goals.

Sagittarians have the innate ability to see their partners weaknesses and faults clearly. The archer's arrow hits its mark when the Sagittarian is called upon to change the negative behaviour patterns of their partner. Unfortunately, this ability does not extend to themselves, and they can remain blind to their own negative traits while perceiving the faults of others clearly.

When their partner needs help, the Sagittarian offers practical advice and enthusiasm, and is genuinely eager to help find a solution. If a solution is resisted or is not immediately forthcoming, the Sagittarian can lose interest and focus on something more rewarding.

Health

Sagittarians can experience difficulties with the hips and thighs, and they need to take care with their insulin levels.

They have strong appetites and while regular exercise keeps their weight down when they are young, they need to guard against weight gain in their later years.

Even when Sagittarians gain weight, they have a firmness about them. They tend to put weight on the hips, thighs and buttocks and, even when quite large, the buttocks do not lose their shape. The men tend to have quite a lot of body hair and they can be prone to baldness.

Sagittarians need to guard against accidents, cuts, bruises and burns resulting from their impatience and occasional clumsiness.

Negative Sagittarius

When negative, Sagittarians tend to exhibit increased clumsiness, both physically and verbally, and they can display an air of arrogance.

Gerry and I used to drink at a hotel that had a piano for the patrons' use. Having a Sagittarian appetite, he would down eight or more glasses of tequila with orange juice and begin to play. The problem wasn't the drink; the problem was that he couldn't play the piano. To be fair, he'd never been near a piano until we discovered this hotel. Together we turned out some of the worst sounds imaginable, until the bar manager appeared in the doorway and ordered us to leave.

It would have been fine had it ended there, but Gerry insisted that we return every Saturday night for months. Every time he reached the eighth tequila, he began to feel creative. We must have been thrown out of that hotel 25 times in a year, yet I have no recollection of us ever being shamefaced.

The negative Sagittarian can also be irresponsible, leaving behind a trail of debris as they focus on some goal as yet unreached. When they end a relationship, they don't spend time agonising over the past. Tomorrow holds another opportunity and they intend to find it.

When negative, these people can attempt to take over their partner's lives. They don't necessarily mean any harm, but they can have all the subtlety of a road train when they think that they know what is best.

Negative Sagittarians can use honesty to suit their own purposes. They have no hesitation justifying their own actions and yet insist upon others detailing their motives. These people have difficulty being monogamous, preferring to seek out novelty through new relationship partners.

Sagittarius lesson

As they are likely to act upon their impulses rather than reflect, those born in Sagittarius have to learn to *know when to move and when to wait*.

The ancient I Ching (Book of Changes) works on the principle that when problems arise there are only two alternatives: to move or to wait. To extend this principle, moving or waiting can be physical, emotional, mental or spiritual. Including these four levels of moving or waiting makes the lesson more complicated than it first appears. Take the example of Fiona, who consulted me about her relationship.

Fiona's partner Warwick had run away when his problems had overtaken him and Fiona wanted to know if it was worthwhile pursuing the relationship. She had been waiting — physically, emotionally and mentally — for five weeks, and she was exhausted with frustration.

Warwick's chart suggested a need for freedom for another nine months. Fiona needed to wait emotionally whilst moving ahead physically, by going out with friends and living her life. Fiona was afraid to move forward mentally, in case she left Warwick behind. It was obvious that Warwick was also progressing mentally, as he dealt with life's lessons. If she was able to wait for Warwick, her patience would be rewarded, for he would most probably return to her once he resolved his inner conflicts.

Capricorn

Capricorn:	December 22 – January 20
Planetary symbol:	The Goat
Glyph:	♑
Element:	Earth
Type:	Cardinal
Ruler:	Saturn

Capricorns are actively practical: their cardinal nature makes them ambitious and their earth sign qualities make them practical enough to work actively towards their goals.

Generally serious, responsible and patient, these people are usually prepared to work hard for their achievements. Being practical, they have little time for fate, preferring to create their fate through effort and perseverance. This is one of the key elements in the typical Capricorn's success. While other signs might await the right opportunity, Capricorns prefer to do something that will move them even slightly towards their desired goals. Naturally, they encounter many obstacles along the way, some of which might have been avoided by waiting for the right opportunity, but their determination usually helps them to succeed in their plans.

Capricorns take their responsibilities seriously and can become critical of those around them who do not share their sense of seriousness, especially in the workplace. An example of this is Ron, who employed me for about a year.

On my last day at this particular company, I arranged for a few bottles of champagne and some cake, which the 10 of us shared in the afternoon. Ron was shocked that we would even consider drinking at the office.

'Hey, Ron, loosen up a bit. It's not as if we're brain surgeons. The magazine will still hit the streets next month,' I said as Ron returned to his office to work. He appeared incapable of letting go of his responsibilities for even a few hours.

Capricorns tend to be serious and responsible even as children, and often seem like old souls in young bodies. Ten-year-old Martin is often embarrassed by his Leo mother and Sagittarian father when in public, as they enjoy themselves without caring about what other people think of them. Martin is even embarrased by the 10-year-old family car and insists that his parents drop him a block away from school so that his school friends won't see him get out of the car.

Capricorn children are often good with money from an early age and it is not uncommon for them to lend money to their parents. Saving comes naturally to Capricorns and they often deny themselves in order to save money for a goal.

Capricorns love structure and they tend to increase the structure or the rules of any situation in which they are involved. This is why politics appeals to the Capricorn type. They are suited to any career that involves administration and organising others by implementing structure, such as law, politics and accountancy. They are astute investors and can be very disciplined financially.

Capricorns often prefer their own company to crowded social situations. They are careful in their choice of friends, being essentially reserved and traditional in their thinking. Capricorns often feel inferior or undeserving and to compensate, they work very hard to justify their rewards.

Reputation is extremely important to Capricorns, and they tend to feel that it is slowly earned and easily lost. They go to great lengths to ensure a good reputation, especially in their first 30 years of life. When they reach their sixties, Capricorns tend to relax a little, feeling that they have discharged their duties and responsibilities adequately. At this point they start the childhood which they did not have time for when they were younger.

In simple terms, Capricorns tend to start life as old people and grow younger in their later years. They can even become a little eccentric in their seventies and eighties.

Capricorns make important decisions slowly, thus reducing the likelihood of mistakes. In a crisis, these people are likely to offer practical, realistic advice and a helping hand. They are slow to change direction, slow to embrace new opportunities and slow to forgive past hurts. They prefer to remain in a difficult situation which is familiar than to risk losing what they have by changing to another potentially unsuitable situation.

'Better the devil you know' is an apt description of the Capricorn attitude to life.

Capricorns tend to be serious and even a little pessimistic about themselves and life's possibilities. I love to tease Angus, a Capricorn friend, about his pessimism with such comments as, 'Oh, Angus. You know those "the glass is half empty or the glass is half full" people? Well, you don't fit either type. You're a "the glass has been stolen" type of guy.'

Capricorns have an innate respect for law and order and for tradition, and they tend to resist change. As parents, they can appear to be stern and strong disciplinarians; alternatively, they can be lax, for they are rarely around the home as their careers consume all of their time and energy.

Being long-term planners, Capricorns appreciate the value of education and a good start in life. They work hard to provide all those things necessary for their children's education or to improve their career prospects.

Capricorns tend to avoid showy displays of wealth, preferring instead to save what they can or to invest in real estate. They can be hoarders, afraid to throw away anything that might be useful later on in life.

They often possess a dry, understated sense of humour, which can go undetected due to their straight-faced delivery.

Relationships

In love, Capricorns tend to be reserved, preferring to show affection only in private. They avoid wild promises and reckless behaviour which could compromise their reputations. They choose their partners carefully, fully aware that a mistake is something they would have to live with for a long time.

Although not very passionate, Capricorns are solid, dedicated and dependable. In fact, they are the perfect partner to replace a negative Sagittarian, according to a Scorpio friend of mine. She described it this way:

'After all the broken promises, the running away from responsibilities and the low boredom threshold of my last (negative) Sagittarian partner, it was great to meet someone who promised rarely but always delivered. Passionate men make great fiction and books are full of them. For my money, give me a dependable man anytime.'

Capricorns prefer to be financially and emotionally independent, and tend to encourage their partners to be independent, too. This is not to suggest that they don't like being in a relationship, but they do need space to fulfil their own purpose and to achieve their goals.

Although cautious in giving their commitment emotionally, once they do, Capricorns do not take their emotional commitments lightly. If they feel betrayed or unvalued in a relationship, they tend to look to theirs career for fulfilment, and in such cases they need to guard against work addiction.

Health

The areas of concern for Capricorns are the knees, the teeth, the bones and the gall bladder. They are prone to skin complaints, including occasional rashes.

Capricorns need to keep up their intake of food as, unlike Taureans and Librans, they do not have a strong attraction for food, especially when under stress. While the Taurean or Libran might seek solace in food in times of stress, the Capricorn is more like to avoid food during stressful periods, depleting their energy reserves at a crucial time.

The negative Capricorn tends to have more difficulties with their bones and their teeth. Soft teeth, which decay early, are often a complaint of this type.

Negative Capricorn

When negative, Capricorns tend to become narrow-minded about life, and they seek ways to ensure that others follow their philosophy of how life should be. As they seek to control people, they can become suspicious of their motives. This suspicion reflects their own hidden motives.

Negative Capricorns can be intolerant of others, morbid, serious and antisocial. They are stingy to the point of embarrassment. Adrian frequently asked waiters to wrap up leftover food for him to take home — not his own food, but that from the next table!

These people can be worriers who constantly fear loss of control. This is especially so in business. The negative Capricorn prefers to do everything themselves, but if they have to delegate work, they usually check up on the job and change it if they feel it was not done the way they prefer.

Negative Capricorns are often in need of a holiday, a rest and a lighter attitude to life. They feel that life has been unkind to them and, in turn, they are bitter.

As parents, negative Capricorns can be very demanding and intolerant of creative endeavours, preferring practical results and realistic goals.

These people tend to suffer from a poor sense of self-worth and, plagued by self-doubt, they limit themselves. They even limit their dreams and aspirations, often condemning themselves to a life of routine and boredom.

Owing to difficult circumstances, Grant was forced to leave school at 15 years of age and had worked in a machinery shop for almost 27 years. He worked hard and was skilled at his trade, but his dream was to be a car mechanic.

He loved cars and spent every available moment around them. I asked him why he didn't seek training in mechanical engineering and he shook his head.

'I'm too old to go back to school now. Those young kids, fresh out of school, would run rings around me.'

'No, Grant. They'd idolise you for your practical experience and you'd be a father-figure to most of them within a month. Besides, you're only 45. It's not as if your blind, with a stick.'

He didn't hear me. In his mind he was too old, so that was it. Yet, with his thorough approach, I'm convinced that he could have built up a fine reputation in a mechanic's business within a short time of graduating.

Capricorn lesson

The lesson for Capricorn is to *be aware of the alternatives in a given situation*. They also need to remember that self-worth can stem from themselves, not just from their achievements. These people can find it hard to accept nurturing from others, as they feel undeserving or that the nurturing comes at too high a price. Capricorns hate to lose control and they are ever aware of situations which might get out of hand.

Richard, a Capricorn friend, was travelling through Amsterdam alone, and he did not speak any Dutch. Nervously, he ventured into a restaurant and ordered a meal. The bill came to 850 guilders, but Richard read it as 1850 guilders. He had only 1200 guilders in his wallet.

He panicked. Shaking, he explained the situation to the manager and his wife, and asked if he could go back to his hotel to collect more money. They agreed and he returned to pay them. During this 10 minutes he felt as though he aged about 15 years. He had visions of spending a month in gaol: the ultimate loss of control.

The Capricorn lesson involves learning to find alternatives outside of the structure they give their lives, to ensure that they are free to grow and develop in many directions.

Aquarius

Aquarius:	January 21 – February 20
Planetary symbol:	The Water Bearer
Glyph:	♒
Element:	Air
Type:	Fixed
Ruler:	Uranus

Aquarius is a fixed air sign, which means that Aquarians relate to the world through thought and can be inflexible in their approach to life. They have strong beliefs about life that they will steadfastly maintain in the face of opposition from others.

Aquarians are usually friendly and are often original thinkers. They possess inventive, even erratic minds and can be described as truly broad-minded. Computing, science, invention, radio and television all appeal to Aquarians as career paths.

With their flair for invention and problem-solving, Aquarians often choose obscure solutions, as the following example illustrates.

My friends and I were holidaying in Fiji, and after a few hours snorkelling we returned to the hotel. The room was hot and still. The four of us were complaining about the heat and the lack of anything but a slow ceiling fan to cool us when Kyle developed a look of fixed purpose. He strode to the small bar fridge, removed the ice-cube tray and emptied its contents into his bathing costume with only a momentary widening of his eyes to suggest the shock of the temperature change. We fell about laughing but, in typical Aquarian fashion, Kyle seemed puzzled that we should find his solution at all amusing.

When Aquarians first meet someone, they scrutinise them carefully. Not to determine their strengths and weakness (as a Virgoan would), but to examine their ideas and beliefs. Aquarians want to know what others think and believe, and why.

Aquarians are usually intuitive people, although not in the traditional way. In place of sitting still and clearing the mind in order to be open to new information, the Aquarian often leaps to the correct conclusion without knowing how they did so.

This is an interesting sign in that it is a combination of tradition and innovation. They seek new approaches to old problems and often have to contend with their inner traditionalist which resists change.

Although very focused mentally on the subjects which interest them, they have a tendency to be absent-minded, especially about the mundane things in life. Imagine a brilliant scientist who cannot record his or her theory on paper until they find their glasses, which are pushed up onto their head.

They are not usually argumentative, nor do they talk for the sake of it. Conversation to these people is for the exchange of ideas, but they argue about principles and ideals which they hold strongly.

Although gentle by nature, Aquarians can become fierce when there is a change to be made or when their freedom is at stake. When fighting a cause, they argue clearly and convincingly, and will undergo great personal sacrifice for the benefit of the group as a whole. They look to the future, pushing for what could be rather than working to maintain the present circumstances. Routine does not appeal to Aquarians, for they enjoy new frontiers and exploring life's possibilities.

Exploring other countries, cultures and philosophies comes naturally to Aquarians, and they can be impatient with those whom they feel are narrow-minded.

A past student of mine, Rodney, told me about the most embarrassing moment of his life, and it involved the broad-mindedness of an Aquarian. In his late teens, Rodney realised he was gay and he began a relationship with another young man. The day arrived when his boyfriend, who lived with his parents, invited Rodney to stay the night. Early the next morning, his friend's mother burst into the bedroom with a tray of tea and biscuits.

'You must be Rodney,' she said, smiling. 'We have heard so much about you. When you're ready, both of you come down to breakfast so Rodney can meet the family.'

Rodney told me that he wanted the earth to open up and swallow him whole. He was racked with guilt about his sexuality, but it didn't seem to be a problem for his friend's mother. She was happy that her son was happy, and she was more than a little curious to chat to Rodney. In typical Aquarian fashion, her curiosity was greater than her prejudice.

Aquarians love to explore new things and as children they are keen to question the world and accepted beliefs. Aquarian children need to limit the time they spend around electrical toys and video games, as Uranus, Aquarius's ruling planet, also rules body electricity. Overexposure to electrical games can accelerate the Aquarian child's electrical or nervous energy, causing them to become easily exhausted and depleted.

Aquarians sometimes like to shock those around them out of their complacency. Elizabeth (an Aquarian) and Tony shared a house together, and when they went shopping at the fruit markets each Saturday, Elizabeth loved to pretend that they were a couple having an argument. What started out as a slight disagreement over some pears would soon escalate into a ruthless slanging match. Stunned onlookers would gather around, wide-eyed, to see how Tony would respond to Elizabeth's outrageous criticisms.

'You disgusting little man. You repulse me, do you know that?' she'd snarl.

'But, darling . . .' he'd plead nervously.

'Shut up, you snivelling excuse for a man. I hate you! You're short and thin and stupid.

Am I speaking too quickly for you, stupid?'

'That's it. Listen you revolting woman . . .' he'd snap.

'Who are you calling revolting?'

'You, bozo. Since when has six pears equalled a dozen pieces of fruit?'

And on it would go, until one of them burst out laughing at the other.

Relationships

In relationships, Aquarians prefer a good deal of freedom and allow their partners the same. They do not like to be possessed by their partners, nor do they become possessive.

Aquarians usually hesitate before making any deep, lasting commitments, as they need to be absolutely certain that it is for the best. Unlike the Libran, who needs to be in a relationship, the Aquarian doesn't care one way or the other about having a close partner. They are more concerned with humanity as a whole rather than with any one particular person. Partners of Aquarians can sometimes feel that everyone else receives more attention from the Aquarian than they do.

A meeting of minds is what attracts Aquarians to a partner. For those who cling to tradition, an Aquarian partner may not be suitable. They can deliberately set out to shock complacent people through their words and actions.

Aquarians are not usually given to physical displays of affection, especially in public. Being the opposite sign to Leo, they are also opposite in their approach to love. While the Leo makes a big production of the courting period, the Aquarian finds conversation and ideas more appealing than romance. In fact, Aquarians can be distinctly unromantic in love, but they are usually steadfast in their commitment once they have given it.

For those who enjoy plenty of freedom to see friends and pursue their own interests, a relationship with an Aquarian might suit them perfectly.

There is a certain detachment about

Aquarians which some people find puzzling. It is not the aloofness of the Capricorn, which stems from a poor self-worth or an overactive sense of responsibility, but a detachment which results from preoccupied thoughts until something outside them demands their attention.

As ideals and beliefs are paramount to Aquarians, a harmonious long-term relationship is usually viable only with someone who shares their beliefs.

Health

Aquarians need to take care of their ankles, calves and wrists, as they can experience problems with these areas at times. They need to ensure good circulation or they may suffer with varicose veins or cold hands and feet.

Body electricity is also an Aquarian concern, as Uranus (which rules Aquarius) rules electricity. Regular exercise and outdoor activity can assist in the re-balance of the fine electrical or nervous energy of the body.

When in poor health, Aquarians often respond well to psychic healing, homeopathy and radionics.

Negative Aquarius

When negative, Aquarians love change for its own sake. They shock those around them for no particular reason and change the direction of their lives haphazardly, having lost any sense of long-term vision.

Negative Aquarians can be tactless and uninterested in learning how others think or feel. They can become rebellious, seeking to dismantle the old ways of doing things without giving sufficient thought to what could replace the present system.

The negative Aquarian can take the form of the radical without a true purpose. These people feel excluded from the group as they don't conform. Instead, they cause havoc among those for whom routine is a comfortable necessity.

An example is Douglas, who found himself in a routine clerical job that was driving him crazy. Instead of simply finding something more suitable, Douglas decided that it would be better if he was forced out of the job, so that he could justify his anger at how ordinary people couldn't accept him.

He started by arriving late for work and leaving early. He took to wearing the most outrageous clothes he could find, including his sister's clothes.

One day, Douglas arrived at 11.15 am and went to lunch at 12.00 pm for two and a half hours, during which time he drank an assortment of wines and spirits, hoping to be asked to leave the job for drinking heavily. Soon after his arrival back from lunch, his supervisor called Douglas into his office. This was it. He was about to be fired. Instead, his supervisor took a different tack.

'Don't think I can't see what you're doing, Douglas. I happen to know that you took an extra 15 minutes for lunch this afternoon and I fully intend to deduct it from your wages.'

Douglas was truly shocked. He could not believe that these people were so tolerant. At the end of the week, Douglas resigned and the managing director commented kindly that 'it takes all kinds to make a world'. It occurred to Douglas that the narrow-minded one in the situation had been him. He had been intolerant of those who chose to live differently from him.

Negative Aquarians can take the word 'eccentric' to new heights. From the person who shares their two-bedroom flat with 50 cats and 23 pigeons, to my uncle Tod, who arranged to have three-phase power connected to his home because he liked the low hum of a particular industrial electrical transformer. 'It helps me to think,' he'd say.

Negative Aquarians have to be careful around electricity, as they can affect electrical appliances around them when they become angry or overexcited.

Aquarius lesson

The lesson for Aquarians involves *seeing life for what it is,* without the blinkers of tradition, *and sharing this knowledge with humanity.*

In astrology, the opposite sign can give

clues about the sign being examined. The opposite sign to Aquarius is Leo, and the lesson for Leo is to express one's individuality. Aquarius has the opposite lesson — to surrender individuality in favour of group effort and group recognition. It involves recognising that each member of a group has something worthwhile to offer the group and that no single person is worth more than another.

Another aspect of the Aquarius lesson involves recognising when traditional values are useful and when they are unnecessary baggage which impedes development or understanding of life.

Part of this lesson involves having faith. Faith that all of us truly want to reach the destination which awaits us all, and faith that the structure of beliefs and tradition is not actually necessary.

In place of fearing the unknown, Aquarians need to learn to understand it by asking the right questions. Sometimes clinging to tradition is merely an excuse for not facing one's fears of the unknown. The Aquarian lesson involves learning to believe that there are answers to all of life's questions, and that to explore the horizon, they sometimes have to leave the shore.

Pisces

Pisces:	February 21 – March 20
Planetary symbol:	The Fish
Glyph:	♓
Element:	Water
Type:	Mutable
Ruler:	Neptune

The glyph for Pisces represents two fish joined together by a cord. Pisceans, like the two fish that symbolise this sign, can adapt to the currents, especially emotional currents. These traits are strengthened because Pisces is both mutable (adaptable) and a water sign (emotional). Pisceans are usually sensitive to the feelings and the needs of others, often sacrificing their own needs to please other people.

The duality of the Piscean nature is symbolised by the fact that the fish are swimming in different directions. These people can be compassionate and patient when others disappoint them, or they can become cold and ruthless, unable to find sympathy or empathy for the needs of others.

I have seen Pisceans offer compassion and service for years at a time without thanks, sometimes even being abused for their efforts. Such was the case with Gina.

Gina nursed her alcoholic husband for five years after a car accident had left him bedridden. In return for her devotion and service, he made Gina the butt of his anger at the world for his condition. When asked why she didn't simply leave him and live elsewhere, she replied, 'But who would look after him? He'd have no one.'

When it was pointed out to her that, if she left him, her husband's isolation would be the result of his intolerance and abusive behaviour, she simply shrugged.

The above example is of the fish swimming in one direction. Ryan exemplifies the fish swimming in the other direction. As a television producer with a film production house, Ryan was living the Pisces lesson; that of turning dreams into reality. Whatever he could imagine, he could create. However, Ryan pursued his dream at any cost, ignoring what he considered petty setbacks — the people involved.

A co-presenter of one television show was experiencing a bout of depression following the death of her mother. Ryan replaced her but, in his Piscean way, did not tell her. She arrived at the studio one day to be told by the make-up artist that she had been replaced.

Pisceans sometimes avoid confrontation, tolerating difficult situations rather than voicing their frustration or disappointment. Thus things appear to run smoothly on the surface, but the problems still exist underneath.

These people are able to make great personal sacrifices if they feel that it is for the common good. They can be quite selfless, in a manner which can be a source of inspiration to others.

Keenly aware of the beauty in the everyday things in life, Pisceans seem to remind those who are constantly busy that miracles are all around them, waiting to be noticed. An example of this is Rachel.

I arrived late one afternoon to find her seated in the garden, staring at a pale pink flower.

'I've been watching it open and do you know something?' said Rachel.

'What's that?'

'I think it knows that I've noticed it, for it has turned its face to me.'

'If you like it that much, why don't you cut it and put it in a vase?'

'Oh, no. It lives out here. I couldn't take it

away from the others and besides, my heart is already brimming with the joy of its colourful face.'

I sat alongside her, the pair of us staring; transfixed by the heady mixture of pink petals and the bright yellow centre, while the sun set and stole the view from us.

Pisceans are romantic and sentimental people, with a well-developed sensitivity for pain in others. They are patient and tolerant with those who need assistance, even if those people don't know it themselves.

Their innate compassion suits Pisceans for work involving animals, for they see that humans have a responsibility to look after all living creatures. Nursing, healing, alternative medicine and the psychic sciences appeal to Pisceans. Spirituality and the study of the purpose of life interests many Pisceans, so it is not unusual to find them immersed in religious studies or spiritual philosophy.

Being sensitive people, Pisceans need encouragement to succeed and, if encouraged, they can excel in artistic and creative endeavours. When visiting Emily, I noticed the house was filled with beautiful paintings. As I stood gazing, I could see that three of the paintings were representations of tarot cards. Without knowing it, Emily's partner, a Piscean, had begun painting a new set of tarot cards. Much of the traditional symbology existed in each painting and I was astounded at the ability of this man. Emily had been encouraging him to paint for many years and, as Emily is a tarot reader, it may have subtly influenced his imagination.

Music, dance, acting and painting usually appeal to Pisceans, and they are better suited to these things than to routine work. Peter is a typical Piscean. A bank manager by day, he paints with water colours whenever he has the chance.

'I must have painted the old windmill at my cottage a hundred times, but I never get tired of it. At different times of the day and through the seasons, it can look completely different.'

His Taurean wife wanted to turn the windmill into a cafe, with a painting of the windmill on the wall. She thought that she could sell about 30 paintings a year and buy the block of land next door in three years. He simply loved painting.

As Pisceans are sensitive to the people and situations around them, they need to take care they don't become depleted of energy or depressed by their surroundings.

Being good listeners, people often confide in Pisceans. They are not always effective negotiators, however, as their need to keep peace and harmony can make them unassertive at times.

Pisceans can have difficulty pursuing their goals because, like fish, they tend to change direction when least expected. If observing a fish swimming in a tank, it appears to move with purpose. Within a short time it frequently changes direction, always with the same sense of purpose. So it is with Pisceans.

Being a water sign, those born in Pisces usually enjoy a view of water, whether it is a river, lake or the ocean.

Relationships

In relationships, Pisceans are romantic and loyal. They tend to place their partners on a pedestal and ignore their faults. They are devoted to those they love and are usually prepared to sacrifice a great deal to ensure their partners' happiness.

Pisceans need to guard against the 'lost dog syndrome'. That is, they tend to collect partners who are lost and in need of love and compassion, then spend the entire relationship depleting their own reserves of energy to help their partners' improve their lives. In some cases, Pisceans will build up their partners' confidence, only to have their partners' leave them for other relationships.

Health

Pisceans can experience difficulties with their feet, including circulation problems, fluid retention, corns or simply unusually shaped feet, which can make finding the right shoes difficult. The mucous membranes and the glands of the body are also areas Pisceans need to be aware of in order to enjoy good health.

Being psychically sensitive, Pisceans need to ensure a balanced, positive work and home environment as their health can suffer if they are surrounded by negativity.

Negative Pisces

Being a water sign, the negative Piscean can be attracted to liquids which help them escape reality, such as alcohol and certain types of drugs.

Negative Pisceans often live their lives waiting for their 'big dream' to come true. The big dream is a clearly detailed existence that will follow a lottery win or their discovery by a talent scout from Hollywood. This is not to say that those who are successful did not start out with a dream, but to point out that the negative Piscean is usually doing little or nothing towards making their dream come true.

Negative Pisceans can become martyrs, sacrificing their lives for the sake of someone who has already squandered their own dreams. Rodriguez was planning to be a world-famous sculptor, but, after abandoning his sculpting course, spent 10 years in an alcoholic haze while his Piscean partner supported him. Being very sensitive, it is easy for negative Pisceans to sink into depression when opposed in their plans for too long or when brutalised by life.

Virginia loved animals and as a child she had five ducks, a wombat and three geese. Her father, a farmer, believed that animals were for selling and eating, and one day he slaughtered one of her ducks and her mother then served it as Sunday lunch.

Virginia cried for three days and sank slowly into a state of depression. She became a vegetarian from that day forward and lived in terror of the next duck being killed. She sat out in the shed with her flock in the wildest storms, comforting them late into the night. No effort was too much where her animals were concerned.

As a result of her father's actions, Virginia's depression lasted a long time. Her family eventually decided that she was a shy, timid person. The real problem, however, was that she was powerless in the face of brutality and insensitivity. Virginia is proof that the negative types are more often made than born that way.

Piscean lesson

The lesson for Pisceans is to *replace selfishness or self-interest with humanitarian interest*. They need to learn that the common good of humanity is greater than the needs of the self.

Pisceans also need to be aware of the difference between those ideas that can be made a reality and those that are simply fantasy. Part of the Piscean lesson involves living out the dream of what they believe their life can be.

They imagine the life they would truly love to live: every detail, from the reflection of their smiling face in the paint of their new car to the heavy scent of jasmine carried on the gentle breeze up the beach as they stand under the enormous fronds of a palm tree.

Now to the challenging part. The task is to make that dream real. Dream it and then be it. When they have sufficient desire to live the dream, they will find the obstacles in their way mere challenges. The lesson of the Piscean is not to be dissuaded by the obstacles.

Once the lesson of their Sun sign has been mastered, the person is able to demonstrate the sign in its positive light, and radiate the individuality of their sign.

The mature Arian demonstrates self-discipline, without rigidity or suppression; a discipline borne of experience and tempered with patience.

The mature Taurean demonstrates patience and tolerance, especially when confronted with differing opinions and beliefs about life.

The mature Gemini demonstrates the decisive mind; quick to examine alternatives, yet always aware of the importance of feelings when making a decision.

The mature Cancerian demonstrates nurturing without expectation or fear of loss. They show us the value of community and family.

The mature Leo demonstrates courage and strength which comes from deep within. From this strength springs compassion and the ability to encourage others to become all that they are meant to be.

The mature Virgoan demonstrates the discriminating mind, always keen to reduce things to their purest form so that we might know their essence.

The mature Libran demonstrates the value of people, music, beauty and love. Theirs is a life filled with optimism and shared with those they love and appreciate.

The mature Scorpio demonstrates desire: the desire to penetrate to the core of life and reveal the truth. When the essence of life is felt deeply, it involves surrender to a power greater than self.

The mature Sagittarian demonstrates understanding, which comes from travel, study and experience.

The mature Capricorn demonstrates a responsible approach to structure and understands the need for structure in order to gain tangible results for our efforts. It is an understanding that the price of peace of mind is effort.

The mature Aquarian demonstrates the benefits of sharing; sharing what they learn with the whole human family so that all may benefit. They seem to understand the saying 'so long as one of us makes progress, we all shall progress a little, and so long as one of us remains in the darkness, we all shall feel his burden.'

The mature Piscean demonstrates compassion for all those who are behind them on the path to enlightenment, and reminds us of the little things that we can do to help others towards their purpose. They show us that we are more than just a human family; we share the path with all the animals and plants and are responsible for those who can benefit from our knowledge.

The glyphs of the signs and the planets

Sign	Glyph	What it represents	Planet	Glyph	Rulership	
Aries	♈	The Ram's Head	Sun	☉	♌	Leo
Taurus	♉	The Bull's Head	Moon	☽	♋	Cancer
Gemini	♊	The Twins	Mercury	☿	♊ ♍	Gemini Virgo
Cancer	♋	Breasts	Venus	♀	♉ ♎	Taurus Libra
Leo	♌	The Lion's Tail	Mars	♂	♈	Aires
Virgo	♍	Female Sexual Parts	Jupiter	♃	♐	Sagittarius
Libra	♎	A Pair of Scales	Saturn	♄	♑	Capricorn
Scorpio	♏	Male Genitals	Uranus	♅	♒	Aquarius
Sagittarius	♐	The Centaur's Arrow	Neptune	♆	♓	Pisces
Capricorn	♑	The Goat's Horn	Pluto	♇ ♇*	♏	Scorpio
Aquarius	♒	Waves of Water	*The alternative glyph for Pluto is sometimes used			
Pisces	♓	Two Fish				

THE HOUSES

A natal (or birth) chart is a chart of the planetary positions at birth, and it is divided into 12 parts called *houses*. Each house represents a different aspect of the person involved. As the year progresses, the sun passes through each house in the chart. By knowing the significance of each house, you can ascertain the most beneficial time to start a new project, a new relationship or a new career; or when to seek new friendships or to expect rewards for career efforts.

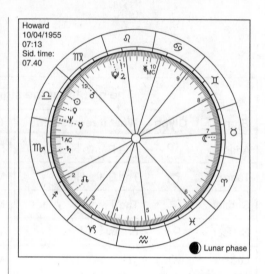

Howard
10/04/1955
07:13
Sid. time:
07.40

Lunar phase

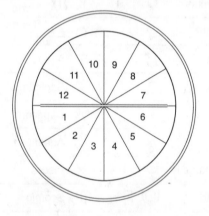

Fig 10

The system of chart interpretation used in this book is the *Placidus system*, named after its inventor Placidus De Tito, a 17th-century astrologer and mathematician. The Placidus system uses an *unequal* house division system, as shown in Howard's chart and in the charts on pages 186, 192 and 193. For illustrative purposes, however, the rest of the diagrams in this book use an *equal* house system.

The unequal house system allows for some houses to be larger than others, for one sign to be on the cusp (the beginning of the house), and for another sign to occupy most of the house, as shown in the fifth house in Howard's chart. When this occurs, the sign on the cusp is usually more significant when examining the house affairs as the cusp is the doorway to the house.

Most astrologers offer the wheel (a chart without interpretation) for an affordable fee when supplied with the date, time and location of birth, as computers have sped up the chart-making process.

Details on how to draw up or delineate a chart manually are not included in this book. If you plan to read charts, or even if you want to see where planets were at a certain time without having to work out a chart, you will need to consult an ephemeris.

An ephemeris is basically a map of all the planetary positions over a number of years. Smaller versions include from one up to 10 years, but most astrologers prefer the full version, which contains planetary positions for 101 years. The following example shows how you can use an ephemeris.

Clare called in for a cup of tea when I was writing one afternoon. She said she was just passing, but I could sense that she had a question. It turned out that she'd met a man she was attracted to and she wanted to know whether they would be compatible. Using only his date of birth, I consulted the ephemeris. William was born on May 11, 1963 and the ephemeris reads:

Sun	Moon	Mercury	Venus
19.35 Ta	14.41 Sg	29.57 Ta	20.17 Ar

Mars	Jupiter	Saturn	Uranus
19.12 Leo	8.22 Ar	22.40 Aq	1.9 Vi

Nept	Pluto	North node
14.9 ScR	9.34 ViR	23.48 Cn

By examining the ephemeris, I could tell Clare that William is a Taurus (Sun 19.35 Ta) with a Sagittarius Moon (Moon 14.41 Sg). I could then tell her where all the planets were when William was born, without the need for his time or location of birth.

A natal chart, such as Howard's (opposite), requires the date, time and location of birth. If you don't have these details, you can still draw up a simple chart, called a *solar chart*. Solar charts are detailed on page 58.

Knowledge of the houses gives you an understanding of when to plants seeds for what you want and when to prepare to harvest the mature plants or goals. The Sun is currently in my tenth house and this is the house of career achievement. By coincidence, I noticed that this date last year and the year before I was signing publishing contracts for books. I noticed the date because I was signing another contract today and had to check the wording of an earlier contract. The sun is in my house of harvest and the contract to publish a book is a part of that harvest.

Intercepted houses are those which contain a sign between two cusps but not touching or crossing either cusp. An example of this is shown in Howard's chart in the sixth house, where the sign of Aries does not cross any cusp. It also occurs in Howard's twelfth house where the sign of Libra does not cross any cusp. Planets found in a sign contained within an intercepted house have more influence than they normally would in a chart. The sign contained within a house is more difficult to access as it has no cusp or 'doorway'.

The *Ascendant* is the cusp or doorway to the first house, and it is very significant in a chart. It details the outer personality of the individual; for example, if someone has a Taurean Ascendant, they may present many of the Taurean qualities in their outer persona. The degree of the Ascendant is important (e.g. 10 degree Taurus), because other planets with the same degree could make a significant aspect. See 'Planetary aspects' on page 165.

The first house

The first house starts with the Ascendant and this makes it an important house. This house shows you how the person projects themselves to others. Their personality and physical characteristics are determined by the first house.

If a planet is found in the first house within 8 degrees of the Ascendant, it affects the personality and physical characteristics, and often the patterns of behaviour. For example, a Gemini Ascendant with the planet Mars 4 degrees from the Ascendant indicates a person with both Gemini and Martian qualities to their personality and appearance. When meeting someone for the first time you are likely to observe their Ascendant characteristics or outer persona.

The second house

This house deals with the things the person values, both within themselves and outside themselves. Attitude towards possessions is shown by the sign ruling the cusp of the second house and the planets contained in the second house.

Financial and emotional security are shown by the second house, and you can determine whether one is more important than the other according to the sign ruling the house and the planets.

The third house

The third house offers insight into how the person relates to siblings and close relatives, but not parents. Early education, including schooling and short trips, is covered here as well.

Self-expression, communication and mental attitude to life are also shown by this house. Speech and writing (short articles or letters) are third house concerns, and if the person experienced difficulties with schooling, check this house for complications. Curiosity about life is also shown in the third house.

The fourth house

The fourth house deals with domestic life and the home, and reveals how the person feels about their parents, especially their mother. This house can indicate whether the person had a stable home life growing up or whether they moved about a great deal. As an adult, the fourth house can show what they want in a home.

An example of this is Peter, whose fourth house cusp is Cancer. Peter loves the privacy of his cluttered little terrace house, which resembles a jumble sale about to be opened to the public. All of the furnishings are from the 1920s and 1930s, yet Peter was born in the 1960s.

The fifth house

The fifth house offers insights into the person's creativity and those things they seek out for pleasure. It also rules short-term love affairs and financial risks, including stocks and investments. Planets such as Jupiter or Mars in the fifth house increase the likelihood of the person taking financial risks.

The father is another aspect of the fifth house, along with how the person relates to children. Leo is the natural ruler of the fifth house, and the Leo lesson of expressing the inner-self through creative endeavours applies to this house.

The sixth house

The sixth house deals with health, diet and attitudes to health. Work is also shown here but not career, which is shown in the tenth house.

Virgo is the natural ruler of the sixth house, being the sixth sign of the zodiac. Exercise and attention to physical wellbeing are shown in this house, along with the person's attitude to being organised in life.

The sign which rules the sixth house cusp can detail the person's attitude to co-workers and their ability to get along with colleagues.

The seventh house

The seventh house deals with partnerships and deep love relationships. Along with love relationships, any close working or one-to-one relationships are governed by the sign ruling the seventh house cusp.

This house illuminates what the person most needs from a partner or from others in general, as the Descendant or seventh house cusp shows the type of people drawn to this person. This house can also indicate what the person looks for in a partner and their attitude to love relationships in general.

In business partnerships where trust is necessary and the relationship develops over a significant period of time, the seventh house can detail how the person relates to others in the partnership. If the person is thinking of entering a partnership, comparison of the intended partners' charts or a *synastry* reading can be of benefit in deciding whether those involved are suitable partners and what complications they can expect when relating to one another.

The eighth house

The eighth house includes sexual desires and partner's finances or things which the partner values. The natural ruler of this house is Scorpio and the Scorpio qualities of delving into oneself or into life and death are shown here.

Investments, insurance and responsibilities regarding the investments of others (including emotional investments) are also included in the eighth house.

Attitudes to sexuality and to sexual desires are shown here, and an example of the eighth house shaping sexual desires is Shane. His eighth house is ruled by Capricorn, and Shane exhibits the typical Capricorn need for structure plus a lack of confidence in his sexuality. He is aloof with his partner and she complains that he always tries to control their finances without negotiating with her first.

The ninth house

The ninth house rules higher education (school education is ruled by the third house). Long-distance travel, ideals and philosophy are also shown here.

An example of ninth house ruling philosophy is Marylin, whose ninth house is ruled by Taurus, suggesting that she feels the need to fit in with accepted beliefs. When she came to me for a reading, she confessed that, as a devout Christian, she was feeling guilty about coming for a reading in the first place.

The need to extend one's mind and to explore ideas, other places and other approaches to life is described by the sign which rules the ninth house cusp.

Publishing and literature are also ninth house matters. While the third house deals with short stories and magazine articles, the ninth house deals with books and with media, including media in other countries.

The ninth house can be used as a guide to suitable higher education and the person's ability to apply themselves to study. It can also indicate whether the person is likely to live overseas for a period of time and it deals with long-distance or overseas communication.

The tenth house

The tenth house represents ambitions and the need to find a place in the world.

In most house systems, the Midheaven represents the beginning of the tenth house. Authority is shown here, both in the way the person responds to authority and how they handle positions of authority. Social status, duty and responsibility are shown by the tenth house.

Career achievements, changes and obstacles are also shown in this house. With power comes responsibility, and the tenth house details how well the person balances power with responsibility.

The eleventh house

The eleventh house represents friends, social life and good causes. The sign ruling the eleventh house cusp details what attitudes the person has towards the world at large, particularly about people from other cultures or those who have differing beliefs about life.

This house describes the person's attitude to societies and groups of people; whether they are happy to belong to groups or whether they prefer to operate alone in life. Whereas the fifth house details personal creativity and how they relate to children, the eleventh house reveals how they deal with humanity at large.

The twelfth house

The twelfth house represents faith; institutions such as hospitals and prisons; and seclusion, either self-imposed or imposed by others. Whereas the sixth house deals with physical health problems, the twelfth house highlights psychological problems.

The qualities of a planet found in the twelfth house tend to remain hidden in the person's nature, and they need to reflect in order to release these qualities.

Sacrifice and atonement are twelfth house

influences, and the person's attitude towards selflessness is shown by the sign ruling this house. Sometimes planets found in this house can show the unresolved issues of a past life.

This is illustrated in Karen's chart, which showed Venus in the twelfth house. Aside from love issues and the challenge of deciding what she valued in life, Venus in her twelfth house represented a female sibling. Karen has one sister who had, as she described it, 'stabbed me in the back a few times in my life'. The sister concerned was represented by Venus and their issues probably extend beyond this lifetime to times long past.

THE SOLAR CHART

The solar chart is one of the simplest charts to draw and interpret. Its most important feature is that it is especially useful when you do not have the person's actual time of birth. Although this method of interpreting charts is not as accurate as a natal chart, it is still surprisingly effective when looking for an overall picture.

To erect a solar chart, you need a *wheel* (see page 196 for sample wheels) and an *ephemeris* (as described on page 12). Next, look up the date of birth and place the Sun in the first house (see figure below). The first house always appears beneath the point of nine o'clock on a clock face. If you don't have time to draw in each planet and explain their significance, simply concentrate on the Sun, the Moon and Saturn. These three give you all the basics.

The Sun represents the light, the Moon reflects the Sun, and Saturn represents the darkness or shadow. The placement of the Sun tells you what lesson the person has come to learn, the Moon placement details the emotional approach the person prefers as a result of their past experiences and memories, and Saturn depicts the obstacles they may encounter as they set out to learn their lesson.

Below is a solar chart for January 4, 1938 showing the Sun, Moon and Saturn.

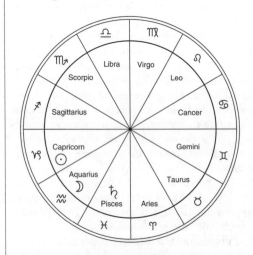

Solar chart for January 4, 1938

THE MOON

The Moon takes almost 28 days (27.3 days to be precise) to complete one cycle. In astrological terms, the placement of the Moon in a chart details how the person deals with life on an emotional level. As the Moon spends only two and a half days in each sign, people born a few days apart can approach life differently as a result of their differing Moon placements.

The Moon in a chart details the mother's influence on the person, as the Moon rules Cancer and the Cancerian lesson involves nurturing.

There are two important points to note about the Moon placement:

1. the sign in which the Moon is placed; and
2. the house in which the Moon is placed.

The Moon in signs

Moon in Aries

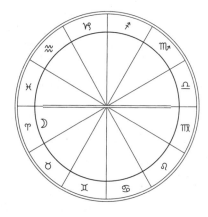

Those with the Moon in Aries tend to be forthright and sometimes emotionally aggressive. They are likely to have grown up with a mother who experienced difficulty showing affection or revealing her soft, nurturing side.

Aries Moon people like to pursue their potential relationship partners and can become dominant in the home. An example of this is Anna.

In the workplace, Anna is quiet and unassuming, but behind closed doors at home she rules with an iron fist. Those outside the family rarely believe her children when they complain that she is too strict.

Aries Moon people are usually self-confident, rebound from emotional hurts quickly and can find it difficult staying in one relationship for any length of time.

Moon in Taurus

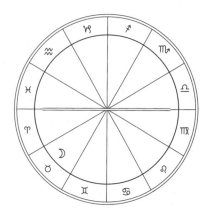

The Moon is exalted in Taurus (see page 74), so this is a good placement for the Moon in a chart.

Taurus Moon people prefer to be in a stable, comfortable relationships, with plenty of material comforts and good food.

Comfort eating is sometimes associated with these people, as they tend to reach for food when things don't look good emotionally. A preference for sweet foods is shown with this placement, along with well-developed patience.

Music is often important to them too, and singers, musicians and those working in the music industry often have this Moon placement. On the negative side, they sometimes find that they place a greater emphasis on possessions than on their love relationships.

Taurus Moon people can be possessive of their partners and their families, and need to guard against stubbornness. They can derive great enjoyment from keeping a garden in later life, as it keeps them connected to the earth. Taurus Moon people are often patient and reliable when raising pets and, like Taureans, they treat their pets like part of the family.

Moon in Gemini

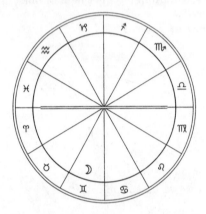

Those with the Moon in Gemini like to discuss their feelings with their partners. They find it easy to invent stories, so short-story writing or magazine journalism can interest them. They need to guard against making up stories when there is no need to exaggerate events. An example of this tendency to exaggerate was shown recently with my son, who has his Moon in Gemini.

During an afternoon party, Max, one of the guests, strolled outside to rest awhile on the lawn. He lay down, closed his eyes and drifted off to sleep. Meanwhile, my son was at the other end of the lawn, playing under the water sprinkler.

Soon my son became bored and decided to shower Max with water. He slowly inched the sprinkler to within range and increased the water pressure. In seconds, Max was drenched. When I reprimanded my son, his excuse was immediate.

'But Daddy, a huge bee was about to sting him and I had to save him.'

To this, the neighbour's four-year-old (a Gemini) added, 'Yes, and a mosquito was about to suck out all of his blood so we scared it away'.

Just as Gemini's love to talk, so it is with those who have a Gemini Moon. A friend with a Gemini Moon and Sun told me recently that her partner has forbidden her to talk during love-making, as she distracts him. Puzzled, I asked her what she actually talked about during the act. 'Oh, anything really,' came the reply.

Those with a Gemini Moon often feel closer to their friends or partners when talking to them on the phone rather than face to face. This placement suggests that the mother was an outgoing person or that she approached her emotions through her mind rather than through feelings.

Gemini Moon people can blow hot and cold emotionally. They can be close to you one day and ignore you the next. Colin was like this and Victoria soon learned to ask 'Who have I got today?' when he seemed to be distant after a period of closeness.

Gemini Moon people can find it difficult to make emotional decisions, as they prefer to ignore their feelings and deal with the alternatives rationally. Preferring not to choose between two alternatives, Gemini Moon people can end up with two relationships, two careers or two of whatever they desire.

When negative, they can be unreliable, promising to do one thing and then changing their minds when a new opportunity presents itself.

Moon in Cancer

This is the Moon's natural placement as the Moon rules Cancer. Cancer Moon people are sensitive, sentimental, nurturing and some-times moody.

The men have a soft side, though it may be well hidden if they are uncomfortable with their emotions. These people can be hoarders, saving things for the day that they might be needed again.

Naturally suited to working in groups, administration and large organisations appeal to those with the Moon in Cancer.

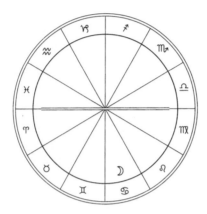

Although sensitive and emotional, these people can be surprisingly forthright when it suits them, and they can present a strong self-image. They have vivid imaginations and are often quite psychic, with vivid dreams at night which can prove prophetic.

It is likely that Cancer Moon people received ample nurturing from their mothers or mother-figures in their early years; if not, the lack of this is keenly felt. Memories of childhood tend to stay with Cancer Moon people. They need to guard against living in the past emotionally, for this drains their creative energy — energy which is better utilised in artistic ventures or creative writing.

Naturally secretive, Cancer Moon people show but a part of themselves at any time, only occasionally revealing their true emotions. They can be like the Moon itself, sometimes reflecting only a little of the Sun's light, at other times fully illuminated.

Being sensitive to the emotional mood of a room, these people react in an instant, revealing their true selves or closing down emotionally.

Unlike the Gemini Moon aloofness which stems from a change of mind, Cancer Moon

aloofness is usually a result of being hurt. These people are sensitive and require careful treatment in order to flourish emotionally.

Moon in Leo

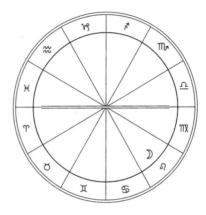

Those with the Moon in Leo are playful, romantic, passionate and of a positive nature. They love a grand romance and enjoy the pursuit of a partner. They are keen to keep the romance and spontaneity alive in their relationships and can go to great lengths to ensure that they are loved and admired by their partner. If seeking a flamboyant relationship, someone with the Moon in Leo is eminently suitable.

Leo Moon people are young at heart and enjoy fancy-dress parties or formal occasions where they can dress up.

At work, these people are usually emotionally buoyant and quick to express themselves with flair and originality. When negative, however, they can be competitive and demanding of attention, like a small child.

This Moon placement suggests a mother or mother-figure who was or wanted to be on the stage. Theatrical leanings or a mother who had an important role upon life's stage are symbolised by a Leo Moon.

Moon in Virgo

Those with the Moon in Virgo prefer a low-key approach to their emotions, as they need to know how they will be received before

the faults and imperfections in others. Their mothers or mother-figures may have been critical of them, leaving them with a poor sense of self-worth.

Moon in Libra

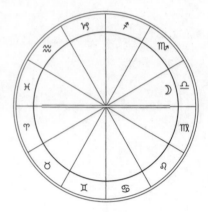

they begin, in case they make fools of themselves.

They usually prefer plain foods and health foods appeal to them. Vitamin and mineral supplements as well as regular exercise are likely to be on their agenda.

Natural observers, they have the ability to learn from the mistakes of others and thus avoid pain and suffering.

Virgo Moon people are suited to any task or career which makes use of their discriminating nature, such as editing, quality testing, design layout or administration. They are usually hardworking, thorough and like to see a job done well the first time.

In love, Virgo Moon people demonstrate their feelings through actions rather than words. Those preferring a partner who is reckless and spontaneous may find the Virgo Moon person a little stolid, as those with a Virgo Moon probably had a mother or mother-figure who was aloof emotionally and not given to flashy displays of feelings. This leaves those with a Virgo Moon preferring a low-key approach in matters of love.

They also tend to be low-key in expressing their feelings and can become distinctly uncomfortable when others fuss over them. Surprise parties are not usually well received by these people.

When negative, they can be critical of themselves and those close to them, demanding perfection and being quick to see

Those with the Moon in Libra enjoy beautiful surroundings, harmonious colours and people who share their love of food and socialising. The Virgo Moon preference for plain foods and routine doesn't suit these people, as they thrive on new conversations, people and situations. They have a keen sense of justice and fair play, and readily fight for the rights of those who are close to them.

Libra Moon people are suited to careers where they can invest their energies in fighting to improve the lives of others, such as the law, social work and community work, or they might prefer a career where they can help others enjoy themselves, such as hospitality, jewellery design or working in an art gallery.

Choosing the right partner is not an easy process for those with the Moon in Libra. They readily make personal sacrifices to ensure the fulfilment of their loved ones and an incompatible partner leaves them miserable, as they make sacrifices without achieving the harmony and happiness they seek.

Libra Moon people usually enjoy the continuous company of their partner and they take pleasure in providing those personal touches that make a house a home.

When negative, these people need to be constantly reassured that they are beautiful and loved, for their sense of self-worth can be realised only through someone else. If others don't value these people, they can find it difficult to value themselves.

Moon in Scorpio

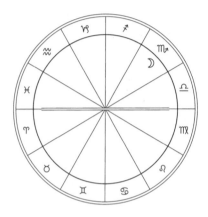

This is a difficult placement, as Scorpio is a fixed water sign, and water is not suited to be fixed in nature. Water flows, evaporates and falls, but rarely does it sit still for too long without stagnating. One way to keep water fixed is to freeze it, and those with a Scorpio Moon can be emotionally frozen because of unreleased emotional pain. When the heart is warmed and the ice melts, the emotions flow once again. After the tears, these people are more open to understanding and emotional healing.

Scorpio Moon people often have very long memories where emotions are concerned. If they have been hurt emotionally in the past, it is probably remembered in great detail. They are likely to have experienced power struggles with their mothers, and these are probably being played out in their adult life with the women around them.

I have observed that these people have difficulty forgiving and forgetting. Anita is a typical case. At 63 years of age she talks about her ex-husband as though he left her yesterday, even though it has been 22 years since she last saw him. Every detail, every frustration, however slight, was detailed with an astounding accuracy, and she simply refuses to forgive the man and reclaim her life.

Those with a Scorpio Moon can usually penetrate to the core of a matter and unravel its hidden content. They are suited to spiritual work where they can uncover the mysteries of life. They usually have an interest in past lives, death, spirituality, secrets and the subconscious mind.

When Scorpio Moon people discover their true strength, they are able to rise above past emotional hurts and accept them as a part of the learning necessary for their spiritual development. They have an innate desire to learn about philosophy or psychology in order to better understand themselves and others. Until they allow their learning to penetrate their heart and not simply remain an intellectual exercise, they can experience recurring emotional obstacles, often in the form of power struggles.

Moon in Sagittarius

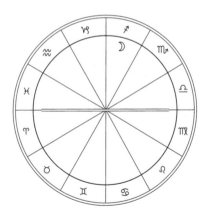

Those with the Moon in Sagittarius can find commitment difficult. Neither emotional nor physical commitment comes easily to these people, yet this Moon placement can force them into situations or careers where they are responsible for the possessions or investments of others.

Sagittarius Moon people usually enjoy plenty of freedom and the thrill of the pursuit where relationships are concerned. They have an innate ability to pinpoint the flaws in their partners and in people around them, but they are often less observant with themselves.

Travel appeals to those with a Sagittarius Moon, as do study and learning, and this learning can take place while travelling or in foreign countries.

These people need to keep an eye on their intake of sweet foods, as they may gain weight around the hips and thighs in their later years. Regular walking can remedy this and offers temporary relief from restlessness.

Those with a Sagittarius Moon may have a mother or mother-figure who was emotionally restless and who encouraged them to achieve, especially through competitive sports. The mother or mother figure probably placed great emphasis upon education and was ambitious for their child.

Their thirst for knowledge can leave these people with little enthusiasm once they have mastered something, and this is also the case in relationships. Once they have learned all that they feel they can from a relationship, they tend to feel restless. This restlessness can be channelled into other areas of their life or into pursuing another relationship.

When negative, those with a Sagittarius Moon may find that they are unable to commit themselves to any one person for very long, preferring their freedom instead. An example of this is Naomi, whose Sagittarius Moon became glaringly obvious as she complained that she couldn't find a man with a deep sense of commitment.

Naomi said she was was keen to settle down, yet at the same time she was saving up for a trip to Europe, where she planned to spend at least two years. When I asked her whether she would consider taking a partner with her if she began a new relationship before she left, she laughed: 'Who wants a man when they're travelling? He'd only slow me down.' When I asked what she might do if she met a suitable man overseas, she replied that if he was truly perfect, she'd tell him to wait for her.

I guess to those with a Sagittarius Moon, the perfect partner is the one who will wait for them while they travel the world.

Moon in Capricorn

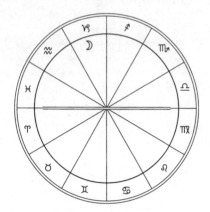

Capricorn is opposite Cancer, the natural home of the Moon, so this placement can be a difficult one.

Those with the Moon in Capricorn often have a mother or mother-figure who was aloof and undemonstrative. She might have been absent as a result of divorce or death, or hard at work when they were growing up, or simply too busy with other responsibilities to nurture them emotionally. It can also describe a mother or mother-figure who was a strict disciplinarian and who worried about her reputation. As a result, they may find that they doubt themselves and deny themselves the emotional nurturing they deserve and need to have. They may consider that they have to earn emotional rewards.

Capricorn Moon people are likely to worry about what others think and feel about them, and they may feel unable to break free of traditional values instilled into them during childhood.

A desire for emotional control in relationships occurs with the Moon in

Capricorn, often leaving these people unable to let themselves go in the presence of another person. Even when they have been in a relationship for some time, they may find it difficult to be emotionally vulnerable before their partner. They tend to choose partners younger than themselves or partners whom they feel they can control.

Capricorn likes structure and those with the Moon in Capricorn like emotional structure. As emotions need to flow to be expressed, structuring and controlling emotions can lead to rigidity. These people desire control over their partners' emotions, fearing that an emotionally unpredictable partner might undermine their own emotional structure. Power struggles often occur in their love relationships because they are emotionally controlling. It's not that they don't feel compassion for their loved ones, it is simply that they lack confidence in their ability to fulfil their partners emotionally.

Capricorn Moon people have a well-developed sense of duty and responsibility. Their early life is often emotionally unrewarding, but in their later years, as their need for structure lessens, they can experience the childhood they never had.

Moon in Aquarius

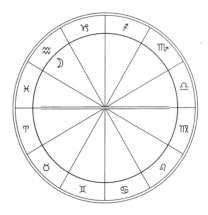

Those with the Moon in Aquarius can display an attraction for long-distance relationships. Keeping in touch with a partner by phone, letter or e-mail is not difficult for these people, as they require plenty of freedom and don't take kindly to being possessed.

An attraction to unusual partners or to those who are devoting their life to a cause or a particular philosophy appeals to the Aquarius Moon person, as does having a partner who comes from a different culture or another part of the world.

The exchange of ideas is important to these people and they enjoy a good conversation. Talking for the sake of it rarely interests them.

As Aquarius is a fixed sign, these people can be quite stubborn, while the air sign qualities of Aquarius mean they often have the need to understand or analyse their emotions and the motivations of others.

Aquarius Moon people may have had an unusual mother or mother-figure. She may have been someone who preferred people outside the family to those within it. She may have experienced frustration at having the responsibility that family life brings with it. This can result in Aquarian Moon types feeling trapped by family life and long-term emotional commitments.

These people tend to be broad-minded and somewhat quirky in nature. Their words and actions can sometimes shock others or leave them puzzled from time to time.

Moon in Pisces

Those with the Moon in Pisces can be idealistic in friendships and relationships. They dream of a perfect world, and yet they can pursue one direction one day and another the next.

It is important to remember that Pisces is represented by two fish, swimming in different directions.

Pisces Moon people often have lives which involve dealing with the opposing emotional forces within. When others gain their trust, they are allowed to glimpse the child within, which may be quite different to the outer persona. This Moon placement increases the romantic tendencies, yet these people can be practical where creative

projects are concerned.

A Pisces Moon often indicates someone with a dream, usually secret, which they plan to fulfil one day.

These people are capable of great sacrifice for those around them and of long-term service to others. This service to others may not be as practical as that offered by those with the Moon in Virgo, but it is done with quiet compassion.

They can pursue music, art or other creative outlets such as dancing, as they manage to find more energy, enthusiasm and discipline for those things beyond the practical in their lives.

Pisces Moon people may need to guard against being emotionally or psychically drained by those around them, as their compassion allows others to take advantage of them from time to time.

When out of balance, the sea restores them, along with music and nature. They often have a great patience and compassion for animals and are fond of working with animals.

The Moon in the houses

Another important factor to consider when examining a natal chart is to note in which house the Moon is placed, as a Pisces Moon in the third house, for example, does not mean quite the same thing as a Pisces Moon in the sixth house.

Those with the Moon in the first house share some of the qualities of Aries, as Aries is the first sign of the zodiac.

These people can be forthright, restless and impulsive. Keenly sensitive to their environment, they may find that they are dominated by their feelings from time to time. Their mothers or mother-figures have shaped their emotional attitudes to life in the early years and to grow beyond those beliefs, they need to question their emotional attitudes carefully, using their minds rather than their hearts to judge what is a balanced point of view.

Moon in the second house

Those with the Moon in the second house share some of the qualities of Taurus, the second sign of the zodiac. These people are likely to be possessive of their partners and of material things. They can be careful in emotional commitments, as they regard their efforts as an investment in their future emotional happiness.

Moon in the third house

Those with the Moon in the third house share some of the qualities of Gemini, the third sign of the zodiac.

Communicating with others is of great importance to these people. Their curiosity makes them keen to study and they enjoy hearing about the lives of others. Routine does not appeal to these people and short projects suit them in the work environment. The Moon in the third house increases the amount of energy they devote to thinking and also it increases their changeability.

Moon in the fourth house

Those with the Moon in the fourth house share some of the qualities of Cancer, the fourth sign of the zodiac.

Their home is important to these people, and it provides a retreat from life when things become overwhelming. They usually have an innate desire for inner peace and security, and their home represents these things to them. They tend to collect memorabilia, especially those things which remind them of past friends and partners or family.

These people are often intuitive and their dreams at night offer them insight into their lives and themselves, as they have a strong link with their subconscious mind through their dreams.

Moon in the fifth house

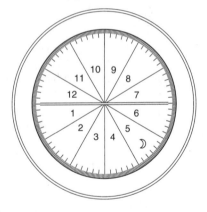

Those with the Moon in the fifth house share some of the qualities of Leo, the fifth sign in the zodiac.

These people are often creative and enjoy the company of others. They sometimes show a tendency to want to be the centre of attention in social gatherings and their playfulness draws others to them socially. They can be romantic and are not afraid to express their feelings when in love. Children appeal to them, as they often retain the enthusiasm of youth.

Moon in the sixth house

Those with the Moon in the sixth house share some of the qualities of Virgo, the sixth sign in the zodiac.

These people are often practical where emotional matters are concerned, preferring a low-key approach to expressing themselves. Continual worry causes problems with their digestive systems, and simple foods are necessary from time to time to relieve the pressure on their digestive systems.

Those with the Moon in the sixth house are often hardworking and unafraid to throw themselves into a task. They have an innate ability to observe others and to know them clearly by their actions rather than their words. Being of service to others gives these people a sense of wellbeing.

Moon in the seventh house

Those with the Moon in the seventh house share some of the qualities of Libra, the seventh sign in the zodiac.

These people have a need for peace and harmony around them, and will go to great lengths to ensure that others are happy. Desire for relationships and partnerships is very strong, and they put a great deal of effort into making these work. They are adaptable to circumstances which involve people who are stubborn or unyielding.

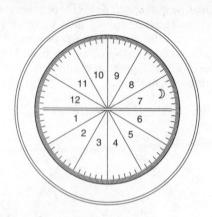

Moon in the eighth house

Those with the Moon in the eighth house share some of the Scorpio qualities, as Scorpio is the eighth sign in the zodiac.

These people are often quite intuitive and can penetrate the surface of a person or a situation to reveal what is beneath it. They stand to benefit from an increase in wealth through marriage, or are likely to be in charge of their partner's material possessions. They may choose a career that involves making decisions around what others consider to be of value, such as assisting people with their investments, either material or emotional.

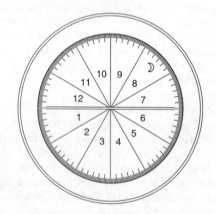

Moon in the ninth house

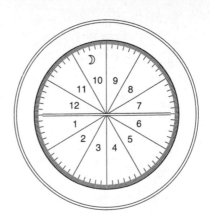

Those with the Moon in the ninth house share some of the qualities of Sagittarius, the ninth sign in the zodiac.

These people can be restless, constantly in search of new opportunities and a deeper understanding of life. They need to guard against learning all they can about their partner and then wanting to move on to another relationship, as this can prevent them from reaching the depths possible within any particular relationship.

They enjoy the outdoors and exercise gives them opportunity to think things through when they have a problem or a decision to make. These people enjoy learning and teaching, and always expand their understanding of life by pushing themselves to do the things they want to do. 'To be all that you can be, you must dream of being more' is the philosophy of those with their Moon in the ninth house.

Philosophy may appeal to these people, even if only from the viewpoint of gathering more information.

Moon in the tenth house

Those with the Moon in the tenth house share some of the qualities of Capricorn, the tenth sign in the zodiac.

These people are likely to be ambitious and to have strong personalities, which they can use to influence those around them, especially when they want others to support them in their endeavours. They are suited to public careers, such as politics, and they need to guard against judging their self-worth by what they achieve rather than who they are.

Moon in the eleventh house

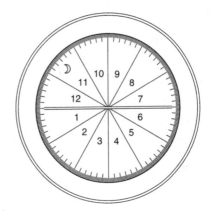

Those with the Moon in the eleventh house share some of the qualities of Aquarius, the eleventh sign in the zodiac.

Friends are important to these people, and their friends are often from different backgrounds and cultures. They are open to new ideas and new ways of approaching life, making them popular and easy to get along with. They find it easy to work towards group goals and to make sacrifices for the common good. As a result, they are suited to being spokespeople for groups.

Moon in the twelfth house

Those with Moon in the twelfth house share some of the qualities of Pisces, the twelfth sign in the zodiac.

These people may need to be aware of the purpose of service and of suffering. Through being of service to others they are able to alleviate some of the suffering which they encounter in their lives. Their natural idealism leaves them suffering when others disappoint them, but they need to try not to let this lead to them hiding their dreams away from others or from themselves.

They have great reserves of strength and compassion for those around them, and they need to be able to replenish themselves spiritually from time to time, through meditation or prayer.

THE PHASES OF THE MOON

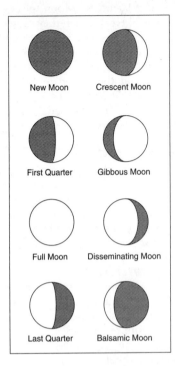

New Moon

Crescent Moon

First Quarter

Gibbous Moon

Full Moon

Disseminating Moon

Last Quarter

Balsamic Moon

Moon phase affect a new project, business or relationship.

To determine what phase the Moon was in on a subject's date of birth, locate the date in the ephemeris and note the Moon sign for that day. If they were born on December 7, 1967, for example, when referring to the ephemeris you will find the following:

Sun	14.10 Sg
Moon	23.57 Aq

In simple terms, this means that the Sun was in Sagittarius and the Moon was in Aquarius when your subject was born.

In a solar chart their Sun and Moon placement would look like the diagram below.

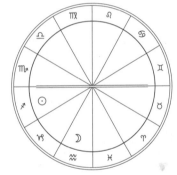

Solar chart for December 7, 1967

When the Moon passes from the New Moon to the Full Moon and back, it affects our moods and emotions. The phase of the Moon at the time we were born is an important factor in our approach to life.

As the Moon waxes (i.e. moves from the New Moon to the Full Moon), there is generally an increasing urge to act upon desires. This can manifest as the urge to start something new, to make a purchase or to initiate a relationship or friendship.

As the Moon wanes (i.e. recedes from the Full Moon to the Balsamic and, finally, the New Moon), the natural inclination is to finish those things commenced in the waxing phase.

In simple terms, the first half of the Moon's cycle deals with personal goals and the second half deals with goals which benefit others. In the same way that the phase of the Moon when we were born affects our approach to life, so too will the

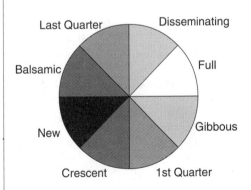

The Moon Phase Wheel

To determine what phase the Moon is in from a natal chart is simple. When the Moon is in the same sign as the Sun, it is a New Moon. When it is in the opposite sign to the Sun, it is a Full Moon. From this you can determine that if the Sun is in Virgo and the Moon is in Scorpio, it is likely that the Moon is a Crescent Moon, because Scorpio is two signs after Virgo so the Moon is between a New Moon and a First Quarter Moon.

New Moon
Those born in the New Moon are likely to be brimming with ideas and enthusiastic about new ventures. Although these ideas are sometimes self-centred, others often assist these people in the fulfilment of their plans. They may prefer ideas to organisation, however, and can lack the pace and discipline necessary to fulfil their plans.

Crescent Moon
Following the New Moon is the Crescent Moon. Those born during this Moon phase are usually self-starters with plenty of new ideas and plans, and they like to include others in their plans.

First Quarter Moon
Those born in the First Quarter Moon are enthusiastic about their ideas and plans, and involve others in these plans. They have a broader outlook than those born in the New Moon phase, allowing for the fact that others might have a different approach.

Gibbous Moon
The last phase before the Full Moon, the Gibbous Moon denotes someone who enjoys public life. These people are less self-centred about their plans, and can easily include and organise others to help fulfil them. They use their charm or charisma to enlist the support of those around them and are capable of seeing what others may gain from helping them.

Full Moon
As the Full Moon reflects more of the Sun's light than any other Moon phase, these people are likely to feel they deserve the attention of others and will seek attention through their personal magnetism.

They are sometimes torn between their own needs and the needs of those around them, as the Full Moon lies at the halfway point between personal goals and goals which benefit others.

Disseminating Moon
Those born in the Disseminating Moon display less desire for the attention of others than the preceding Moon phases, especially those born in a Full Moon. Disseminating Moon people can see the benefits of working with others.

Third Quarter Moon
As the Moon appears to wane or recede in its cycle, so too does the light it reflects and the energy it radiates. Those born in the Third Quarter are more conscious of others when making plans and find it easier to follow the directives of others than the earlier Moon phase types.

Balsamic Moon
Those born during the Balsamic phase experience long periods of reflection throughout life, or periods where little seems to drive them forward.

This phase gives an awareness of the bigger picture and these people are able to sacrifice their personal desires in favour of group desires or goals. If they don't do this willingly, life repeatedly tests them, to make them realise the good they can offer others when they release their personal goals.

Balsamic Moon people often benefit those who follow them. This may be in the form of leaving for others something that will further their understanding of life or develop their creativity.

Part 3

The Planets

The planets are celestial bodies that orbit the Sun. The word 'orbit' comes from ancient Greek and means 'to wander'. Each planet takes a different length of time to orbit the Sun according to its distance from the Sun. The orbit of each planet is set by its distance from the Sun, the size and mass of the planet and the Sun's gravitational field.

The inner planets are those between the Earth and the Sun. These are Mercury and Venus. The outer planets are those which orbit the Sun at a greater distance than the Earth. These are Mars, Jupiter, Saturn, Uranus, Neptune and Pluto.

Due to their shorter orbit, the inner planets complete a cycle more rapidly than the outer planets. The times taken to complete one orbit of the Sun are listed below.

Mercury	88 days
Venus	225 days
Mars	687 days
Jupiter	12 years
Saturn	29.5 years
Uranus	84 years
Neptune	165 years
Pluto	248 years

The Moon orbits the Earth at one complete orbit every 28 days.

When a planet is retrograde in a chart, this means that it appears to be travelling backwards compared with the Earth. In truth, retrograde planets are travelling in a different orbit from the Earth's orbit and can give the appearance of travelling backwards when they are travelling more slowly than the Earth in its orbit of 365¼ days, or one year per orbit of the Sun.

When a planet is retrograde in a chart, its influence is lessened. For example, a retrograde Mercury would lessen the mercurial quickness and encourage the person to think before speaking or to reflect upon what they have heard or seen before reacting.

The Sun and Moon are never retrograde, but all the planets are retrograde from time to time. For example, Mercury is retrograde up to four times per year for around 23 days each time.

Jupiter has a 12-year cycle, meaning that every 12 years Jupiter returns to the same position as your birth chart, Saturn returns every 29.5 years, and so on. For more information on the effects of each returning planet, see 'Many Happy Returns' on page 146.

Planetary influence

Each planet exerts an influence wherever it is found in a chart, but this influence varies according to the planet and the sign in which it is found.

As each planet has a sign over which it rules, its influence in that sign is both strong and usually unimpeded. In certain signs a planet is exalted, in detriment or in fall, and to interpret the chart opposite, below is a description of terms.

Rulership: Each planet rules one or more signs, and when found in such a sign, the planet exerts a strong and unimpeded influence.

Exaltation: When a planet is exalted in a sign it exerts its greatest influence in that sign.

Fall: When a planet is in its fall it is opposite the sign of its exaltation and its influence is diminished.

Detriment: When a planet is in its detriment it is opposite the sign which it rules. Its influence is diminished due to the opposing forces of its nature and the nature of the sign in which it is found.

The basic rule is that a planet is always strongest when in its own sign, and next strongest when it it is exalted. Its influence is weakened when in detriment or fall.

STRENGTHS OF THE PLANETS

Sign	Ruler	Planet exalted in this sign	Planet's fall	Detriment
♈ Aries	♂	☉	♄	♀
♉ Taurus	♀	☽	♅	♇
♊ Gemini	☿	—	—	♃
♋ Cancer	☽	♃	♂	♄
♌ Leo	☉	♆	—	♅
♍ Virgo	☿	☿ and ♇	♀	♆
♎ Libra	♀	♄	☉	♂
♏ Scorpio	♇	♅	☽	—
♐ Sagittarius	♃	—	—	☿
♑ Capricorn	♄	♂	♃	☽
♒ Aquarius	♅	—	♆	☉
♓ Pisces	♆	♀	☿	♇

MERCURY

The planet Mercury is about the same size as the Moon and it completes its cycle every 88 days.

Mercury rules the signs Gemini and Virgo, and the third and sixth houses are its natural positions. In Gemini, Mercury increases eloquence and enhances the ability to translate thoughts into words rapidly. In Virgo, Mercury steadies the hands so that they might perform great work, such as playing the piano or performing surgery.

In mythology, Mercury was the messenger of the gods, whose winged sandals and helmet assured him great speed. In astrology, Mercury represents communication, adaptability, the reasoning powers of the mind and analysis.

The negative qualities of Mercury include indecision, scepticism, criticism and restlessness of mind. Mercury rules the mind, communication and, to some degree, writing. The Egyptian equivalent of Mercury was Thoth, who was scribe to the gods, carefully recording all that they deemed worth relating to man.

Mercury in the signs

Mercury in Aries

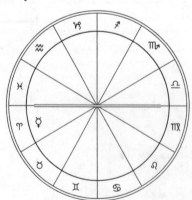

Those with Mercury in Aries tend to be quick-minded, impatient and eager to share their ideas with others. They need to be aware of the power of their words, as they can be verbally abrasive from time to time. They can motivate others with their enthusiastic approach and need to ensure that they have time to complete a project before they commit to it.

Mercury in Taurus

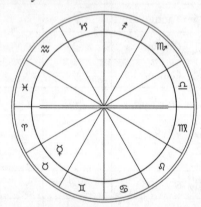

Those with Mercury in Taurus are usually careful in their choice of words and they prefer to have more time than most to consider the various possibilities before making a commitment to something. They learn better through direct experience than through theories and study.

Mercury in Gemini

Those with Mercury in Gemini usually possess quick minds and can switch from one concept to another easily. When deciding between alternatives, they rapidly seek out all the possible outcomes of any given scenario. However, they can lack the tenacity to see their choices through to their conclusions.

Their quick-mindedness lends itself to humour and also to impatience with slower minds. These people need to guard against

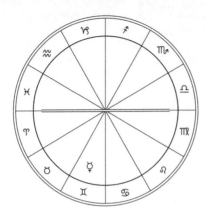

taking on too much at one time, for this placement can find them more committed in words than in action.

Mercury in Cancer

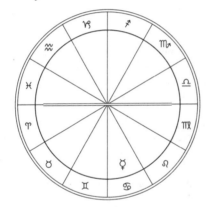

Mercury in Cancer tends to improve the memory, especially for sentimental details and for childhood events.

Storytelling and public speaking comes naturally to these people, especially if the topic arouses the emotions of their listeners. They are able to adapt easily to the opinions and ideas of others in a subtle and tactful manner.

These people often experience periods of confusion between thoughts and feelings as they attempt to make sense of why they feel the way they do about themselves and about life.

Mercury in Leo

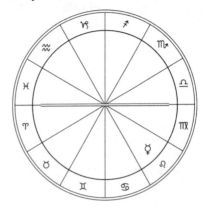

Those with Mercury in Leo are convincing communicators, whether as actors or simply in their day-to-day lives. Naturally creative in both verbal and written expression, they can become so enthusiastic about what they are saying or writing that they have difficulty knowing when to stop.

People with this placement are natural organisers and usually possess strong and ambitious minds, but they can be quick-tempered. They enjoy the company of children, as they are childlike themselves, and are usually creative. They need to guard against gambling, as Mercury is quick to decide and Leo is fond of taking risks.

Mercury in Virgo

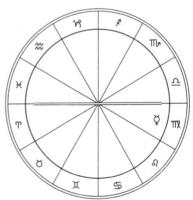

Mercury is exalted in Virgo, which means it is at its peak of positive influence when in this sign.

Those with Mercury in Virgo usually possess clear, logical minds and are scientific and practical in their approach to things. They are good judges of character and often possess a discriminating outlook.

A keen interest in diet and natural living is shown here, and they need to be aware of becoming puritanical or over-discriminatory in their diet and exercise routine. An interest in science, chemistry anatomy and physiology are likely with Mercury in Virgo.

Mercury in Libra

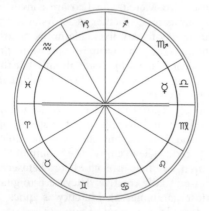

Those with Mercury in Libra usually enjoy a well-balanced mind and a gift for public speaking or singing.

These people are persuasive and capable of turning an argument in their favour quickly and smoothly. However, they can sometimes become confused, identifying with both sides in an argument and agreeing with each point of view. This placement can sometimes indicate an inability to make decisions easily.

Mercury in Scorpio

Those with Mercury in Scorpio are perceptive and tend to arrive at the answer to a problem through an intuitive process rather than by following logical steps. They are attracted to the psychic sciences, research

and hidden truths which require mental determination.

Mercury in Scorpio gives a sharp tongue which lends itself to sarcasm. This, combined with the ability to know intuitively a person's weak points, means these people know what to say to achieve the greatest effect.

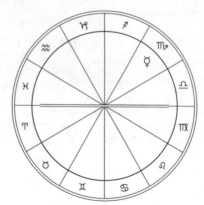

People with this placement can be adept at locating problems with mechanical things, owing to their combination of intuition and the ability to focus their attention for long periods of time. An example of this placement is Derek, whose career involves emergency mechanical repairs on refrigerated trucks, with time-sensitive cargo demanding urgent attention.

With a background in engineering and a reputation which finds him very much in demand, he is regularly rushed out to stranded semi-trailers to locate and repair the mechanical problems. He often locates the problem within minutes, unlike the other mechanics who may have to spend several hours trying to locate a fault.

Mercury in Sagittarius

Mercury in Sagittarius indicates a quick mind with an interest in philosophy or religion and in other cultures. Travel to explore other cultures is common with those who have this placement.

To be able to complete those things they start, these people need to learn to

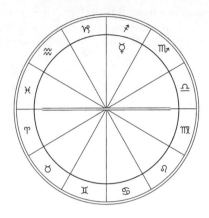

an air of authority that comes from careful study of the subject they are dealing with. These people usually resist conversation for the sake of it, as they prefer to use words sparingly and only for a useful purpose.

Scientific, methodical and tenacious mentally, they move slowly and diligently towards their desired goals. This makes them suitable for detective work, science, chemistry and mathematics.

Mercury in Aquarius

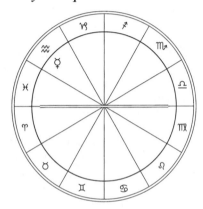

concentrate, for they have a tendency to start new things continuously, regardless of what is still in progress. They also need to develop tact, as they often speak their minds without first thinking of how their words will be received.

Teaching comes naturally to people with this placement, as they are able to find a simple way to express complicated subjects.

Mercury in Capricorn

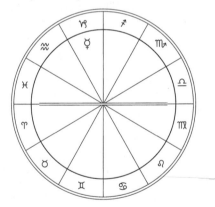

Those with Mercury in Capricorn are usually careful planners, able to plot long-term courses, especially with regard to their careers. They have methodical minds and are slow to assimilate new information, but they retain what they learn for a long time.

As speakers or writers they tend to lend a sober quality to their words and they possess

Those with Mercury in Aquarius are quick-minded and sometimes eccentric in their thinking. They can arrive at the correct conclusion without following the expected path of thought. They tend to exhibit a bizarre or quirky sense of humour and they stick to their beliefs and ideas despite opposition from others.

Although idealistic, they are practical in their application of their ideals and stubbornly refuse to compromise their beliefs. They usually have a wide variety of friends and acquaintances who share their intellectual approach to life.

Mercury in Pisces

Those with Mercury in Pisces have vivid imaginations and strong intuitions. Their writing is gentle, perhaps poetic, and they are inclined towards music as a career.

Being very sensitive to others, they are tactful in their handling of those around

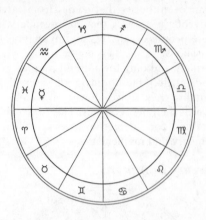

them, and this suits them to working with nurturing those who are unwell.

When faced with obstacles, these people tend to seek an escape through books, movies or music, and they can use these mediums to express themselves. Although gentle in word and manner, they can be subtly persuasive, guiding others towards their desired goal.

Mercury in the houses

Mercury in the first house

Those with Mercury in the first house are usually eager to start new projects, although they are not always able to complete what they begin. They can be highly strung and restless of temperament.

Eager to say what they think, these people can find it difficult to listen to others, especially when Mercury is retrograde. Mercury is retrograde about four times a year for around 23 days each time, and this is often a period of confusion with regard to communication. Letters are delayed, phone calls are not returned promptly and so on.

Mercury in the second house

Those with Mercury in the second house enjoy a balanced, well-ordered environment. Like those with Mercury in Taurus, their surroundings are important to them and they put a great deal of effort into ensuring their surroundings are comfortable.

These people enjoy music and often possess good singing voices. They usually have sound financial skills.

Mercury in the third house
As Gemini rules the third house, this placement is somewhat similar to Mercury in Gemini. It increases communication abilities, although it can also increase the critical nature of some people, especially when retrograde.

Those with Mercury in the third house have the ability to write magazine articles or short stories; in particular, children's stories. They find it difficult to read or write longer works, and when reading longer works they tend to juggle two or three at one time as they have restless minds.

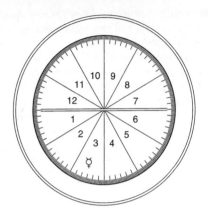

This is a good placement for teachers and these people are keen to study many different subjects throughout their lives.

Mercury in the fourth house

Those with Mercury in the fourth house often have strong communication with their mothers or mother-figures. This usually indicates a talkative or Mercurial mother.

These people also have an interest in early childhood teaching, antenatal classes or working in birthing centres.

An example of this placement is Vivienne, who decided to teach antenatal classes after having her own children. She is dedicated to her work and to the positive influence mothers can have over their children in the first few months of life.

Like Mercury in Cancer, these people can be quite communicative in the home, even though they may not appear that way outside the home. This is a good placement for those who teach at home or use their home as a base for communication.

Mercury in the fifth house

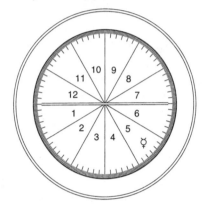

Mercury in the fifth house enhances creative communication. People with this placement find that they can communicate their ideas and inspirations easily. They can inspire others and, as teachers, enjoy encouraging their students on to greater levels of achievement.

Like those with Mercury in Leo, people with Mercury in the fifth house have a tendency to become involved in love affairs that are brief but romantic.

These people usually encourage the creative qualities in their children. When retrograde, however, they tend to stifle their children's creative expression or ignore their children altogether.

Mercury in the sixth house

As Virgo rules the sixth house and Mercury rules Virgo, this is a good placement for Mercury.

Those with Mercury in the sixth house often show a well-developed interest in health and physical wellbeing. They are suited to work where they can be of service to others by communicating the benefits of a balanced diet and regular exercise; for

example, natural or alternative therapies, osteopathy and naturopathy.

These people are usually good with their hands and work with a sense of precision which stems from a need for perfection. This placement can also indicate a tendency to depletion of the nervous system.

When retrograde, Mercury in the sixth house can detail a preoccupation with health and wellbeing, bordering on hypochondria. These people can become obsessed with their own health, demanding the constant service and attention of others. They can also be insensitive to the needs of those around them.

Mercury in the seventh house

Those with Mercury in the seventh house usually have a good rapport with their relationship partners. They prefer quick-minded partners and enjoy engaging in light-hearted banter.

These people are well suited to work that involves promoting other people, especially if the person they are promoting is their relationship partner. They are able to negotiate effectively in situations where two people or parties are in conflict or have differing needs, as Mercury in the seventh house enables them to see both sides of an argument.

Mercury in the eighth house

Those with Mercury in the eighth house have an innate ability for research. Journalism appeals to them, as do various types of investigative research.

They are able to discover other people's secrets with relative ease, but need to curb this tendency with their partners. Although they may excuse it as wanting to know the needs of their partners, partners of those with this placement can find it invasive.

Mercury in the ninth house

Those with Mercury in the ninth house enjoy learning. Travel is often for learning purposes with these people, and they make friends wherever they go. The appeal of other cultures and languages helps them to learn the ways of life and languages of the places they visit.

They make skilled and talented teachers,

Mercury in the eleventh house

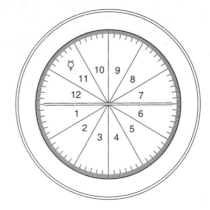

as they have the ability to simplify complex issues without diminishing the content or essence of the subject.

Mercury in the tenth house

Those with Mercury in the tenth house usually have good presentation skills when delivering talks or representing an organisation as a part of their job. Like those with Mercury in Capricorn, they are rational and often pragmatic. Their communication abilities mean they are suited to a wide variety of careers.

This placement also improves their hands-on skills and these people are comfortable both with mechanical things and intellectual concepts.

Those with Mercury in the eleventh house enjoy having friends from a variety of backgrounds and cultures. They relish a good discussion, even when they are opposed in argument.

Like those with Mercury in Aquarius, they make excellent spokespeople for organisations, as they enjoy mixing with people from all walks of life and from different cultural backgrounds. Quick-minded, they are able to solve problems by approaching them from an obscure viewpoint.

Mercury in the twelfth house

Those with Mercury in the twelfth house are usually able to read others quickly and easily. Their analysis is a combination of logic and intuition. Like those with Mercury in Pisces, they have vivid imaginations and can inspire others through the written or spoken word.

Able to keep their own counsel, these people are drawn to those who need support or help. This suits them to work in psychology, nursing, counselling or as a clairvoyant. They tend to be slow to push themselves forwards owing to self-doubt.

VENUS
♀

The planet Venus completes its cycle every 225 days. Venus rules the signs Taurus and Libra, and the second and seventh houses are its natural positions.

Venus represents harmony, affection, love, beauty and teamwork or cooperation. Its position in a chart details that which a person values in life — in themselves, in others and in material things.

In mythology, Venus was the goddess of love, beauty and harmony. The harmony Venus represents applies to voice, colour, tone and personality. The placement of Venus in a natal chart indicates the areas in which the person needs to develop an awareness of others and of what others are able to offer.

Venus in the signs

Venus in Aries

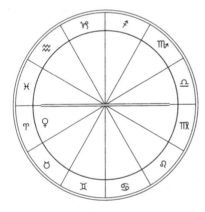

Those with Venus in Aries tend to be impulsive in love. They enjoy pursuing their intended partners with all the passion that Arians can muster. They have a tendency to be somewhat selfish, however, and they can be impatient when it comes to their partners' feelings and needs.

These people often have an affinity with wood, whether it be working with wood or simply appreciating different timbers.

Venus in Taurus

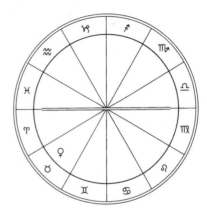

As Venus rules Taurus, this is a positive placement. It increases the Venusian qualities of appreciation of food, music and beauty.

Those with Venus in Taurus value material possessions. In love, they are affectionate and sensual, loyal and patient. They enjoy their physical comforts and can be stubborn when it comes to change. These people enjoy food and tend to overindulge from time to time.

Nature appeals to these people, as does music, and they often have pleasant singing voices.

Venus in Gemini

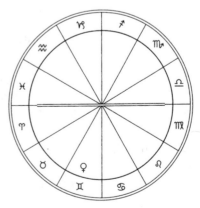

Those with Venus in Gemini are quick to express themselves, yet gentle in their choice of words. They are natural writers, speakers and entertainers.

These people tend to fall in love with someone for their mind, and connect with their partners through conversation, unlike those with Venus in Taurus who prefer to connect through touch. People with Venus in Gemini tend to spend more time talking to their friends on the telephone rather than meeting with them face to face.

Venus in Cancer

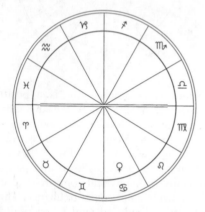

Those with Venus in Cancer tend to be gentle and nurturing, and intuitively know when others are in need of support. They enjoy nurturing their friends and partners, but can become moody and frustrated when others are not as sensitive to their needs in return.

People with this placement are suited to nurturing children or those in need of tenderness and a little doting attention. They enjoy reading and watching movies, as they often possess strong imaginations and can be quite sentimental. They tend to collect anything which they deem to have sentimental value, such as photographs and memorabilia.

Venus in Leo

Those with Venus in Leo are romantics in the grand tradition. Loyal and affectionate, they need to guard against being more in love

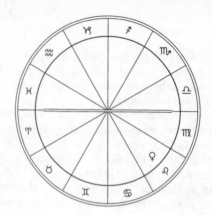

with the idea of love than with their partners.

People with this placement maintain a childlike creativity throughout their lives and they enjoy the company of children. They are naturally expressive, suiting them to a career in acting or entertainment. They can be extravagant where beautiful things are concerned. 'I simply couldn't resist it' is a phrase often used by those with Venus in Leo. They can be vain on occasion.

Venus in Virgo

Those with Venus in Virgo prefer a low-key approach to their emotions. They detest a scene or a fuss being made of them and tend to be critical of those they love. They may describe it as wanting to improve their loved ones, but it is easily interpreted as withholding love due to perceived imperfections.

In their homes they are usually neat and tidy, preferring clean lines and simple, subdued colours. They are usually attracted to partners who appear healthy, natural and down-to-earth. Finding the right time and the most appropriate expression of their love is very important to these people, but often for them there is no right time, leaving their feelings unexpressed.

Venus in Libra

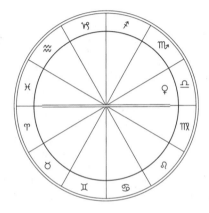

As Venus rules Libra, this is a beneficial placement as it increases the Venusian appreciation of beauty, of friends, and of harmony in clothing, colours and music. These people often present themselves in a harmonious fashion, making them appealing to others.

Their need to be in a relationship at all times is strong, so life as a single person is very difficult for them to endure. They tend to have a mental picture of their ideal partner and, when in a relationship, can gently push their partner towards the ideal they have in mind.

Disharmony in their environment can be very stressful for these people, leading to health problems such as digestive disorders. When their environment is harmonious, they blossom and thrive.

Venus in Scorpio

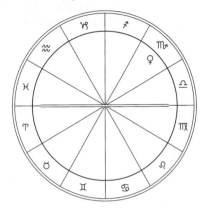

Those with Venus in Scorpio tend to have magnetic personalities, and they can be jealous and possessive. The Scorpio intensity means these people are attracted to love affairs and liaisons that are charged with passion and surrounded by secrecy.

With emotional maturity comes the ability to temper their sexual desires with self-control, or even channel their sexual energy into creative projects. Theirs is a passion which craves expression, and physical expression is often preferred to the written word.

Venus in Sagittarius

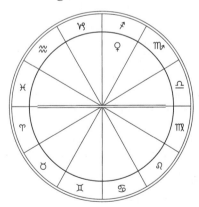

Those with Venus in Sagittarius are usually optimistic about life and love, and they have a tendency to idealise love. They are not usually suited to domestic life, preferring to travel or to pursue a career. They are attracted to partners from whom they can learn.

People with this placement need to guard against becoming overweight in their later years, because they continue to eat as much as they did when they were younger, but without taking the same amount of exercise.

Venus in Capricorn

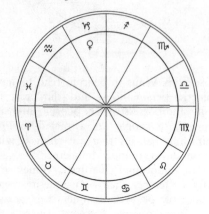

Those with Venus in Capricorn are cautious in love, slow to commit themselves, yet steadfast once they have given their commitment. They can be aloof emotionally and may have difficulty expressing the depth of their feelings for those they love. They feel that love must be earned, and until they overcome their feelings of inadequacy, they can keep those close to them at a distance.

These people are patient and have a well-developed sense of responsibility for their loved ones. They prefer to express their feelings of affection through actions rather than words. These actions can include working hard to provide those they love with a comfortable home and financial security.

Venus in Aquarius

Those with Venus in Aquarius can seem to be somewhat detached emotionally. They can feel more at home with a group of people than spending time solely with their partners.

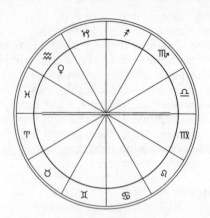

Freedom is of paramount importance for people with this placement. They resist being possessed in relationships and prefer partners who are also their friends. Friendships are more valuable to them at times than relationships.

Friends or partners from different cultural backgrounds appeal to those with Venus in Aquarius, and it is rare to find all their friends gathered in one place at one time. These people usually have a wide variety of friends who do not normally mix in the same circles.

Venus in Pisces

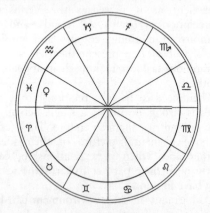

Those with Venus in Pisces are usually gentle, compassionate people who are often attracted to lost, troubled or problematic partners. Their innate compassion and sensitivity draws them to people that society does not accept or understand. They often have well-developed psychic abilities, especially where their friends or partners are concerned. They are prepared to undergo great personal suffering and deprivation for their partners. An example of this is Claire, who financially and emotionally supported her husband Russell, an alcoholic, for nearly 20 years. Despite persistent attempts by her children to get her to leave him and start her life afresh, Claire stayed with Russell until his death.

Venus in the houses

Venus in the first house

Those with Venus in the first house tend to be friendly and outgoing, exuding the Venusian attractiveness and generosity. Others find these people attractive and easy to get along with, and are willing to help them achieve their goals.

People with this placement usually appreciate beautiful things, but may need to guard against selfishness when Venus is negatively aspected.

Venus in the second house

Those with Venus in the second house usually have a weakness for material possessions. They have difficulty resisting beautiful clothes, jewellery and expensive restaurants, and tend to indulge their need

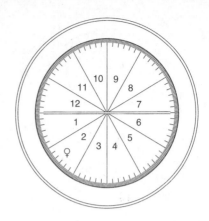

for pleasure. They need to develop an awareness that money and material things may not always be forthcoming, as they tend to live for today and not plan for tomorrow.

This is a positive placement for a melodic singing voice.

Venus in the third house

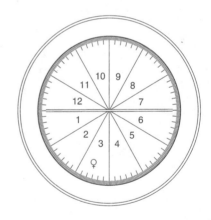

Those with Venus in the third house tend to be cheerful and optimistic. They express themselves in a clear and positive manner, and they usually have an untroubled relationship with brothers, sisters, neighbours and colleagues at work.

Venus in the fourth house

Those with Venus in the fourth house love to surround themselves with beautiful, creative and artistic things, and their homes usually

radiate a feeling of warmth and harmony, particularly as they grow older. They love their families and put a great deal of effort into ensuring harmony in their family life.

Venus in the fifth house

With the fifth house ruling short-term love affairs and Venus ruling love, this combination can emphasise the tendency towards many short-term affairs or, at the very least, make people with this placement very attractive to the opposite sex.

These people often have beautiful and creative children, and usually make sound decisions regarding financial investments.

As teachers, these people are able to express themselves in a creative and harmonious manner which makes the subject more appealing to the student.

Those with Venus in the sixth house are usually well-liked at work by fellow employees and by management. If they are managers, they are usually tactful in their handling of subordinates.

These people recognise that work and the work environment needs to be enjoyable and harmonious for optimum results to be achieved, and they often put extra effort into ensuring that their surroundings are harmonious. An example of this is Virginia, who worked as a receptionist at a healing centre where I rented rooms some years ago. Virginia always arrived with a large bunch of flowers which she arranged in vases in each practitioner's room. It was a cheerful gesture which lifted the energy of the centre and those working within it. In a way, Virginia was healing the healers.

Venus in the seventh house

This is a good placement for Venus, as Venus rules Libra, the seventh sign of the zodiac and the natural ruler of the seventh house.

Those with Venus in the seventh house enjoy harmony in long-term love relationships. They sometimes benefit materially and emotionally through marriage. These people are usually well-liked or or even favoured by the public. It is a beneficial position for singers, actors and artists.

admitted into care with senile dementia. Although Marjorie had five brothers and sisters, the burden fell to her.

Venus in the ninth house

Venus in the eighth house

Venus in the eighth house increases the sexual desires and can bring conflict between the Venusian love of harmony and the Scorpio (the eighth house ruler) sexual desires. This placement can give rise to sexual and emotional power struggles in love relationships.

People with this placement often find themselves responsible for their partners' finances or for the material possessions of others. This can include the settling of finances after the death of someone close to them or being responsible for someone who no longer has all their mental faculties. An example of this is Marjorie, who found herself in charge of her mother's house and financial affairs when her mother was

Those with Venus in the ninth house are usually sympathetic and kind, with a desire to learn things which may benefit others. They seek harmony in the application of philosophy, which makes them suitable for positions where they can act as an intermediary between people of different cultures or religions.

Travel is often a natural part of their lives or careers, and these people often benefit from travel or from moving away from their place of birth. Benefits can include new relationships or job offers. Venus in the ninth house smooths the path for these people when they travel, creating harmonious circumstances and opportunities.

Venus in the tenth house

Those with Venus in the tenth house enjoy financially comfortable circumstances, often as a consequence of a successful career. This placement grants these people a smooth and harmonious path upwards in their careers and in the eyes of the world.

These people are often public favourites. With their harmonious voices and appearance, they are well-suited to being the public face of a product or an organisation.

Venus in the eleventh house

Those with Venus in the eleventh house are likely to be assisted in the pursuit of their dreams and plans by their friends. They put others at ease with their acceptance of the differences in people and their non-judgmental natures.

When Venus is negatively aspected, these people may find that their friends can impose upon them and then cast them aside when they have served their purpose.

Those with Venus in the twelfth house choose to avoid life in the public eye, preferring their own company instead. They are often drawn to working in hospitals, prisons or to a life of seclusion in a monastery or convent.

The twelfth house tendency to keep things hidden can lead these people into love affairs which last a long time but are kept secret. An example of this was Gordon, who died suddenly of a heart attack in his late fifties.

As a company director, Gordon travelled overseas and interstate regularly, but these trips were not all they appeared to be, as his funeral proved. The arrival of Carol, a long-term lover from interstate, and Arena, another lover from overseas, shocked and confused his family, who had no idea that he was involved with these women.

MARS
♂

The planet Mars completes its cycle every 687 days. Mars rules the sign of Aries and its natural position is the first house.

In mythology, Mars (or Ares) was the god of war. This planet represents courage, action, aggression, desire and impulsiveness.

Mars prompts action and encourages people to rise to a challenge, or to push through obstacles rather than negotiate solutions. For Mars, there must be a clear winner and loser in any given situation.

Mars in the signs

Mars in Aries

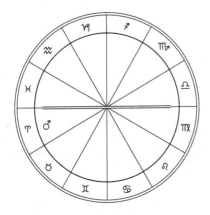

Those with Mars in Aries usually possess excess physical energy and they don't tire easily. They are enthusiastic and prefer to look forward to goals than to resolve past issues. They can lack patience and prefer acting on impulse to carefully planning things in advance. These people tend to be headstrong and can find it difficult to sympathise with others.

Mars in Taurus

Those with Mars in Taurus have enthusiasm and energy, but it is tempered with Taurean stability, enabling them to finish what they start. This placement encourages them to

work within a deadline on projects. These people can be possessive and are not afraid to work hard for material things. They need to guard against valuing people in terms of their material possessions.

Mars in Gemini

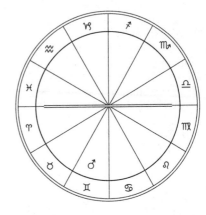

Those with Mars in Gemini are usually sharp-minded and, when out of temper, they can be quite scathing and sarcastic. The Martian energy and impatience combined with the Gemini quickness of mind make them formidable opponents in an argument.

Mentally restless, these people often try to tackle too many things at once. They need to be more aware of how they intend completing a project before they commence it. They make excellent debaters, but they need to be more aware of the power of words. They can run on nervous energy and deplete their nervous systems from time to time.

Mars in Cancer

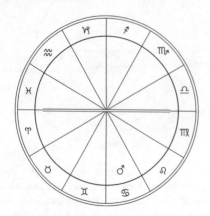

The Mars aggression can be internalised when Mars is in Cancer, causing self-criticism and nervous tension affecting the stomach. These people are moody: soft and nurturing one minute, aggressive and independent the next.

This placement adds enthusiasm to imagination and encourages these people to act on their dreams to make them real. They often defend their homes and families vigorously if they perceive a threat from others.

Mars in Leo

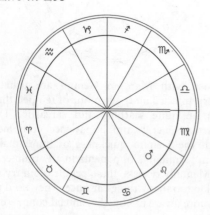

Those with Mars in Leo are enthusiastic, creative and competitive. They can be possessive of the limelight, refusing to share the attention with others.

If their creative energy is channelled effectively, these people can be talented artists or craftspeople, but they need to guard against constantly competing with others, or being driven to success through addiction to work.

Mars in Virgo

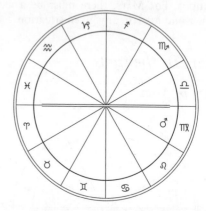

Those with Mars in Virgo are hardworking and energetic, but they tend to take responsibility very seriously and worry about the outcome of projects and situations. They usually complete the projects they start.

Excess worry and spicy foods tend to disagree with their digestive systems, so plain foods are recommended, along with some quiet time every day.

Mars in Libra

Those with Mars in Libra can be a combination of tact and force, leading others where they want them to go in a gentle and subtle manner.

These people are alternately industrious and lazy, as the Mars energy dissipates quickly when in the Venusian sign of Libra. This placement can make this type the peacemaker one day and the warmonger the next, so they must take care to

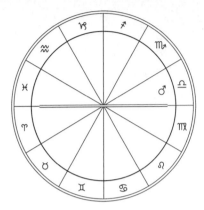

notice the consequences of their words and actions.

Mars in Scorpio

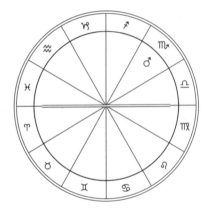

Those with Mars in Scorpio are strong-willed, focused and sometimes stubborn in the pursuit of their goals. They have a tendency to brood over past hurts and need to learn to control their tempers, as they can lash out when angry.

Sexual desires propel them to act without thought of consequences until they learn self-discipline. Desire is often a big part of their day-to-day lives and they usually have a magnetic personality which triggers the desire within others.

Mars in Sagittarius

Those with Mars in Sagittarius usually enjoy plenty of freedom and lots of challenges.

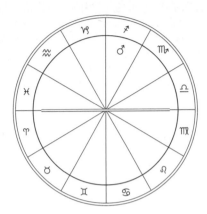

They are optimistic, enthusiastic and argumentative, with an abundance of physical energy to be expended.

Walking is of great benefit to these people, as they find that they are better able to solve problems when they are outdoors walking. Sports and outdoor activities appeal to them and they thrive on goals and challenges. This placement increases the Sagittarian tendency towards clumsiness, so these people need to be extra vigilant physically and verbally.

Mars in Capricorn

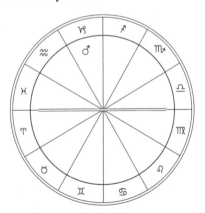

Those with Mars in Capricorn are realistic, hardworking and ambitious. They prefer to learn through direct experience and are loath to accept directives from those around them. There is a tendency for their tempers to flare up when things don't go their way.

As small children, these people are independent and responsible; as parents, they expect their young children to be self-reliant very early in life.

Extended periods of stress can lead to skin allergies or irritations. Time spent outdoors in a garden can relieve stress for those with this placement.

Mars in Aquarius

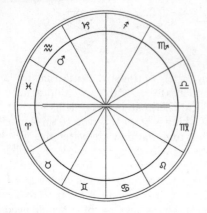

Those with Mars in Aquarius tend to have sharp minds and can argue clearly and vigorously. However, they are more likely to fight for a cause than for themselves. This placement reduces the Mars competitiveness through the natural Aquarian sense of fair play.

These people are often prepared to seek other cultures through travel and they experience a restlessness and a need to relocate from time to time.

Mars in Pisces

Those with Mars in Pisces start out with the best intentions, but they can lose sight of their goals along the way. They are better starters than finishers, so partnerships in business or creative endeavours help to ensure their success. The Mars restlessness coupled with the Piscean tendency to dream can leave these people with energy but lacking in purpose. The Mars energy can be channelled into creative pursuits, such as careers involving music, painting or writing.

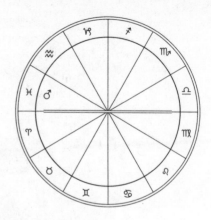

Mars in the houses

Mars in the first house

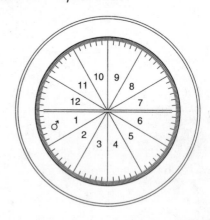

As the first house is the natural position for Mars, this placement increases the physical energy and the need for physical activity. Although natural organisers, those with Mars in the first house tend to be impatient with others and eventually insist on doing everything themselves. They are usually self-confident and have an air of purpose about them. They need to be careful about accidents to the head or headaches.

Mars in the second house

Those with Mars in the second house work hard for material possessions and are motivated by material gain. They can be competitive where financial opportunities

are concerned. They need to learn to value abilities as much as material things.

Mars in the third house

Those with Mars in the third house are quick-minded and analytical. They can be impatient, and need to learn how to deal with those in their immediate environment who oppose their plans. This placement can describe difficulties with siblings in the early years which, if not resolved, can lead to workplace conflicts in adult life.

Mars in the fourth house

This placement increases the desire for a secure home and for independence. As a result, these people usually leave their parents' home when quite young, in order to establish a home of their own.

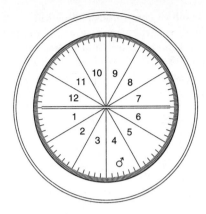

Those with Mars in the fourth house have a need to experience powerful feelings and they must guard against creating conflict or drama in order to experience the heady sensation of profound loss, grief or pain. They can also be more aggressive behind closed doors at home than they are out in public.

Mars in the fifth house

Those with Mars in the fifth house are creative and always ready to take a risk. Whether it is in business or at the casino table, they love the thrill of gambling.

As parents, these people can be autocratic and they need to ensure that they don't encourage rivalry among their children. I have seen parents do this believing that it helps a child to achieve their best, but sensitive children often become less confident as a result of continuous competition.

These people have sound leadership abilities, as long as they accept feedback from those they are leading. They love challenges and enjoy the opportunity to be heroes occasionally.

Mars in the sixth house

Those with Mars in the sixth house are hardworking types who much prefer being busy to being idle. They can be hard taskmasters, expecting others to work to their exacting standards.

They are usually mechanically minded and enjoy puzzles and working out how things fit together. They need to watch their digestive systems, especially their intake of hot, spicy foods.

Mars in the seventh house

This placement is opposite the natural house for Mars (the first house), which means that conflict can arise due to impatience with others. These people need to learn to value the opinions of those around them, especially their relationship partners. They seek active and enthusiastic partners who have the Mars qualities in abundance.

Mars in the eighth house

An increase in sexual energy is associated with Mars in the eighth house, along with the ability to delve deeply into research projects.

Management of the financial affairs of others, including the affairs of their partners, is shown with this placement. These people need to be aware of when their need to control their partners' finances is required and when they are simply being over-controlling.

Mars in the ninth house

Those with Mars in the ninth house are usually enthusiastic and will fight for their beliefs. They need to guard against pushing others into believing what they believe, however, as this placement can make them zealous.

These people are restless to travel the world and to learn new things. They can experience conflict between their urge to visit foreign places and to learn new things and their attachment to their current beliefs.

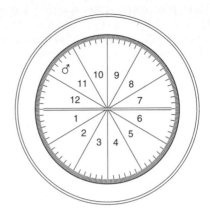

As new ways of living life are shown to them, they are torn between wanting to embrace the new and their need to convert the locals to their own way of life.

Mars in the tenth house

Those with Mars in the tenth house are self-made men and women whose Mars energy is directed towards their careers. They are practical and reliable, preferring to oversee things than to do all the work themselves.

Good organisers and leaders, these people are ambitious to make a name for themselves in the world, but their tenth house Mars energy can make them insensitive to the needs of others as they pursue their goals.

Mars in the eleventh house

Those with Mars in the eleventh house are attracted to friends who have the energy and enthusiasm to explore life. This can lead them into trouble from time to time, so they need to learn good judgment before acting upon their impulses.

These people collect friends from all walks of life. They enjoy being challenged by their friends, in areas such as competitive sports and so on.

Mars in the twelfth house

Those with Mars in the twelfth house can become frustrated that their energy and their desires are expended without concrete results. The Mars energy needs to be directed towards understanding the human condition, or these people can seek a short-cut to personal fulfilment through misuse of their Mars energy. This may involve drugs or alcohol.

This placement can suggest karmic difficulties with a father or a brother, or with men in positions of power and responsibility.

These people are often emotionally intense and need to maintain a sense of emotional and spiritual balance through meditation or yoga.

JUPITER
♃

The planet Jupiter is the largest of the planets and it completes its cycle every 12 years. Jupiter rules the sign Sagittarius, and the ninth house is its natural position.

Jupiter is a planet of expansion — the expansion of ideas, of projects and of the physical body. Considered a lucky planet by early astrologers, Jupiter brings benefits and foresight wherever it is placed in a chart.

Jupiter in the signs

Jupiter in Aries

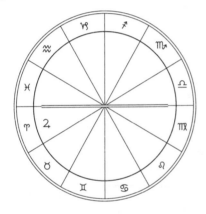

Those with Jupiter in Aries are likely to be energetic, enthusiastic and somewhat impatient. This placement gives them confidence in themselves and an urgency to get on with things when they know that there is a challenge at hand. They have the courage of their convictions and leadership positions appeal to them. They need to guard against leaving a job half done in favour of starting something new.

Jupiter in Taurus

Those with Jupiter in Taurus have to be careful with their possessions. As Jupiter is expansive and loves to experience new things and Taurus loves to hold on to things, these people can accumulate more than they ever need.

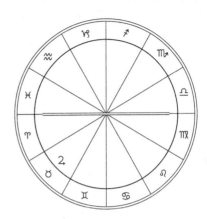

This placement can indicate someone who hoards things that they will not use, but cannot seem to release. This is also the case for health, and this placement is likely to increase the person's weight. Both the planet Jupiter and the sign of Taurus share a love of sweet foods, so these people may need to watch their weight in later years.

This is a good position for singers or public speakers, as Jupiter opens or expands the throat, the Taurean area of the body. These people often have pleasant speaking voices.

Jupiter in Gemini

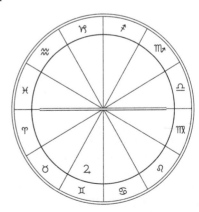

Those with Jupiter in Gemini sometimes have short attention spans, preferring short articles to books, or a conversation to a short article. These people often start a new book before completing the current one, as they are eager for knowledge. They are convincing speakers.

As Jupiter rules Sagittarius and Gemini is opposite Sagittarius in the zodiac, this is not the best aspect for Jupiter. The expansiveness of Jupiter and the nervous energy of Gemini make for a restlessness mind and, sometimes, a lack of thoroughness. When problems arise, assistance from siblings or from those in their immediate environment is likely.

Jupiter in Cancer

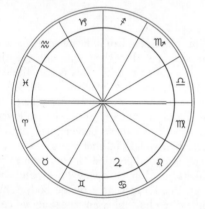

Jupiter is exalted in Cancer, making it the most favourable position for Jupiter in the zodiac. Ancient astrologers decided that Jupiter was exalted in Cancer because Cancer is the sign of feelings and emotions, and the purity of Jupiter can turn emotion into devotion.

This placement suggests great protection from the mother or mother-figure during the formative years. These people enjoy a balanced home environment and receive support from those in the home.

On the negative side, they may need to guard against drinking to excess when they feel trapped by too many commitments. Jupiter loves the freedom to explore and those with this placement can feel torn between the urge to nurture those around them and the need to be free to explore life.

Jupiter in Leo

Those with Jupiter in Leo love children and enjoy expressing themselves. This is a good placement for a career in the theatre or on life's stage, as these people have an individual creativity which they need to express.

This placement increases the tendency to pursue love affairs (the fifth house rules affairs as distinct from relationships, which are shown in the seventh house) and these people may need to learn more about commitment before they can settle down to one deep relationship.

Jupiter in Virgo

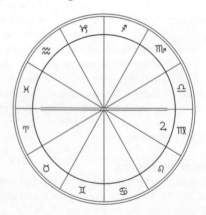

There is a conflict when Jupiter is placed in Virgo, as Jupiter is expansive and Virgo is discriminating. Jupiter wants to accept all available opportunities whereas Virgo wants to narrow the opportunities down to one perfect opportunity. This creates inner friction in people with this placement.

Those with Jupiter in Virgo are often valued in the workplace and can usually see better ways to do things at work. They enjoy good health, as Jupiter increases their desire to exercise and Virgo places a great emphasis upon physical health. When in Virgo, the Jupiterian tendency to increase weight is kept in check.

Jupiter in Libra

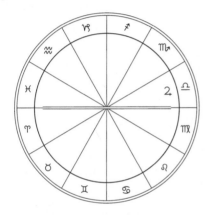

Those with Jupiter in Libra enjoy sweet foods and may need to guard against gaining weight on their hips and thighs as they mature. Their enthusiasm makes them attractive to others and they tend to be outgoing and easy to get along with.

They value their friends and put a great deal of energy into maintaining their relationships and friendships. They are able to encourage and inspire those around them and they usually enjoy being surrounded by beautiful things.

Jupiter in Scorpio

Those with Jupiter in Scorpio can quickly penetrate to the core of a person or a situation. It is a good placement for counsellors or detectives as it heightens the ability to scrutinise a situation. They are also

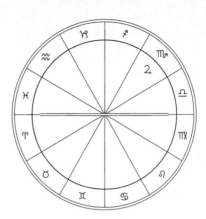

suited to any career in which they can help others, as they have the ability to show others the way.

These people are endowed with great presence and are convincing actors or public speakers. Jupiter's expansiveness can fill an auditorium and Scorpio's depth can capture the essential emotion that the speech or play requires.

They need to guard against dissipating their energy in the pursuit of sex, drugs or alcohol, ignoring their path in life and losing the gift of far-sightedness that Jupiter brings.

Jupiter in Sagittarius

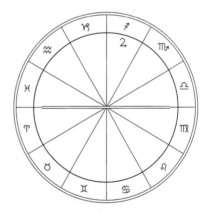

As Jupiter rules Sagittarius, this is a positive placement. These people relate easily to Sagittarians as they share some of the Sagittarian qualities. Those with Jupiter in

Sagittarius are usually generous and tolerant of others, and have an interest in religion or philosophy. Learning interests them and they seek careers where they will always be learning something new.

Naturally ambitious, these people have the ability to impress others and, as a result, those around them often push them forward in their career. When opportunities present themselves, those with Jupiter in Sagittarius are usually the first to see them. They have natural leadership abilities and prefer to be in charge. They thrive on goals and challenges, as long as these do not demand too much commitment from them.

Jupiter in Capricorn

This is a difficult placement, as Jupiter's enthusiasm is stifled by Capricorn's love of structure. While Jupiter wants to be free to choose whatever opportunities are suitable, Capricorn believes that there are only a few opportunities and that it is best to make the most of what they have at present. This means that people with this placement search for new frontiers yet feel insecure or uncertain when out at the cutting edge.

Those with Jupiter in Capricorn display good self-control and are able to organise others easily. Both Jupiter and Capricorn love to be in charge, but Capricorn increases their seriousness and their belief that if they want a job done well, they had better do it themselves.

Although Jupiter likes to cut corners from time to time, its placement in Capricorn means these people like to complete things thoroughly the first time. Whenever they cut corners, they find themselves held accountable and obliged to complete the task again. When they are content to work within a structure, success comes more readily. This often occurs as they mature.

Jupiter in Aquarius

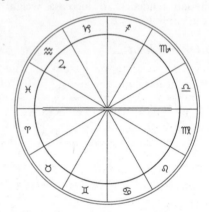

Those with Jupiter in Aquarius value their freedom. They enjoy travelling to foreign countries to learn about other cultures and enjoy the philosophies practised by other cultures.

These people usually have inventive minds and are open-minded when encountering people with different beliefs. They can be effective go-betweens when different groups of people come together and are excellent spokespeople for groups.

Humanitarian causes appeal to people with this placement and they need to feel that what they contribute benefits others more than themselves. They often have friends from all cultures and all walks of life, as they enjoy being part of the larger community of humankind.

Jupiter in Pisces

Those with Jupiter in Pisces have a desire to study and to learn about metaphysical issues, and healing or helping others also appeals to

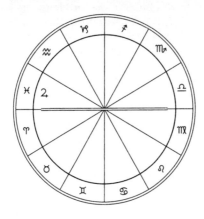

them. They tend to be less focused upon material possessions and more interested in life's purpose than other placements, and need to guard against being drained emotionally or psychically by those around them as this leaves them unable to pursue their own purpose in life.

They can be an inspiration to others, especially in small ways as opposed to grand gestures. Receiving recognition for their efforts is not as important for these people as achieving the desired results for others.

Jupiter in the houses

Jupiter in the first house

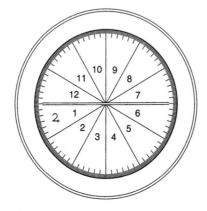

Those with Jupiter in the first house are usually generous and optimistic. They exude

a certain confidence in themselves and this helps others to have confidence in their leadership abilities.

These people enjoy the outdoors and they may gain weight in their later years if they do not maintain a regular exercise routine. They need to guard against becoming egocentric and overindulging in food, drugs or alcohol.

Jupiter in the second house

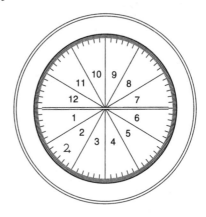

This placement can assist with financial security and gives those with Jupiter in the second house confidence in their abilities. They are usually hardworking and enthusiastic when tackling problems, but they need to guard against taking unnecessary financial risks.

Jupiter in the third house

Those with Jupiter in the third house are natural teachers, as they are easily able to comprehend complex matters and simplify them while retaining the essential theme. They usually get along well with those in their immediate environment, who assist them when they need help. Writing, teaching and travelling appeal to these people as they are both physically and mentally restless.

Jupiter in the fourth house

This placement can suggest a financial inheritance from parents, or that their parents assisted them greatly when they were children. They prefer a large or spacious home, and they are usually excellent hosts. Financial security is shown here, especially in later life, and these people rarely lack a comfortable home environment.

Jupiter in the fifth house

Those with Jupiter in the fifth house derive a great deal of fulfilment from their children, as they retain a childlike creativity and enthusiasm into their later years. They are natural risk takers and can gain by speculating with business, stocks and shares if Jupiter is well aspected.

Jupiter in the sixth house

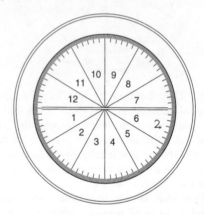

This placement combines the Virgoan (sixth house ruler) preference for a healthy diet and simple food with the Jupiterian love of excess, taming it to bring about balanced health through moderation. When negatively aspected, the Jupiterian excesses can hold sway, increasing the weight and causing problems with the liver and the digestive system.

People with this placement are usually held in high esteem by coworkers and they have a tendency to work too hard on occasion.

Jupiter in the seventh house

Those with Jupiter in the seventh house may benefit socially through marriage or a long-term partnership. This placement often attracts positive and sympathetic marriage or relationship partners, and these people are likely to marry more than once.

When Jupiter is negatively aspected, these people can be restricted by their marriages or relationship partners, and if they divorce, they are loath to remarry.

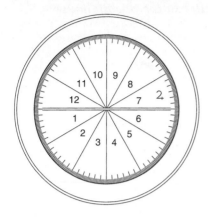

Jupiter in the eighth house

Those with Jupiter in the eighth house can display an interest in life after death and in the psychic sciences. They may benefit financially through marriage, partnerships or legacies. They are often natural counsellors, as they can penetrate the depths of human nature and understand what they find. Psychology and psychiatry interests them. When Jupiter is negatively aspected, they are likely to pursue sex without commitment.

minded and tolerant of others, and can easily rise to positions of power in learning institutions or charities. In their careers, they are often role models for others, and their rewards usually come later in life.

Jupiter in the tenth house

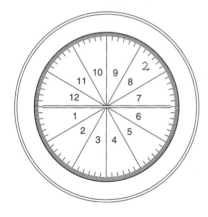

Jupiter in the ninth house

As Jupiter rules the ninth house, its influence is particularly strong in this placement. Those with Jupiter in the ninth house are often noble in outlook, with strong religious or philosophic tendencies. They enjoy travel and other cultures. They are usually broad-

Jupiter in the tenth house is a very positive placement for a successful career. These are people of character, integrity and honour, well deserving of the esteem in which they are held by others. They are forward-thinkers who take their responsibilities seriously, making decisions which benefit those in their profession and in society generally.

Jupiter in the eleventh house

Jupiter in the twelfth house

Those with Jupiter in the eleventh house often rely upon their friends to help them out in times of need. They usually have influential friends and associates who benefit them in life.

Naturally popular, they are suited to organising social situations and groups of people. They usually have a strong desire to help those in need, especially those in other countries and cultures.

Those with Jupiter in the twelfth house achieve success in hospitals, laboratories and prisons, as the twelfth house rules these areas. They are also suited to a monastic life, especially if it involves helping the poor and the sick. If they don't involve themselves directly in chartitable acts, they usually donate to organisations that conduct this type of work. These people have a talent for turning enemies into friends and for resolving conflicts which cause complications between people later on in life. They need to guard against having too much faith in life's possibilities without a grounding in reality.

SATURN
ħ

The planet Saturn completes its cycle every 29.46 years. Saturn rules the sign of Capricorn and the tenth house is its natural placement.

Saturn brings caution, uncertainty, duty, responsibility, patience and wisdom based upon practical experience. It also brings a sense of limitation and frustration through frequent disappointments.

Saturn rules the father or the father-figure. The traditional role of the father is to teach the child what is expected of them by those in the community — the rules and codes of behaviour. Although most young children find such rules and codes restrictive, they often realise how beneficial these are as they mature. A fair code of conduct allows for community cohesion.

The placement of Saturn in a chart shows the father's influence and reveals some of the restrictions the person can expect throughout life.

Saturn in the signs

Saturn in Aries

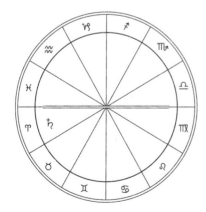

This placement gives a sense of enthusiasm and perseverance. Although sometimes impatient, they are in the process of learning that freedom is the result of patience and self-discipline. As they mature, their impatience and enthusiasm are tamed and concentration upon their desired goals helps them achieve what they seek.

These people need to learn to put others first sometimes, as they can be quite selfish. They can experience headaches or knocks to the head from time to time, as Saturn brings restrictions and Aries rules the head.

Saturn in Taurus

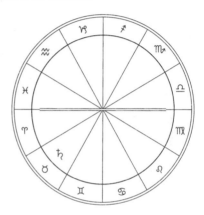

Those with Saturn in Taurus are usually hardworking and careful with their money as they know how hard it was to earn. They are patient, slow to embrace change and sometimes determined to the point of being stubborn. They are long-term planners and tenacious in the pursuit of goals.

The lesson with this placement is to value people rather than possessions. Sometimes these people can derive security from material possessions as a replacement for a much-needed connection with other people.

Saturn in Gemini

Those with Saturn in Gemini are usually serious about their studies. They understand the value of learning and can apply themselves to study in a disciplined manner. They are careful in their choice of words and capable of methodically overturning

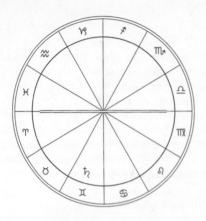

another's viewpoint through systematic thinking.

As writers and teachers they excel, but they must guard against cynicism or bitterness when things don't work out as they planned.

Saturn in Cancer

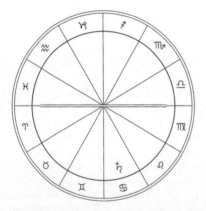

Fear of loss or of financial impoverishment is a motivating force for those with Saturn in Cancer. They conceal their feelings from those around them and demonstrate their love by worrying about their friends and family. As parents they can be over-protective and suffer from feelings of inadequacy. They can experience difficulties with giving and receiving affection, for although soft-hearted, they can be hard to reach emotionally because of their hard exteriors.

Saturn in Leo

Those with Saturn in Leo are usually self-confident with a natural flair for organising others. They work hard on creative projects, realising that inspiration is only a small step towards the finished product. They often display an overdeveloped sense of duty and responsibility, and can find it difficult to let go of control. They are usually strong-willed and tend to hold their creative expression in check, producing a finished product that is unadventurous but widely accepted by others.

Saturn in Virgo

Saturn in Virgo strengthens the organising and analytical tendencies, and people with this placement tend to prefer their lives to be neat and orderly. Although hardworking, they often prefer to work alone, as they only let down their guard when others are not present.

Often critical of themselves and of others, they tend to work hardest when they are worried about something. They seem to do their best thinking when their hands are busy. This placement increases worry about their health.

Saturn in Libra

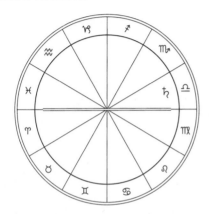

Those with Saturn in Libra usually have a well-developed sense of justice and responsibility. This placement can indicate that the father or father-figure possessed a strong sense of fairness, which he passed on to his child. Cooperation with others could be a testing ground for their beliefs about justice and fairness, particularly in relationships.

Saturn in Scorpio

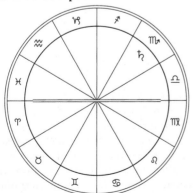

Those with Saturn in Scorpio often display a depth of character which others find difficult to penetrate. These people can usually keep a secret and are adept at discovering the secrets of others. This placement indicates an ability to assist others to make decisions about their possessions or those things which are valuable to them. It also increases the courage to face life's obstacles and shows a relentless desire to succeed.

Saturn in Sagittarius

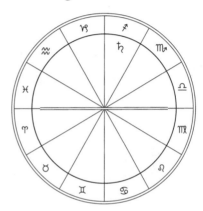

Those with Saturn in Sagittarius are usually good teachers and organisers. In their early years, they may struggle with the need to earn the respect of others and the desire to be free to explore life in all its myriad forms. As they mature, they tend to be given postions of responsibility in their careers, as they realise that sacrifices must be made to achieve goals. These people are independent, even when they are young children, and they have a philosophic turn of mind.

Saturn in Capricorn
Those with Saturn in Capricorn are natural organisers who take their responsibilities very seriously. They find it hard to rest when there is still work to be completed. They are hardworking, preferring to earn their rest and relaxation. They tend to value achievement over happiness and need to guard against taking life too seriously. Mark is an example of this placement.

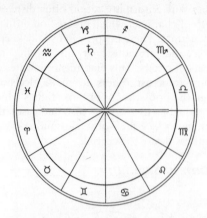

Mark loved to play golf, but was uneasy if he felt that he hadn't earned the time off to play. In order to play a guilt-free game each Sunday afternoon, he started work early and finished late, six days a week. 'Loosen up a little,' I would say to him and his response was invariably the same each time: 'It's all very well to have a good time — when you can afford to do so'.

The lesson for this placement is to be aware of how they can be of service to others.

Saturn in Aquarius

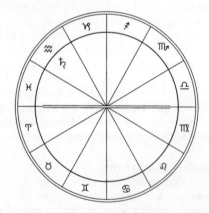

Those with Saturn in Aquarius usually possess a commonsense attitude to life. They can be fixated upon their own ideas and goals, ignoring the needs of those around them. They tend to make friends who share their serious interests and they must guard against becoming too critical of their friends. Early in life they tend to be conservative in their choice of friends, but as they mature they become more tolerant and open-minded in this regard.

Saturn in Pisces

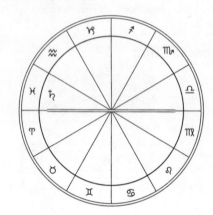

Those with Saturn in Pisces can be torn between their need to dream and their desire to make their dreams real. They are naturally sensitive to the needs of others and are capable of great self-sacrifice when required. This placement can suggest a life of karmic atonement. This may be in the form of self-sacrifice so that others can achieve their desired goals.

Power struggles with the father or father-figure are suggested with this placement. Their fathers may have restricted their ability to pursue their dreams and make them real. These people need to be careful not to use drugs or alcohol when faced with obstacles, as their perseverance is usually rewarded.

Saturn in the houses

Saturn in the first house
Those with Saturn in the first house can appear aloof at first meeting, and they usually warm to people slowly, especially if Saturn is the rising planet (i.e. the first planet after the Ascendant). They often feel inadequate and can become despondent

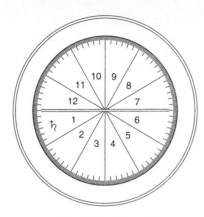

when opposed in their plans. They possess a poor sense of self-worth, typically because the father or father-figure has not valued them or shown them that they are loved.

Saturn in the second house

Those with Saturn in the second house have a tendency to put possessions before people. They have difficulty trusting or relying on others, and turn to material possessions for security and comfort.

These people work hard for the things they desire and financial success is the result of their tireless efforts. However, they need to be aware of their true worth and to allow others to value them for who they are rather than for what they do or achieve. Sometimes they become suspicious when love is offered without any apparent effort required on their part.

Saturn in the third house

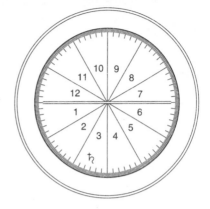

Those with Saturn in the third house work hard for knowledge and are prepared to read the driest and most uninspiring books to gain the knowledge they seek. They retain what they have learned and often possess an orderly mind.

These people can feel misunderstood by their families and may have spent their childhoods observing rather than participating. They are precise in their choice of words, for they are aware that others remember what they say, and they are careful with their reputations.

Saturn in the fourth house

Those with Saturn in the fourth house experience restrictions in their home life in their early years. This is often due to the father or the father-figure. In some cases the father is absent and the restrictions are financial.

These people can become hoarders, their homes cluttered with unnecessary possessions. This is often the result of a fear of scarcity.

They need to be careful with their stomachs when stressed, as ulcers are common. Effort put into making the home a cosy and nurturing environment goes a long way to reducing stress and enhancing their lives.

Saturn in the fifth house

Creative and emotional frustration accompanies this placement, perhaps due to the father or the father-figure. Saturn in the fifth house can detail a father who restricted artistic expression or who perceived his child to be a burden rather than a joy.

These people need to guard against becoming too restrictive with their own children, as this may lead to feeling that parenthood is a burden or a chore. They can lose sight of the joys of parenthood, as they sometimes spend too much time concentrating on the responsibilities.

They have an innate desire for the respect of others, which they need to earn rather than demand. It is important that they earn the respect of their children, otherwise they can expect little or no real contact with their offspring during their later years.

Saturn in the sixth house

Those with Saturn in the sixth house tend to work hard in their jobs, exuding an air of competence and diligence. As managers or employers they can be hard taskmasters, expecting others to work to their own exacting standards. They are hardworking employees, resting rarely and worrying constantly.

An example of this is Sophie, who is an accountant for a small company. She described lying awake at night worrying about budget blow-outs and the lack of proper care given to costing new materials. I was unable to impress upon her that it was not *her* money she was worrying about, and that her employer seemed unfazed by the whole situation.

Overwork sometimes leads to health difficulties, particularly digestive problems. These people need to maintain a healthy balance between work and play.

Saturn in the seventh house

Those with Saturn in the seventh house tend to be cautious where relationship commitments are concerned, as they know that once they have made a commitment they are unlikely to leave the relationship, even if they are unhappy. These people can feel insecure if their partners start to change or grow. They work hard to maintain the status quo in a relationship, as their relationships are often more about security rather than growth.

Saturn in the eighth house

Those with Saturn in the eighth house are usually self-disciplined, sometimes to the point of denying themselves a social life. Sexual relationships can suffer as they pursue financial security.

At work, they usually hold positions which involve making decisions or taking responsibility for things which others value. This includes handling other people's finances and advising on relationship issues. These people are often prepared to work hard and they can be very disciplined financially.

Saturn in the ninth house

Those with Saturn in the ninth house have a patient and steady approach to all things philosophical. They are natural teachers and lecturers, but need to guard against ridiculing those who do not share their beliefs about life. They have great powers of concentration and thoroughly research those subjects that interest them. These people can experience difficulties travelling purely for pleasure, but travel that is work- or study-related appeals to them.

Saturn in the tenth house

This is a good placement for career success, as those with Saturn in the tenth house know the value of perseverance and tend to be self-reliant. They are attracted to positions of power, but need to remember that with power comes responsibility. This desire to be successful in the eyes of others can be the result of a father or father-figure who was too engrossed in his own life or career to notice his child in their formative years.

Hence these people can seek the attention that was denied them as children.

People with this placement need to be aware of their tendency to ignore family life in favour of career, for this can lead to estrangement from their children, particularly in their later years.

Saturn in the eleventh house

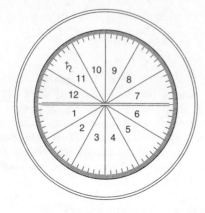

Those with Saturn in the eleventh house screen their friends carefully, preferring long friendships to short-lived acquaintances. In their younger years, they may prefer friends who are a good deal older than themselves. They are drawn to groups with a serious

rather than a social purpose, and are often prepared to work hard so that others benefit.

Saturn in the twelfth house

Those with Saturn in the twelfth house tend to crave solitude. They yearn for inner peace and can find this through meditation and service to others. They often feel they owe a debt to others and that service offered with humility can repay that debt.

This placement can suggest that in past lives, they have been enemies with their present fathers, leaving them with a deep-seated lack of trust that requires resolution in this lifetime.

URANUS

♅

The planet Uranus is four times larger than the earth and its orbit takes 84 years. It has an eccentric orbit, with its poles pointing towards the sun during its orbit due to the 98-degree angle of the poles. This makes it move forward in its orbit while rotating sideways.

Uranus rules the sign of Aquarius and the eleventh house is its natural position. Uranus is exalted in Scorpio, in detriment in Leo and at its fall in Taurus.

Uranus rules the circulatory system, the body electricity and the ankles. It is associated with eccentricity, original thinking, electricity, technology, astrology, space travel, freedom and unpredictability. Uranus is also associated with intuition, but a sudden flash of awareness rather than the more subtle forms of intuition associated with Neptune or the Moon.

Uranus increases originality of thought and its negative aspects can lead to rebellious urges and the need to destroy that which represents stability and conformity. The function of Uranus is to bring about sudden change, in order to awaken a deeper understanding of life. The change can be chaotic at first, but to see life from a new perspective it is sometimes necessary to remove familiar things.

Uranus increases the need for independence and the humanitarian tendencies. Those with strongly placed Uranus in their charts have a well-developed sense of altruism.

Uranus in the signs

Uranus in Aries
Those with Uranus in Aries are original and independent, full of energy and ambition. They are courageous in the face of adversity and often have an affinity for mechanical or electrical devices. Abrupt and impulsive, they can act and speak without thought for how

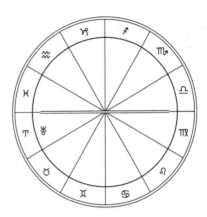

others will feel. This can lead to conflict with those around them, though they intend no harm. They are restless, quick to start new projects and just as quick to give up projects when new opportunities present themselves.

Uranus in Taurus

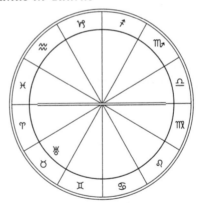

Uranus in Taurus increases the Taurean stubbornness, making these people alternately stubborn and changeable. They desire new and unusual material possessions, yet are happy to let them go when change requires them to do so.

Single-minded, they are practical in the pursuit of their ideals. When Uranus is negatively aspected, they may experience unexpected financial fluctuations from time to time. Uranus is in its fall in Taurus as Taurus loves stability and Uranus seeks change. This conflict can cause inner tension.

Uranus in Gemini

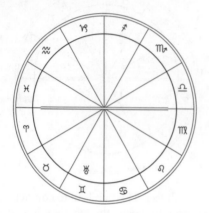

Those with Uranus in Gemini are original in their thinking and can pursue two lines of thinking at one time. They can solve problems while concentrating on unrelated subjects, as their minds are alert and adaptable. They are quick to understand new concepts and are talented writers. They have highly charged nervous systems and become exhausted periodically when they attempt too many things at once.

Their personalities are usually quite dissimilar to those of their siblings yet this is not a handicap if Uranus is well aspected. When negatively aspected, these people can experience a lack of acceptance from their families, friends and colleagues. This is often due to their eccentric behaviour.

Uranus in Cancer

Those with Uranus in Cancer have highly developed intuitions and can develop their intuitive abilities, particularly with prophetic dreams. They can be torn between their thoughts and their feelings, especially where home and family are concerned.

Their nervous dispositions can lead to difficulties with the digestive system. Their restlessness may tax those close to them, leading to temporary or even permanent

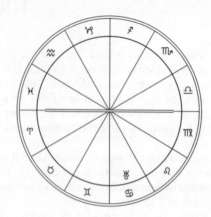

separation from loved ones. They possess strong imaginations which can benefit their careers and day-to-day life, and they are protective of family members.

Uranus in Leo

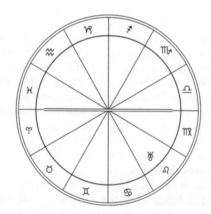

Those with Uranus in Leo are very determined people with a well-developed sense of self. They can be rebellious and impatient when contradicted. They are natural leaders and organisers.

They can be creatively original and are suited to careers in the media and public life. As teachers, they can make any subject more interesting with their unconventional approach. They are strong-willed and assertive, and can benefit from a more gentle approach to others when pursuing their goals.

Uranus in Virgo

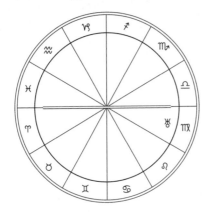

This placement increases the scientific and mechanical mind of Virgo, and these people have keen business abilities. They are capable of presenting realistic solutions to problems and prefer to rethink their ideas before proceeding. These people can improve accepted methods and procedures with their practical inventions and solutions.

They have an interest in natural healing and psychic healing, and they need to guard against becoming hypochondriacs if Uranus is negatively aspected. A negatively aspected Uranus in Virgo can lead to unusual ailments, most often brought on by stress and worry.

Uranus in Libra

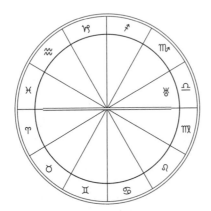

Uranus in Libra increases the idealistic Uranus temperament and enables these people to be more cooperative than the other Uranus placements. They can experience a need to please their partners *and* a desire to be free to pursue their own lives, resulting in erratic behaviour from time to time. This stems from the fact that although they want relationships, they don't necessarily want the responsibilities that come with being part of a couple.

They often possess creative imaginations and keen intuitions. They are also generous with their time and energy when their friends need help or support.

Uranus in Scorpio

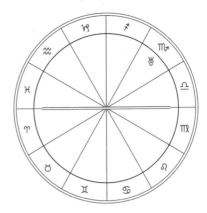

Those with Uranus in Scorpio have exceptional investigative powers and good concentration. As Uranus is exalted in Scorpio, it has added power when found in this sign. These people can appear calm and unruffled on the surface while experiencing turbulent emotions within, and these inner feelings need expression to ensure inner harmony.

They are forceful and determined, but need to guard against stubbornness, as Scorpio is a fixed sign and Uranus increases stubbornness wherever it is found in the chart.

When negatively aspected, those with Uranus in Scorpio can direct their energies into unusual sexual pursuits for the sake of novelty. This results in depletion of energies and often their habits are concealed from those close to them.

Uranus in Sagittarius

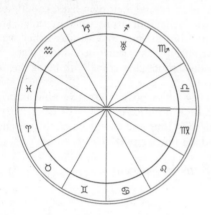

Those with Uranus in Sagittarius are optimistic, enthusiastic and unconventional in their thinking. They are broad-minded and tolerant of the opinions of others.

Keen students, they can approach education as an opportunity to uplift humanity, and they seek ways to improve traditional methods of teaching. They enjoy travel because it gives them further opportunities to learn.

When negatively aspected, these people can become narrow-minded, preferring to disrupt old methods of education or religious beliefs without thought as to what will replace them. Revolutionary in their approach, they need to gain a deeper awareness of the right of others to hold different beliefs about life.

Uranus in Capricorn

This placement shocks Capricorn out of its love of routine and fear of things new or different with periodic opportunities for change. These people are ambitious and have a strong sense of responsibility. They are original with business ideas and their powers of organisation and perseverance help them to succeed with their plans.

They are restless and yet they fear change,

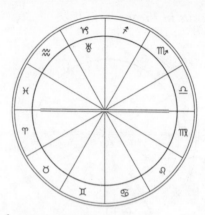

preferring to remain in familiar surroundings. This dilemma can result in stomach and digestive disorders unless they allow some change to take place within their lives. They are torn between the need to do things according to tradition and the desire for change.

Uranus in Aquarius

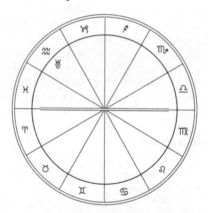

Aquarius is the natural home of Uranus, and these people are original and humanitarian in their approach to life. They are usually kind, friendly and decidedly independent. They can be inventive, especially when it comes to problem solving, as they have the ability to think of unusual solutions to problems. They are intuitive, seeming to leap mentally to the correct conclusion rather than feeling what is right.

They are unselfish, generous and

sometimes need to guard against being used by those around them. They may experience problems with their ankles or their circulatory systems if their health deteriorates.

Uranus in Pisces

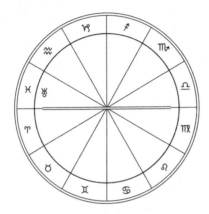

The erratic effects of Uranus are slowed when in Pisces, and these people are creative, inventive and intuitive, although they tend to lack confidence in themselves. Their humanitarian tendencies mean that those close to them may sometimes feel ignored, and they need to develop an awareness of their immediate environment. They are regularly faced with possible change and uncertainty, and must learn to differentiate between imagination and reality.

When negatively aspected, these people seek drugs or alcohol to escape reality, which affects their health and increases their tendency to be clouded in their thinking.

Uranus in the houses

Uranus in the first house

Those with Uranus in the first house are often quick-minded and unconventional. They are impatient for change, preferring to lead rather than follow where new ideas are concerned.

Their appearance can seem odd or eccentric, for they are usually too concerned with ideas and concepts to care about the

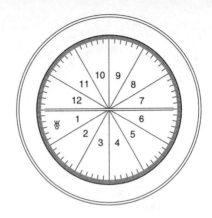

way they look. They are restless and usually open-minded. If Uranus is within 5 degrees of the Ascendant, these people can expect sudden changes throughout their lives.

Uranus in the second house

Those with Uranus in the second house enjoy money for the opportunities it offers them, especially the freedom financial security brings. Sudden unforseen financial losses and then gains are associated with this aspect, regardless of advice given or taken, as Uranus offers change as a way to develop the soul.

Uranus in the third house

Those with Uranus in the third house possess quick and curious minds. Unconventional thinkers, these people are natural speakers or writers. They experience strong urges to

travel and may cut ties with their families at some point in their lives.

When Uranus is well aspected to the Sun or the Moon, it increases psychic abilities, particularly clairvoyance, as Uranus rules ethereal energy and the third house deals with communication. If afflicted (squared the Sun or Moon), Uranus in the third house can indicate quarrels with siblings or neighbours and an unsettled mind. This placement can also suggest unusual occurrences during short journeys.

Uranus in the fourth house

Uranus in the fourth house can describe an unusual relationship with the mother or mother-figure and an unsettled home environment in the early years. Sometimes these people fare better when they have moved away from their original home environments, for they can experience antagonism from siblings and neighbours in the early years.

They prefer to be free of responsibilities, particularly those related to home or family. This placement increases interest in psychic development. These people can feel misunderstood by those close to them in their homes and communities.

Uranus in the fifth house

Uranus in the fifth house increases originality and creativity, and encourages the pursuit of unusual hobbies and interests. These people can become engrossed in their mental pursuits and ideals, ignoring the needs of their children in favour of the greater community.

As parents, they can encourage their children to undertake unusual creative ventures. This is not a good placement for success involving financial risks as Uranus brings sudden change and any gains can soon turn to losses.

Uranus in the sixth house
Uranus in the sixth house can indicate a need for freedom and space, particularly in the work environment. These people often see new and original ways of doing things at work and can become frustrated when those around them don't implement the suggested changes. They enjoy unusual

work, especially if it involves irregular hours, but must guard against nervous depletion. These people prefer working alone and can appear abrupt or impatient with coworkers.

This placement can indicate unusual health problems which respond rapidly to alternative treatments, including etheric rebalancing or psychic healing.

Uranus in the seventh house

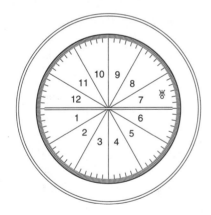

Those with Uranus in the seventh house enjoy unusual relationships. They are drawn to friends who are independent, unconventional and sometimes even radical.

This placement can indicate a hasty marriage or periodic sudden changes in relationship circumstances. These people can feel misunderstood by their partners, or may prefer a great deal of freedom and space in their relationships.

Uranus in the eighth house

Those with Uranus in the eighth house usually have a deep interest in the occult (hidden knowledge) and intuitive dreams at night. They have an unusual approach to sex, and are likely to die suddenly rather than as the result of a prolonged illness.

These people may benefit financially through an inheritance or legacy. They may receive sudden material increases through relationship or business partners.

Uranus in the ninth house

Those with Uranus in the ninth house have inventive and original minds. They are often idealistic and yet they can be realistic and effective when it suits them. When badly aspected, they can become ruthless idealists, pursuing their goals at any cost.

This placement suggests unusual incidents while on long travels, resulting in adventures or disasters, depending on how Uranus is aspected. These people are independent and their religious or philosophical beliefs can be unorthodox.

They are generally far-sighted, enabling them to pursue careers which lead to worldwide travel to quench their thirst for knowledge. They are keen students and unconventional yet inspiring teachers.

Uranus in the tenth house

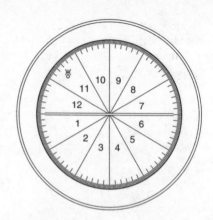

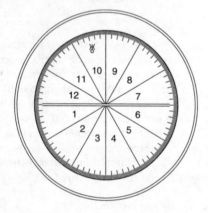

Those with Uranus in the tenth house can experience a need for freedom in their careers to pursue their own directions. Their inquiring minds can traverse the accepted boundaries of their fields, leading to discoveries and improvements which benefit others.

They are humanitarians and will work hard for a worthwhile cause. Although independent, they are usually hardworking and ready to accept any changes in career direction that life may present to them.

Uranus in the eleventh house

This is the natural placement for Uranus, and these people attract unusual friends and acquaintances. Although humanitarians, they can become radical if aroused, acting

with complete disregard for those whose ideals conflict with their own.

Friendships can bring positive or negative changes into their lives, depending on how Uranus is aspected. When Uranus is positively aspected, their friends can help them in pursuit of their goals. When Uranus is negatively aspected, selfish motives underlay friendships and these people can become financially or emotionally drained through the actions of their friends.

Uranus in the twelfth house

Those with Uranus in the twelfth house often feel alone. They can be secretive and aloof, which only increases their feelings of isolation. They are naturally intuitive and inventive, especially with chemicals and science.

This is a good placement for studying the psychic sciences, and they must be careful to maintain the balance of their etheric bodies, as they can become drained from time to time. They need to ensure regular rest to maintain good health, as sudden health problems appear periodically with this placement.

NEPTUNE

Ψ

The planet Neptune completes its cycle every 165 years. Neptune rules the sign of Pisces, and its natural placement is the twelfth house.

In Roman mythology, Neptune was the ruler of the sea (his equivalent in Greek mythology was Poseidon). The sea symbolises emotions and those with strong Neptune chart influences are usually attracted to the sea.

Some of the qualities of Neptune include dissolving, creativity, spiritual understanding, compassion, sacrifice and universal love and understanding.

Some of the negative aspects of Neptune include delusion, escapism through alcohol, drugs or dreams, and fear and avoidance of responsibilities in the physical world.

Neptune's purpose is to dissolve self-interest in favour of humanitarian interest. Neptune dissolves to enable something new to take its place. Neptune's effect is a gradual one, breaking down the residue of anger, grief, attitudes and pain, or stealing away the minutes of your life if you live in its negative aspects and avoid your growth and development. Neptune rules the feet, the glands of the body and the toxic build-up of waste in the body.

Neptune in the signs

As Neptune has an elliptical (non-circular) orbit, it does not travel through each sign at the same rate. Periodically it moves in a retrograde motion (i.e. it appears to move backwards compared with the earth's orbit), which means it may enter a new sign one month then return to the previous sign for weeks at a time. If the person was born in a year when Neptune moves from one sign to another (e.g. 1942), check an ephemeris or the natal chart to confirm which sign Neptune falls in.

Neptune moved through Aries from 1861 to 1874 and through Taurus from 1874 to 1887. As it is extremely unlikely that anyone reading this book would have been born during this period, I have not included these placements.

Neptune in Gemini (1887–1901)

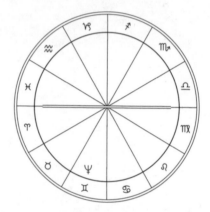

Those with Neptune in Gemini possess quick and perceptive minds, and have an inner restlessness which propels them towards new situations and experiences. They can be gifted speakers with the power to sway public opinion.

When Neptune is negatively aspected, these people become shrewd manipulators of those around them, using the Gemini gift of words with the Neptune intuition to know when to speak to sway those they seek to control.

Neptune in Cancer (1901–1915)

Those with Neptune in Cancer tend to be intuitive and sympathetic to the needs of others. Their intuitive abilities are easily developed, and psychometry (the act of reading the energy left in objects by those who have owned or handled them) and dreams are sources of psychic information.

When negatively aspected, these people tend to be self-indulgent and retreat from life through alcohol, drugs or dreams.

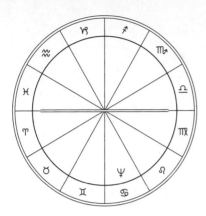

Neptune in Leo (1915–1929)

Those with Neptune in Leo are usually warm-hearted and generous. They enjoy socialising and can pursue creative projects successfully. They have the ability to teach creative disciplines in an inspiring manner.

The arts or the entertainment industry appeals to them and they can enjoy success in these areas if they curb their tendency to dream about success rather than actively pursuing their goals.

When negatively aspected, these people dream of being treated like royalty and can ignore those who support them as they indulge their dreams and fantasies.

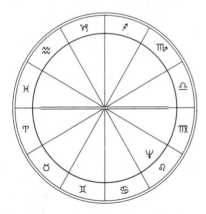

Neptune in Virgo (1929–1942/43)

Those with Neptune in Virgo have a practical approach to their creativity. They tend to approach the psychic sciences with scepticism, requiring proof before they trust. When Neptune is negatively aspected, these people do not believe in the psychic sciences even when faced with proof.

They have an affinity for natural therapies and herbal medicine, along with an interest in diet. They are attracted to nursing and medicine as a career. They need to guard against hypochondria and undiagnosable ailments. Meditation can restore good health.

Neptune in Libra (1943–1957)

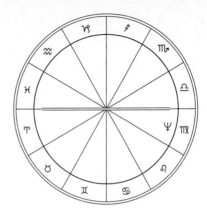

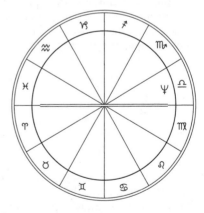

Those with Neptune in Libra have an innate need to help others achieve peace and harmony. These people enjoy music and beauty. They need to guard against confusion resulting from conflict between their thoughts and their intuition of what is right in a given situation. They seek spiritual union in their relationships and need to remain aware of the practical effort and sacrifices that may be required to maintain such a relationship.

Neptune in Scorpio (1957–1970)

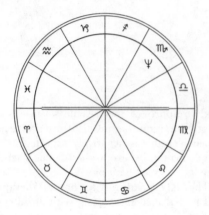

Those with Neptune in Scorpio are sensitive to those around them. This is a positive placement for spiritual growth. These people have an innate desire to delve into life's mysteries through science and the psychic sciences. They are emotionally intense and need to remain aware of the effect their desires have upon them and their life paths.

When negatively aspected, Neptune in Scorpio fuels a desire for sex, drugs, alcohol and sensual pleasure, with a complete disregard for spiritual development. If those with a negatively aspected Neptune do not discipline their desires, they can suffer the consequences. This placement is one of extremes — spiritual discipline or sensual gratification leading to self-destruction. Scorpio is a sign of absolutes and although Neptune is subtle in its effects, when in Scorpio it demands to be fixed in its purpose, as Scorpio is a fixed sign.

Neptune in Sagittarius (1970–1984/85)

Those with Neptune in Sagittarius are philosophical in their approach to life. They have an interest in many religions, but prefer

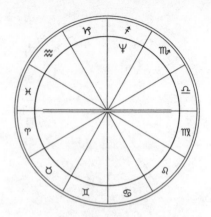

to take a little from each one rather than follow one particular belief dogmatically. Travel offers these people great opportunities for learning and fulfilment.

When negatively aspected, these people can lose their desire to explore life and other cultures, preferring instead to cling to the beliefs they were raised with rather than risk 'losing their way'.

Neptune in Capricorn (1985–1999/2000)

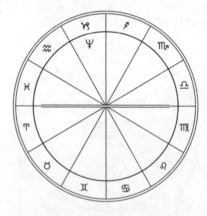

Those with Neptune in Capricorn are deep thinkers, drawn to such careers as detective work or scientific studies. They have the ability to combine the Neptunian humanitarian aspects with the Capricorn far-sightedness, enabling them to form detailed long-term plans to achieve goals which have far-reaching effects in the world.

In business, they can combine their intuition with their practical application to achieve profitable results. These people realise the value of establishing a world community with a structure that will benefit everyone. At first they may choose to establish such a community through business dealings, but this is followed by more social interaction.

Neptune in Aquarius (2000–2015)

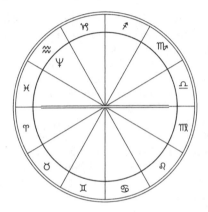

Those with Neptune in Aquarius will have strong humanitarian ideals and will pursue the concept of a global village where we are all responsible for the welfare of one another. They will be likely to study the control the mind has over matter, especially the human body. This placement may assist with inventions, as it will increase the ability to solve problems in a creative manner.

Neptune in the houses

Neptune in the first house
Those with Neptune in the first house are usually psychically sensitive and this makes them prone to mood swings according to the energy surrounding them at any given time. Without any spiritual understanding they can become confused by their moods,

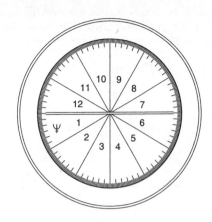

for which they can see no apparent cause.

These people have a tendency to be romantic and are often impractical in their approach to achieving their goals and desires. Neptune in this position is about dissolving the sense of self.

Neptune in the second house

Those with Neptune in the second house tend not to be too concerned about their finances, which fluctuate, sometimes wildly. They appreciate beautiful things but are often careless when it comes to looking after their cherished possessions.

Neptune in this position is about dissolving the sense of what belongs to self and what belongs to others. If Neptune is negatively aspected, these people may be dishonest in acquiring money and material possessions. If this occurs, they are likely to experience the loss of material possessions from time to time as they learn their lessons.

Neptune in the third house

This is a good position for Neptune as the psychic abilities are given expression in a practical manner. Clairvoyance, automatic writing and clairaudience (the psychic ability to hear the voices of spirits) can be developed with practice and discipline. However, without practice or with little discipline, the clairvoyant abilities merely confuse these people, and they have difficulty discerning what is intuition and what is simply a fear or hope.

Neptune in the third house is about dissolving attitudes and karma involving siblings and close family. As children, these people need to be encouraged to exercise in order to stay connected to their physical bodies and not become lost in dreams and fantasies.

Neptune in the fourth house

Those with Neptune in the fourth house usually experience insecurity and discomfort in the home. As children, they may have had a parent who did not fulfil their responsibilities in the home and, as a result, they escaped into dreams in order to create the perfect home environment within themselves. An example of this is Angela, whose father was a chronic alcoholic.

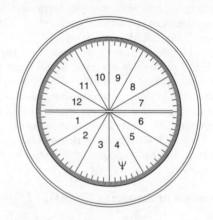

Angela's childhood was spent in chaos as her father drank away all the available funds and periodically became violent. When his violence escalated, Angela and her mother and sister were forced to seek accommodation elsewhere, usually at a local charity for days at a time.

In response to her situation, Angela created the perfect home within herself, unaffected by the reality of her situation. As an adult, she had moved home six times in the past five years, each move occurring with little or no planning.

Neptune in the fourth house is about dissolving past attitudes to the home and encouraging a stable and harmonious home environment based in reality and not in the imagination.

Neptune in the fifth house

This is a positive placement for creative endeavours, as Neptune offers inspiration and the fifth house deals with creativity and self-expression. Acting, singing or earning a living through the arts are signified with this placement.

Short-term love affairs, often secret, are shown with Neptune in the fifth house, and these can be the result of romanticising the partner and then not approaching the relationship realistically. Instead of dealing with a problem in an existing relationship, these people are likely to begin another relationship or an affair which fulfils their

need for romance. Sometimes this placement can suggest unrequited love.

Neptune in the fifth house is about dissolving the need for self-centred creativity and encouraging people to focus their creative energies upon others, including their children. The children of people with this placement can demand unusual amounts of love and attention, as Neptune seeks selfless effort and sacrifice.

Neptune in the sixth house

This placement increases the psychic abilities and encourages their use in a practical manner. Those with Neptune in the sixth house work hard and make great sacrifices for their ideals. The sixth house Virgo rulership (although in opposition to Neptune's natural twelfth house Pisces

qualities), lends a practical, earthy reality to Neptune. These people are especially sensitive to the emotions of those around them and need to ensure a balanced and harmonious work environment to maintain good health.

Neptune in the sixth house is about dissolving past attitudes to work and health, encouraging a balance between physical and spiritual needs. Exclusion of the spiritual needs can result in undiagnosable ailments, exhaustion and psychic disturbance, but favouring the spiritual needs can lead to a decline in energy and health. These people respond well to natural therapies, the elimination of certain foods from their diets, and vitamin and mineral supplements.

Neptune in the seventh house

Those with Neptune in the seventh house are often found searching for the ideal partner. They put a great deal of energy into seeking the perfect 'soul mate', hoping that this person will fulfil them. Instead, they can find partners who are likely to deceive them and who shatter their illusion of the perfect relationship.

People who are regularly deceived often participate subconsciously at some level. Neptune in the seventh house dissolves dreams and illusions regarding relationships. In place of the illusions, these people have the opportunity to develop close, loving relationships based in the real world, although this requires great sacrifice from time to time with this Neptune placement.

An example of this placement is Giselle, who came to me for a synastry reading (i.e. a careful comparison of two people's charts to ascertain compatibility and discord between them) for herself and her boyfriend. When I commented that he didn't appear to have a great deal of commitment to one relationship, she cried, 'The cad! He's married with two children and we've been having an affair for two years now . . . and he's still no closer to commitment than he ever was.'

'What makes you sure that he wants a commitment?' I asked.

'We've discussed it, often, but he just doesn't change.'

'You seem to be having doubts about this relationship.'

'It was fine until he told me that his wife was pregnant again. This means that he'll never leave her.'

Giselle dreamed of the perfect relationship but the current reality was far from the dream. Neptune in her seventh house was dissolving her illusions about partnership.

Neptune in the eighth house

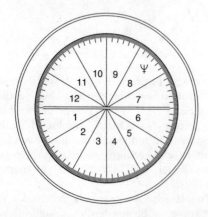

As the eighth house deals with the possessions of others and Neptune represents the dissolving of attitudes, this placement can represent the dissolving of attitudes to other people's possessions. This placement also dissolves attitudes to joint resources and to sex. It encourages these people to make sacrifices for the common good of the group.

Those with Neptune in the eighth house are usually psychic, especially regarding other people's needs. Their psychic abilities are in constant demand, whether they have consciously developed them or not, as others seek them out for help in re-balancing their energies spiritually.

Neptune in the ninth house

Those with Neptune in the ninth house are drawn to philosophy and higher learning. They prefer unplanned and unstructured travel, and need to guard against fixed opinions regarding religion or spirituality as this placement can lead to religious fanaticism.

These people have a talent for locating opportunities for spiritual learning or advancement when travelling. An example of this is Hugo, who stopped for a bite to eat and ended up deep in conversation with a monk in a roadside cafe. Wherever Hugo travels, he arrives at a location at the precise moment some mystical or spiritually significant event occurs, and he gathers the information offered to him. It is never planned by him, but life seems to place him where he needs to be at the very moment he would learn the most from a given situation.

Neptune in the ninth house is about

dissolving attitudes to religion and spiritual philosophy, and encouraging tolerance for the beliefs of others.

Neptune in the tenth house

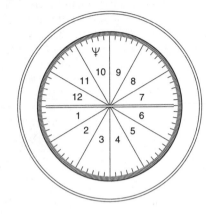

Neptune in the tenth house can assist with career success if these people have a career in the psychic sciences, nursing, or in a charity organisation. These people are idealistic and are attracted to a career which improves the lives of others. Although others may appreciate their efforts, these people often doubt themselves. This can be the result of a father or father-figure who did not encourage or show them how to find their place in the world.

Neptune in the tenth house is about dissolving past attitudes to career and to the importance of gaining a reputation in the eyes of others. It encourages the devotion of energy towards showing others that beyond material needs there is a spiritual purpose which offers everyone the peace and fulfilment they seek.

Neptune in the eleventh house

These people are humanitarian in nature and can spend a great deal of time and energy supporting their friends and acquaintances in their times of need. They attract Neptunian types of friends who share their need to dream.

If Neptune is well aspected, their friends assist them to fulfil their dreams, but when

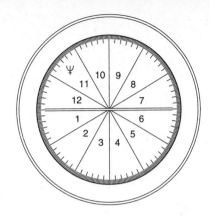

negatively aspected their friends deceive them and dissuade them from their purpose, often by draining their emotional and psychic energy or through drugs and alcohol.

An example of this occurred with Helene, who spent five years saving to start her own business. Three months before she was to leave her job, an acquaintance started his own business and borrowed half of her savings, with the promise of great returns within a short time. His business failed and Helene is still saving for her goal, 15 months later.

Neptune in the eleventh house is about dissolving attitudes to those in need. It encourages people to define their goals and their purpose, and to ensure that others do not dissuade them from achieving their goals.

Neptune in the twelfth house

Being the natural ruler of the twelfth house, Neptune increases the need for forgiveness, love and understanding. A sense of distance or isolation accompanies this placement, and this offers an opportunity to focus concentration upon deeper matters, including psychic and spiritual development.

The twelfth house deals with confinement, in the form of institutions, hospitals, monasteries or prisons, and Neptune in this house increases the tendency to work in these places or to be confined to them. Sometimes these people seem confined even though physically they are free.

Service is another aspect of the twelfth

house, and Neptune also relates to serving others in order to restore balance for past actions. Those with Neptune in the twelfth house can expect many opportunities to be of service in order to atone for past actions that caused pain or suffering to others. If this service is not given freely, confinement may be required to restore the balance. The confinement may be in the form of ill health, depression or a prison term. It may simply be the sacrifices required by a partner or a family member over a period of time.

Neptune in the twelfth house is about dissolving past-life karma and encouraging a oneness with humanity through spiritual awareness.

PLUTO

The planet Pluto completes one cycle every 248 years. Pluto rules the sign of Scorpio and its natural placement is the eighth house. Pluto has an elliptical (non-circular) orbit, which means that it spends only a relatively short time in some signs compared with others. For example, Pluto moved through the sign of Cancer for 24 years (July 1913–October 1937), yet it passed through Scorpio in just over 11 years (November 1983–January 1995).

Pluto is a planet of transformation. Transformation sometimes requires a death of the old to make room for the new and Pluto assists with this type of regeneration.

Pluto also rules obsession and compulsion, destruction and conflict. The Pluto conflict goes deeper than the power struggles of Mars, to revenge and vendetta.

The effect of Pluto is to assist with spiritual growth in any way that is necessary. Pluto often brings great change with it and the wise course of action is usually to surrender to the change. The change may take the form of loss, enlightenment, a serious accident, a psychological breakthrough or even death.

In mythology, Pluto ruled the underworld and, in everyday terms, it still does. Drugs, weapons, smuggling, prostitution and spying are some of the things ruled by this planet.

When Pluto brings change to your door, there really is no choice but to accept it. Although Pluto destroys situations, it also offers new opportunities in place of the old. Pluto forces people to look within at the darker side of themselves so that they can take responsibility for those fears and desires which lurk in the shadows.

Pluto in the signs

Pluto moved through Aries from 1822 to 1851 and through Taurus from 1851 to 1882. As it is extremely unlikely that anyone reading this book would have been born in this period, I have not included these placements.

Pluto in Gemini (1882–1912)

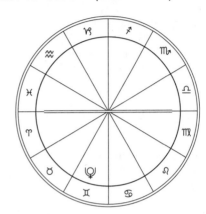

Those with Pluto in Gemini have the ability to communicate directly and to penetrate the defences of others with words. This placement increases the journalistic tendencies, making it difficult to keep a secret from these people. They enjoy reading thrillers and mysteries. An interest in psychology and a mind which is restless for knowledge and capable of studying many and varied things are also Pluto in Gemini qualities.

Pluto in Cancer (1912–1938)

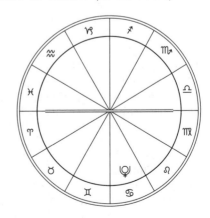

Those with Pluto in Cancer are offered an opportunity to learn as a result of family turmoil. They may be cut off from their families through death or divorce, or simply through the Cancerian tendency to hide away from anything that doesn't look or feel pleasant. Pluto insists that these people face their family issues, which often manifest as family power struggles. Issues surrounding home, country, family groups, and emotional stability and security stemming from a feeling of belonging are challenged when Pluto is Cancer.

Pluto in Leo (1938–1957)
Those with Pluto in Leo can expect to be tested in terms of their creative expression and their sense of self. Against all odds, these people pursue their goals, especially creatively. They can also expect to be tested by their children, who may challenge their

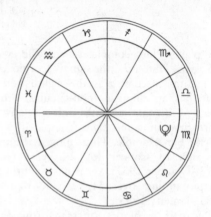

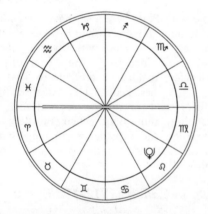

beliefs and their way of life. When challenged, these people need to be aware of an innate urge to want to crush and to dominate their loved ones. The lesson is one of surrendering to the current circumstances offered by Pluto. If they do crush or dominate their offspring, they may win the battle but lose the trust of those they love.

Pluto in Virgo (1957–1972)
Those with Pluto in Virgo are usually analytical and tend to be more aware of diet and physical health than most other placements. They are often demanding, especially of themselves, and they need to guard against expecting the same standard from others as they do from themselves.

When Pluto is negatively aspected, these people can seek out drugs and chemicals to alter their reality or to smooth their paths through life. Pluto in Virgo suggests an all or nothing attitude to self-awareness. They are either very strict or escapist when it comes to being aware of who they are.

Pluto in Libra (1972–1984)

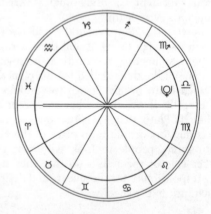

Those with Pluto in Libra have a desire for justice, inner peace and harmony. Relationships and partnerships can be a battleground until they surrender to the idea that negotiated solutions ensure lasting harmony. Until they learn this, they tend to experience difficulties in hearing their partner or being heard by them. Those with this placement may continually test their relationship partners' commitment to them and to the relationship, as they can be jealous.

Cooperation and compromise are required with this placement, and these people may have to lose all that they value in order to realise their own true worth and the value of harmonious agreements between themselves and others.

Pluto in Scorpio (1984–1995)

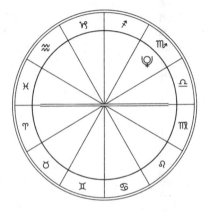

As Pluto rules Scorpio, those with this placement have an innate need to know the truth of a matter. This is because Pluto brings transformation and Scorpio desires to understand the essence of people and situations. Naturally intuitive, they know when others are attempting to deceive them and they are swift in their retaliation for broken trust.

These people have a talent for research and are interested in the psychic sciences, past lives and reincarnation. Psychology, hypnosis and pathology fascinate them, as does tracing the family tree.

Those with this placement have deep courage and a will of steel when it comes to facing the darker side of themselves or others. When negatively aspected, they dissipate their energies in the pursuit of alcohol, drugs and sexual conquests.

These people have very long memories for emotional hurts and can be ruthless in their need to even the score. They have a strong sense of justice and unless there is a strong amount of air (Gemini, Libra or Aquarius) in the chart, reason and logic can be dominated by emotional urges.

Pluto in Sagittarius (1995–2010)

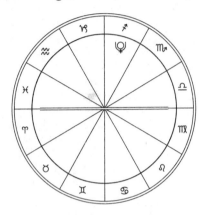

Those with Pluto in Sagittarius have a need for honesty and can be ruthless in their exposure of people who are deceitful. Naturally philosophical, they seek to discover the essence of any philosophy or religion before giving it their total commitment.

The lesson here is to transform the higher mind, clearing it of all confusion or false beliefs. Those with Pluto in Sagittarius challenge philosophies or religions which ask for faith and offer scant explanation in real terms. They travel far in search of higher learning and their innate desire for understanding can produce clarity of thinking.

Pluto in the houses

Pluto in the first house

Those with Pluto in the first house are usually strong-willed with great powers of attraction and repulsion. They can draw people and opportunities to them without apparent effort, and repel people and situations that they don't want to be involved with, again without effort.

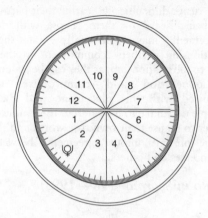

These people can experience powerful emotional swings and are often hesitant to reveal themselves to others. Defiant when pushed, they are determined to live life their way and to go at their own pace.

People with this placement need to become aware of the effect they have upon others, as their Pluto first house nature can make them intense and sometimes inconsiderate of others. When they decide that they don't like someone, they usually ignore them completely.

The lesson for these people is to use their courage and independence to transform their outlook and to fulfil what they perceive as their unique destiny.

Pluto in the second house

Those with Pluto in the second house can be emotionally and materially possessive, and they need to guard against unethical conduct in the pursuit of material things. They believe that material security brings emotional security. If they cling to this belief, life strips away their material base from time to time, to allow them to find inner security.

They can appear stubborn, defensive and slow to change. They usually possess inner strength, patience and perseverance.

The lesson for these people is to transform their attitudes to material things and to people. They are in the process of learning to value people above material things, and this lesson may be painful from time to time as they lose those material possessions they value. They are also learning the value of the opinions of others in reaching balanced conclusions.

Pluto in the third house

Those with Pluto in the third house often possess penetrative minds, which collect data and piece together puzzles, whether physical or mental. They have an innate need to discover how the physical world works and to label or classify the world as they have come to know it. To do this they observe patterns in physical and mental occurrences.

The third house communication influence makes these people powerful speakers and writers, able to put great emotional force into their communications. In extreme cases they can become compulsive talkers, as the third house restlessness becomes a channel for the Pluto force.

Journalism or short-story writing appeals to them if Mercury is well aspected, as they possess minds capable of penetrating to the core of a matter and expressing it in clear and concise terms.

There may be power struggles with close relatives or siblings, or they may assist those close to them to transform their beliefs about life.

Pluto in the fourth house

Those with Pluto in the fourth house can experience turmoil in their home life, especially in their early years, as they strip away all those things they have become dependant upon for emotional security. There may be power struggles with one or both parents and, if Mars is also in the fourth house, this may take the form of a parent who is tyrannical at home but the opposite in public. The need for emotional security can be intense, contributing to mood swings and subtle manipulations to control the source of emotional security. They feel an unquenchable hunger for emotional nurturing which can dominate their lives. It is unquenchable because they must fulfil themselves from within, not from without.

These people swing between their emotional dependency upon others and their need to find people who depend upon them emotionally and whom they can control.

When circumstances disintegrate, they find the inner strength to face any crisis. When they discover their inner strength, they can nurture others without fear of loss or the desire to control.

They are usually intuitive and imaginative, and need to guard against using their imagination to feed their fears. The lesson here is to find an inner security that is not dependant upon a home or comfortable surroundings.

Pluto in the fifth house

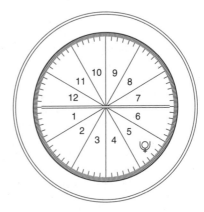

Those with Pluto in the fifth house have the ability to focus great attention and energy in creative endeavours, leaving the finished product with a magnetic energy and attraction. If they are unable to channel their energy into something creative, it may find a release through sex in love affairs or brief liaisons.

The children of these people can open up a deeper understanding within their parents, as this placement suggests a child from whom the parent can learn a difficult but valuable lesson.

These people need to be in charge of their own destinies and to shape their lives with their wills. They have to guard against being self-centred. In a positive sense, this placement can show great reserves of energy for creativity, a deep love of children, a magnetic personality and a need to protect those close to them. In a negative sense, these people can become attention-seeking, competitive and wilful where compromise is required.

Pluto in the sixth house

Those with Pluto in the sixth house are often keen to delve into the problems of others in order to help restore balance, and this placement indicates careers in psychology, natural therapies and healing. These people usually have a keen sense of touch, enabling them to locate physical health problems through touch, massage and so on.

They usually have the ability to organise people and situations effectively without the need for continual recognition. They have keen analytical minds which quietly categorise those around them. Their powers of analysis are very strong and their self-analysis can lead to self-criticism if they are not careful. To avoid this continual self-criticism, they sometimes fill their waking hours with work and other obligations, preventing any thought of themselves.

When negatively aspected, these people can be extremely critical, using Pluto to strip away the masks that others wear while avoiding any self-examination. Their own self-criticism has already stopped them from doing or creating anything which might be criticised and this criticism of others can lead to criticism from others in return.

The lesson here is one of tolerance and self-sacrifice in order to benefit others. The sacrifice often involves hard work and they

need to guard against becoming obsessive with work standards.

Pluto in the seventh house

Those with Pluto in the seventh house often experience emotional turbulence in relationships. They seek to control their relationship and/or business partners, and until they learn to listen and cooperate, relationships can involve continual struggle.

They attract emotionally strong partners and seek to control them. In the positive sense, these people can be very intense in their love for those close to them and they must guard against jealousy.

The lesson here is to learn how to be equal in relationships with others. These people can be compulsive in their need to be in relationships and in their approach to them, leading to situations where one partner dominates the other. They have a strong desire to be liked and needed by others.

They can benefit from being aware of the importance of time alone as well as time spent with others. Time spent alone can give them the opportunity to reflect upon the state of their relationship with themselves and with others.

Pluto in the eighth house
Those with Pluto in the eighth house are usually intuitive, with the ability to penetrate to the core of a person or a situation. This is the natural house for Pluto and this

placement makes for very intense people, as they combine Pluto's need to transform and the eighth house desire to strip away that which is superfluous in life.

They can be 'all or nothing' people, who throw themselves into situations or ignore their surroundings. They make good investigators and can intuitively understand people quickly and accurately.

These people seek out intense experiences in life — where most of us hold back because of the risks involved, they walk boldly into the fire.

When pushed, these people can be vindictive and unrelenting in seeking personal justice. They can be dogmatic and stubborn and emotionally manipulative through emotional withdrawal. When they seek answers they leave no stone unturned and they are capable of facing the darkest parts of themselves with courage and determination. They can also be very secretive.

The lesson with this placement involves stripping away all the layers of conditioning to reveal the essence within. To find and nurture that spiritual essence or core is of paramount importance for spiritual growth and development for these people.

Pluto in the ninth house

Those with Pluto in the ninth house have a strong thirst for knowledge and are prepared to travel far to enhance their understanding of life. Theirs is a deeply philosophical or religious nature and they need to guard against becoming fanatical about particular beliefs.

The psychic sciences appeal to them, as does any study that requires intense focus and dedication. They need to understand life and to know where they belong. They believe that their destiny is unique and they seek the freedom to pursue their destiny. Universal truth features strongly in their lives and in their search for meaning.

Their enthusiasm for what they discover about life leads them to want to convert others to their points of view, and they need to guard against becoming too zealous in their philosophical approach. When others resist their approaches, they can feel alienated.

They are capable of grasping the essence of a situation very quickly and they value honesty and openness. They are also intuitive and capable of rising above the smaller details to keep an awareness of life's 'big picture'.

The lesson with this placement is to strip away the day-to-day responsibilities in order to glimpse the purpose of life.

Pluto in the tenth house

Those with Pluto in the tenth house have magnetic personalities which suit them to positions of power. If they use this power irresponsibly, power struggles usually follow, resulting in destruction.

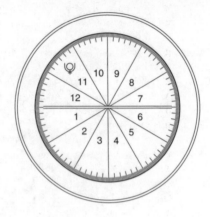

The tenth house Pluto power struggle involves controlling society or being controlled by it. These people can feel restricted and made powerless by society, or they can place too much emphasis upon career and status. Thus they can justify any and all actions on the basis that 'it was in the interest of the company/country' etc.

When things don't go their way, these people withdraw. They are good organisers and pragmatic in their approach to goals. They are usually ambitious and occasionally anxious. They need to guard against being hypocritical when it suits their purposes and autocratic in their handling of subordinates.

The lesson with this placement is to learn to establish one's individuality or authority within a group or a society. This may be in the form of social responsibilities and in the negative sense, it can involve manipulating the system to get to the top.

Pluto in the eleventh house

Those with Pluto in the eleventh house can be idealists, and they are effective representatives for groups who support a cause. They are dedicated to human equality and are often charismatic.

They are intuitive and sensitive to the needs of any group with which they are involved and they can be convincing speakers when discussing the group's objectives. They can be eccentric and erratic in behaviour, sometimes deliberately so, in order to ensure that they are not a part of the majority.

They have an innate need to reform themselves which sometimes manifests as a need to reform others or society. They need to see others' beliefs in action to judge their effectiveness before dissecting them and casting aside important aspects of their philosophy. They also need to develop awareness of when their ideas are an improvement upon the traditional way and when they are simply a reaction to the acceptable path. Pluto in the eleventh house can lead them out of the mainstream and into a life of isolation if they don't accept any of the ideas and concepts of those around them.

The lesson with this placement is to strip away any outmoded understanding of life. They may do this by rejecting the beliefs accepted by their parents and peers and they usually review their own beliefs periodically.

Pluto in the twelfth house

Those with Pluto in the twelfth house have the ability to delve deeply into themselves and into the mysteries of life. Naturally intuitive, they gravitate towards those who are most in need of transformation, such as people with physical or mental health problems. They have the ability to locate the source of a physical or emotional problem quickly through the use of energy rather than words.

They may undergo periods of isolation in order to replenish themselves physically and spiritually, and if they don't do this willingly, life arranges these times of reflection for them. They are at their best when supporting the downtrodden and are often more assertive when negotiating on behalf of others than they are when only their own needs are involved.

These people are naturally psychic and deeply private. They seem to understand that to keep a secret from others, first you must keep it from yourself. Pluto in this house dissolves the sense of self or ego, leaving these people with a weakened sense of identity.

When negatively aspected, these people can feel restricted by the sacrifices required of them throughout life and may sink into a quiet state of depression or despair. To remedy this, they need to spend time among those who are more in need than themselves and yet who still struggle towards realising their goals.

The lesson here is to tear away the physical in order to reveal the spiritual. These people are learning to see beyond the physical circumstances to understand the spiritual causes and consequences of their actions.

Part 4

A Deeper
Awareness

MANY HAPPY RETURNS

A natal chart shows the position of each planet on the day of a person's birth. These planets move through the zodiac (and the chart) and eventually return to the same position they were at the moment of birth, but at different times from one another because of the different lengths of their orbits.

When a planet completes a cycle, it can have a profound effect upon us, and knowing when this will happen can help us to prepare for change and growth.

The Sun completes one cycle every 365 days. This is called a *solar return* or, more commonly, a *birthday*. The Moon or *lunar return* occurs every 28 years, and at 14 years of age the progressed Moon is opposite the natal Moon (as it has completed half its cycle), causing opposition to the mother or mother-figure. This enables us to break free of maternal influence and become independent.

Saturn completes one cycle every 29.5 years. At almost 15 years of age we experience a *Saturn opposition* (the halfway point of the cycle). This urges us to challenge those things our fathers represent so that we can become independent of paternal beliefs about life.

The *Saturn return* at 29.5 years is marked by a period of seriousness and reflection upon life, friends and career. This is the time when many women consider the alternatives of having a family and pursuing a career, and many men seek a long-term partner and consider settling down to family life. If already in a long-term relationship or career, the Saturn return is a time to reconsider whether this is the most suitable path for long-term fulfilment.

A second Saturn return occurs at 59 years of age, and at this time we reflect upon our lives and our career achievements.

Jupiter completes a cycle every 12 years. The *Jupiter return* is a time when we feel invigorated and enthusiastic about pursuing new goals and challenges. It is a positive time.

The *Uranus return* occurs at 84 years. *Uranus opposition* occurs at 42 years of age. Each point where Uranus squares (i.e. at 90 degrees to the return position), opposes or returns to the position it was at our birth indicates a time of change. These ages are 21, 42, 63 and 84 years.

At the age of 21, we are considered mature in the eyes of society. We reconsider our life paths at 42 years, often acting out of character and forcing changes to our life direction. The *Uranus opposition* can take the form of leaving a long-term partner. Stefan is a classic example. Three weeks after leaving his wife of 20 years, I saw him driving a red sports car, his passenger a very young woman.

Another *Uranus square* occurs at 63 years, again a period of change. This is a time of preparation for retirement.

As *Neptune* and *Pluto* spend different periods of time in each sign, there is no set age for their squares and oppositions. Neptune returns at 165 years and Pluto at 248 years, so these returns are not significant here.

One of the most important periods for change is between the ages of 28 and 30, when the Saturn and lunar returns fall close to one another. Few people come through these returns unchanged, and they have the potential to help us shed much of our emotional and physical baggage for the journey ahead.

PLANETARY RETURNS

Solar	1 year
Jupiter	12 years
Lunar	28 years
Saturn	29.5 years
Uranus	84 years
Neptune	165 years
Pluto	248 years

THE MOON'S NODES

The Moon's nodes are of great significance in astrology; in fact, some astrologers read only the Sun, Moon and the Moon's nodes in chart interpretation.

The *south node* ☋ can be seen as a bowl, which contains our past experiences and understanding from previous lifetimes and the early years of our present lifetimes; the *north node* ☊ is like a pair of headphones, through which the universe directs us towards our fulfilment.

The north and south nodes are always opposite one another. For example, if your north node is in Taurus then your south node must be in Scorpio, its opposite sign.

The north node is the path ahead of us whereas the south node represents our footprints. The south node is the foundation upon which we can explore our north node. Those who choose to dwell in the familiar territory of the south node are unlikely to find fulfilment in life. Deep fulfilment comes after we have explored and understood the lessons of our north node.

While the north node points to the qualities we need to develop in order to become complete, the south node shows us which negative qualities we need to release. As children, we usually live in the familiarity of our south nodes. It is only as we mature that circumstances encourage us to develop our north node awareness. While some people never release themselves from the familiarity of their south node patterns, most of us have an awareness of our north node obstacles and opportunities by the time we reach our mid thirties.

The Moon's nodal placement moves backwards through the zodiac at the rate of about one sign every 18 months. Consequently, every person born in this 18-month period will have the same Moon's nodes. For example, from March 30, 1969 until October 16, 1970 the Moon's north node was in Pisces, so all those born during this period will have their north node in Pisces and their south node in Virgo.

The following table lists the Moon's north nodes for the 20th century. If someone was born on a day when the Moon's node moved from one sign to the next and you don't have an exact natal chart, simply read the description for both signs and decide which one better describes the person in question.

The Moon's north nodes

January 1, 1900	— December 28, 1900	Sagittarius
December 29, 1900	— July 18, 1902	Scorpio
July 18, 1902	— February 5, 1904	Libra
February 6, 1904	— August 24, 1905	Virgo
August 25, 1905	— March 14, 1907	Leo
March 15, 1907	— September, 30 1908	Cancer
October 1, 1908	— April 20, 1910	Gemini
April 21, 1910	— November 7, 1911	Taurus
November 8, 1911	— May 27, 1913	Aries
May 28, 1913	— December 14, 1914	Pisces
December 15, 1914	— July 3, 1916	Aquarius
July 4, 1916	— January 20, 1918	Capricorn
January 21, 1918	— August 10, 1919	Sagittarius
August 11, 1919	— February 26, 1921	Scorpio
February 27, 1921	— September 16, 1922	Libra
September 17, 1922	— April 4, 1924	Virgo
April 5, 1924	— October 23, 1925	Leo
October 24, 1925	— May 12, 1927	Cancer
May 13, 1927	— November 29, 1928	Gemini
November 30, 1928	— June 18, 1930	Taurus
June 19, 1930	— January 6, 1932	Aries
January 7, 1932	— July 26, 1933	Pisces
July 27, 1933	— February 12, 1935	Aquarius
February 13, 1935	— September 1, 1936	Capricorn
September 2, 1936	— March 21, 1938	Sagittarius
March 22, 1938	— October 9, 1939	Scorpio
October 10, 1939	— April 27, 1941	Libra
April 28, 1941	— November 15, 1942	Virgo
November 16, 1942	— June 3, 1944	Leo
June 4, 1944	— December 22, 1945	Cancer
December 23, 1945	— July 11, 1947	Gemini
July 12, 1947	— January 28, 1949	Taurus

January 29, 1949	—	August 17, 1950	Aries
August 18, 1950	—	March 6, 1952	Pisces
March 7, 1952	—	September 23, 1953	Aquarius
September 24, 1953	—	April 13, 1955	Capricorn
April 14, 1955	—	October 31, 1956	Sagittarius
November 1, 1956	—	May 20, 1958	Scorpio
May 21, 1958	—	December 8, 1959	Libra
December 9, 1959	—	June 26, 1961	Virgo
June 27, 1961	—	January 14, 1963	Leo
January 15, 1963	—	August 2, 1964	Cancer
August 3, 1964	—	February 20, 1966	Gemini
February 21, 1966	—	September 9, 1967	Taurus
September 10, 1967	—	March 29, 1969	Aries
March 30, 1969	—	October 16, 1970	Pisces
October 17, 1970	—	May 5, 1972	Aquarius
May 6, 1972	—	November 22, 1973	Capricorn
November 23, 1973	—	June 12, 1975	Sagittarius
June 13, 1975	—	December 29, 1976	Scorpio
December 30, 1976	—	July 19, 1978	Libra
July 20, 1978	—	February 5, 1980	Virgo
February 6, 1980	—	August 25, 1981	Leo
August 26, 1981	—	March 15, 1983	Cancer
March 16, 1983	—	October 1, 1984	Gemini
October 1, 1984	—	April 21, 1986	Taurus
April 22, 1986	—	November 8, 1987	Aries
November 9, 1987	—	May 28, 1989	Pisces
May 29, 1989	—	December 15, 1990	Aquarius
December 16, 1990	—	July 4, 1992	Capricorn
July 5, 1992	—	January 21, 1994	Sagittarius
January 22, 1994	—	August 11, 1995	Scorpio
August 12, 1995	—	February 27, 1997	Libra
February 28, 1997	—	September 17, 1998	Virgo
September 18, 1998	—	March 18, 2000	Leo

Aries north – Libra south node

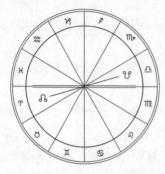

Those with an Aries north node are in the process of learning about self-confidence and the importance of pursuing goals. Often these people fall into their past-life pattern of pleasing others instead of forging ahead in pursuit of their own goals. Although they are usually adept at creating harmony by mediating between warring factions, while they continue to do this fulfilment eludes them.

Fulfilment for these people comes from being who they are regardless of how others react. Life constantly tests them by creating situations where they are forced to think for themselves, until they realise they are indeed capable of achieving things that they only previously dared dream about.

An example of this placement occurred with Rosemary, whose Libra south node found her depleting her reserves of energy in her attempt to keep harmony in her 17-year marriage to John. One day John arrived home to declare that he was moving out to live with his new girlfriend. Rosemary was devastated.

After a period of grief, however, Rosemary realised that she had to pick herself up and start building a new life. After working at several part-time jobs, she spent three years studying and is currently pursuing all of her newfound goals, including acting, travel and a career. John is so impressed with the changes in Rosemary that he asked if he could come back and make a new start. She laughingly told me her reply: 'No, John. I've done all the ironing of men's shirts I intend doing in this lifetime.' It was hard for her to stick to her decision at first, but the promise of her Aries north node called her onwards to a confident life ahead.

To truly discover themselves, these people need periods of time alone. Although they enjoy their own company, they can fear being alone as their south node past experience is of finding themselves through others. As they develop a sense of themselves, they can become overly assertive, until they find a balance between the Libran sense of harmony and the Arian sense of individuality.

Taurus north – Scorpio south node

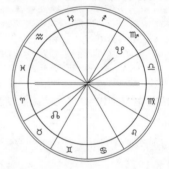

Those with a Taurus north node are in the process of learning about the stability and pleasure offered by material things. These people can find themselves falling back into past-life patterns of desire and the need to please their partners sexually, without acknowledging their own emotional and sexual needs.

In simple terms, the Taurus north node is about building a set of values to live by. If these people fall back into their Scorpio south node there are constant power struggles, crises and emotional instability as they struggle to learn about moderation. An example of this is Craig.

Craig displayed a destructive pattern in his love relationships of which he was unaware. Whenever he started a new relationship, he would begin to push his partner away from him. In a subtle but forceful manner, he continually tested his partners' emotional limits until they left him, usually never to speak with him again.

At the end of each of his relationships, Craig moved forwards into his Taurus north node, building stability and self-confidence until the next relationship. However, as soon as he began a new relationship, his destructive tendencies surfaced once again.

The Scorpio south node is often evident in clandestine meetings and affairs, or in a hidden agenda and a struggle for power. When living in the Scorpio south node, these people find it almost impossible to receive pleasure from their partners, as this might give their partners some small amount of control over them.

When slighted, those with a Scorpio south node can respond with deadly accuracy, pursuing their opponent relentlessly while ensuring that they appear to be innocent when the score has been evened.

As they move forward into the Taurus north node, they find stability, contentment and abundance. They discover that these are available for everyone, so they need not feel threatened when others seek these things as well.

Gemini north – Sagittarius south node

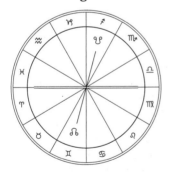

Those with a Gemini north node are in the process of learning about society and the benefits of a community. After lifetimes of independence they are learning to value the opinions and beliefs of those around them.

With a Sagittarius south node these people occasionally feel restless and they resist inclusion in community events as they fear that responsibility stifles them. Co-operation with others benefits them greatly when they are able to leave behind their fear that society or the community may restrict them. Perhaps in past lives these people lacked the ability to cooperate with others and, because of this, they lacked the feedback that others offered them.

Those with a Gemini north node need encouragement to include themselves in group activities, in order to realise that many different viewpoints can sometimes lead to a greater understanding of a situation or a concept.

At first they tend to want to be the group leader and become frustrated when others don't follow them. Before they can lead successfully they need to learn how to listen to others and to heed the advice of those who have more experience. This proves very difficult for Gemini north node people, but in time they come to see that all situations can be viewed from several different angles, and that more balanced decisions are made after considering every possible angle.

Diplomacy and communication skills need to be carefully developed to assist these people to express what they have learned from previous lives. Education is usually important to these people for them to feel acceptable to others and to society. Higher learning is greatly valued by these people in the first half of their lives, and they can be condescending to those who do not have a university education.

An example of the Gemini north node is Marla. As a child of 10, Marla emigrated to Australia from Russia with her parents and her two sisters. She looked forward to starting her new life until she realised that the language barrier caused what seemed like insurmountable obstacles. Her parents spoke very little English and her sisters were so confused and frightened by their new environment that they became almost mute after they arrived. It was left to Marla to learn the new language and to communicate for the whole family. Anytime a stranger appeared at the front door or there were some forms to fill out, Marla was summoned to sort out any possible misunderstanding.

At first Marla resented the responsibility, but later she realised the opportunities that mixing with the community offered. New friendships were forged and a friend's mother discovered that Marla wanted to resume playing the piano. An old pianola was delivered and sheet music arrived almost weekly. Slowly it occurred to Marla that her new community actually wanted her to be happy and that when she communicated her needs to them they responded. In turn, when the community required help, Marla responded with all she could offer. She is now a social worker, specialising in the integration of immigrant communities.

Cancer north – Capricorn south node

Those with a Cancer north node are in the process of learning about nature, emotions and the importance of nourishing others. Nurturing others spiritually, emotionally, mentally and physically is the purpose of those with this nodal position. With their Capricorn south node, these people feel their responsibilities keenly, and they tend to focus on practicalities rather than emotions.

In their past lives, they were in charge of others and their hunger for prestige and social position is still evident. They prefer being served to being of service to others, and life continues to thwart them in their attempts to be admired and powerful.

Money and material possessions are a stumbling block now and they have to learn to value feelings and family above profit.

Each time they revert to their Capricorn south node inclination to hoard money and material possessions, they experience emotional and spiritual emptiness until they reach out for emotional fulfilment.

These people have a tendency to take advantage of those close to them, especially financially, and the justification used here is that 'business is business'. Any material or financial advantage can weigh them down or slow their progress towards mastering the Cancer north node lesson until they learn that others require nurturing and not an acquisitive friend.

These people often grow up with poor role models for nurturing and have to draw upon their own resources to find the wellspring. They must learn to give nourishment as well as receive it. This is very hard at first, as their rigid past-life attitudes have to be cast off before they can truly allow others to become close to them. When these people learn to nourish others they discover that giving is receiving. It doesn't matter whether they nurture one or 100 people, but rather that they do so. An example of a north node in Cancer is Georgina, a friend of mine.

Georgina grew up in a home where nurturing was virtually nonexistent. Her mother resented the limitations a child placed on her life, and Georgina soon realised that money and position were more important than family responsibilities.

As an adult, Georgina joined the public service and started to work her way up to a position of power and prestige. No fulfilment came from these efforts, so she left and started her own business. She soon established a good reputation and a certain amount of prestige accompanied her career. Still it was not enough, so Georgina sold the business and moved away from her friends and associates.

Georgina married and had two children, although she never saw herself as a mother. Rather, she described herself as a career person, a manager, a leader. At first she resented the lack of freedom motherhood brought with it, but slowly she started to develop her Cancer north node, realising that as she nurtured her children, she too felt nurtured.

Georgina's career urges once again surfaced, but this time she chose a career that involved nurturing others. She started to grow crops organically, as this was the purest type of food she could imagine. Now, in growing food for others, she has both a career and an outlet for her nurturing. It is interesting that the sign of Cancer rules the stomach and what Georgina grows ends up nurturing through the stomach.

Leo north – Aquarius south node

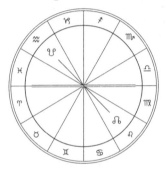

Those with a Leo north node are learning about their inner strengths. They are learning how to express who they are and to overcome their easygoing attitudes in favour of creating the lives they want for themselves.

To teach them about their inner strength, life arranges for them to face problems alone, without friends to support them. As they confront their hurdles, they need to ensure that their energy is not misdirected into self-pity. When they overcome their challenges alone they are better equipped to show others how to do the same. They can become a beacon of light to all those around them who have yet to face their own tests in life.

Overcoming self-doubt in order to become a true leader is part of the Leo north node lesson. The past-life Aquarian desires to enlist the help of friends fails to make any difference when facing tests in the present life, as these people may seek the advice of others, but rarely do they take it.

Self-discipline brings results, but with their past-life Aquarian experiences of being free to do whatever they choose, these people avoid situations where others discipline them. Until they learn about self-discipline, much of their energy can be wasted on creative projects that are never completed.

Independence versus purpose is the struggle here. The purpose cannot be fulfilled until the need for independence is laid to rest. The Aquarian south node sense of fairness and equality stands them in good stead for leadership positions when they have decided upon a purpose in this lifetime.

These people thrive on competition, but do not seek the advantage over others. A goal which is not won fairly is worthless to them. Real strength includes compassion for others. At first these people avoid competition, as it appears unfair that only some win. Later they realise that achieving personal goals need not adversely affect others, in fact it can sometimes inspire others to do the same.

The Aquarian south node need for freedom to pursue individuality can hinder these people in their early years. Yet as they are left alone to face life's tests, they begin to recognise their true strengths. Eventually they can start to express their individuality creatively and with confidence.

Sometimes these people live an independent life regardless of whether they are married or in a long-term relationship. They keep others at a distance and fear losing their freedom or their individuality to a relationship.

The Leo north node offers great success in life when they have learned about their inner strength and the value of sharing who they are with the world. This nodal position shows us the inventor, creating anew from what is around them and expressing a concept or idea in a fresh manner.

Virgo north – Pisces south node

Those with a Virgo north node are learning about developing a clear understanding of themselves and of life. Past-life experiences have seen them depend upon others and avoid facing life squarely; in this lifetime they must learn to discern who and what deserves their time, attention and efforts.

When they fall back into their Pisces south node, these people endure a life of confusion and emotional chaos from which they hope to be rescued by others. Instead, others are relying upon them for support and their Pisces south node makes it hard to say 'enough is enough'. Escaping through daydreams, drugs and alcohol only brings more problems, and this north node challenge forces them towards clarity of mind and a perceptive understanding of how life really works.

Past-life experiences of being of service to others and of being persecuted or not acknowledged have left a trace of martyrdom within these people, and the Virgo north node prompts them to ask themselves 'Is it really worth it?' when they set out on a path of self-sacrifice.

The Virgo north node points these people towards health and healing, including nursing, medicine, natural therapies and dietary approaches to health.

The Pisces south node sometimes produces health problems resulting from psychic disturbance or an imbalance between the physical and spiritual bodies. Finding a balance between the two can show them the path to true healing.

These people often lack confidence in themselves and have to be pushed at first. They can picture their goals completed perfectly, but fear that such a high standard is impossible. They need to learn self-discipline as their Virgo north node is practical enough to make their dreams a reality if they can overcome their Pisces south nodal pull towards being content to dream the dream rather than experience the reality.

Don't dream it, be it is the lesson here. Although they can be critical of others when others fail to achieve their goals, they can have a different set of rules for themselves, preferring to believe that others have never had it so hard. Peter, a friend whose north node is in Virgo, has developed a system to allow for his Pisces south node.

I phoned to invite him for lunch one day and he declined, as he had booked two days of 'absolute self-pity, followed by an evening of wallowing'. After I stopped laughing, he assured me that by setting aside time specifically for self-pity, he was able to be more effective in his day-to-day living. He then invited me to attend and I politely declined as I was aware that one's wallow does not a summer make!

Happiness comes from being of service to others rather than hoping that others will serve them by removing their past sorrows. Service, efficiency and attention to detail are things to be developed by those with a Virgo north node.

An example of this lesson occurred to me (I have a Virgo north node) in London in the late 1980s when I worked as a clairvoyant in a psychic centre. Despite my years of experience, I spent the first few weeks in a state of confusion. The centre was a profitable business and the manager was strict about the length of time each reading was to last. Cassette tapes were C30s (15 minutes each side) and C60s (30 minutes each side) and the readings lasted 15, 30 or 45 minutes, according to the cost.

We were instructed to start the tape as soon as the client sat down and to complete the reading as soon as the tape stopped. I baulked at the idea of stopping the reading according to time and the manager often enquired sarcastically, 'What do you want for £20 — their life story?'.

He was teaching me that structure is important. My longest reading previously had taken three hours and 20 minutes, mostly due to the fact that I was unassertive and could not bring myself to say 'Enough!'. I maintain that I can now give a better reading in 60 minutes than I ever did in twice the time.

Libra north – Aries south node

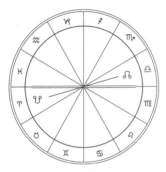

Those with a Libra north node are learning about self-sacrifice and the importance of other people in their lives. The Aries south node past-life experiences of putting themselves first and doing whatever was necessary to get what they wanted has to be curbed in order to learn the lesson of the Libra north node.

Listening to others is very difficult for those with an Aries south node, and they can change their minds at will with little awareness of how it will affect others. Competitiveness, single-mindedness, selfishness and vanity are evident here, but all these things leave them empty and hungry for someone to share life with, something that only their Libra north node can offer them.

The lesson here involves learning to give rather than to receive, and although those with an Aries south node often have a full heart, they can find it difficult sharing their fullness with others. Love is without value until it is given away and this is part of the lesson for the Libra north node.

Goals and challenges call these people forwards, but emptiness awaits at the achievement of each goal. It is the journey and not the outcome which is truly important, and someone to share the journey can make all the difference when the goals have been reached.

The Aries south node is filled with memories of competition and achievement, yet in this lifetime those things offer scant fulfilment. The lesson is to realise that competition must now give way to cooperation. Until they learn this, they find themselves alone with their achievements.

This nodal lesson is even more evident in relationships. Their tendency to compete with their partners or to discount their partners' feelings, wants and needs in favour of fulfilling themselves leads to arguments, which their Aries south node enjoys, as it appears as a contest to be won. An example of the Libra north node is Roxanne.

Roxanne resisted what she described as 'losing myself in a relationship' by remaining fiercely independent. She was so independent that her partner, Carlos, sometimes wondered if he was in a relationship with her at all. She was scornful of his neediness, and in fact shrank from the neediness of all those around her.

After ending her relationship with Carlos, Roxanne had a series of relationship disasters, which led her to decide that she wanted to be alone, as she felt that relationships weren't worth the effort.

Finally, Roxanne fell in love with a man who was as independent as she was. She was thrilled with the idea of two people who didn't need one another, but were happy to spend time together when it suited them. In time, however, she discovered that Nicholas seemed to have very few needs indeed and that she could not find a way to increase his happiness.

When she first spoke of her need to please Nicholas, I had to remind myself that I was hearing this from Roxanne. What had started out as a challenge — to please Nicholas — was rapidly becoming a source of great pain for Roxanne. Being faced with her own need to conquer her partner and still remain independent highlighted to her the futility of the loneliness that results from continual competition with others. She was starting on the path towards sharing and cooperation, the Libra north node lesson.

Self-love must give way to love of others with this nodal position and self-sacrifice is required as an expression of unselfish love for others.

Scorpio north – Taurus south node

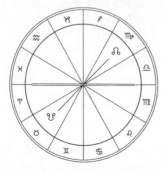

Those with a Scorpio north node are learning about the need to surrender to changes within. These changes relate to their understanding of life.

The Taurus south node carries a set of beliefs about life which these people stubbornly cling to, despite evidence that life is different from their perceptions. They must surrender their need for ownership — possessions and the pursuit of material things can consume much of their waking hours, yet bring them limited fulfilment.

They want to possess their partners, their families and all those things they desire but do not yet own. It is not sufficient for them to admire or appreciate something without desiring to own it.

The lesson here is to discard the need for material things in favour of emotional and spiritual experiences. Their Taurus south node past-life tendencies to pursue physical and sensual pleasures and material comforts,

and their stubborn refusal to pursue spiritual goals, weighs these people down until they cut all ties with the past.

The Scorpio north node lesson is not subtle, for it involves absolutes. One cannot carry material baggage on a spiritual journey, for material possessions demand one's attention; attention which is needed for the journey.

These people often seek positions of authority and their lives can revolve around material possessions, but none of these things brings them fulfilment. When they surrender their material desires, life offers to transform their understanding of themselves and of life. They need to surrender all attachments (including any attachments to other people) in order to develop an inner sense of self-worth.

If these people become too enmeshed in the material world, life may remove the attachments which block their path to spiritual fulfilment, forcefully if necessary. This can take the form of a ruined business, the loss of personal belongings and even the loss of family, leaving them alone in later life.

It is often only when they experience life without all their material comforts and burdens that they can truly realise who they are. An example of the Scorpio north node occurred with Andrew.

Andrew had been a pilot for many years, flying internationally and enjoying all the material comforts that his career offered him. He was married with two children and spent his spare time tinkering with his motor car collection. His was a comfortable life.

Life remained comfortable until his regular health check-up revealed that he had heart problems, which signalled the end of his career as a pilot. In the two years that followed, his life spiralled out of control, to depths even he couldn't believe. His wife left with the children and the house was sold. The stock market crashed and wiped out most of his investments, forcing him to sell his beloved cars.

Andrew's confidence, which depended upon his career and social standing, was shattered and he sank into a deep depression. A failed business venture and a series of heart operations used up all the money he had left. When he arrived for his first reading, he had been homeless and living in his car for a week.

'What did I do to deserve this?' he asked me in a shaky voice and, when I heard his story, I wanted to cry with him. It was a purging of all those things which held him from his spiritual purpose in this lifetime.

At first he was unable to comprehend that he would not return to the materially comfortable life he had left behind and that instead he could discover a much more worthwhile treasure within himself. For too long Andrew had valued things outside himself more than his spiritual purpose, and the north node encouraged him to move forward as his south node dried up.

Andrew's greatest growth occurred when he released his attachment to the material baggage and began on the path of growth offered by his Scorpio north node.

Sagittarius north – Gemini south node

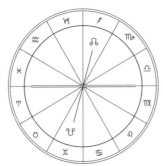

Those with a Sagittarius north node are learning to understand universal truth. To do this they must to release the need to please other people's perceptions of life. It involves a process of releasing accepted community attitudes in favour of searching for universal truth.

So keen are Gemini south node people to be acceptable to others that they tell others what they believe they want to hear, then convince themselves that they too believe it. However, at some later point they may be witnessed telling someone else a different version of their beliefs about life with equal conviction. They feel unable to express themselves or to verbalise their beliefs about life.

Until they pursue their Sagittarius north node, these people can expect to spend their lives trying to determine what is acceptable before giving their opinion, for they fear the disapproval of others. When they pursue the Sagittarius north node they cease to care what others think of them, as they realise that truth is more important than the opinions of others.

These people need to develop a longer attention span, for they can become distracted easily. Higher learning appeals to them in later life, especially if they pursue their Sagittarius north node. Many of the negative Gemini traits need to be weeded out, including the tendency to gossip and to categorise things and people without sufficient thought.

When a balance is struck between the Sagittarius north node and the Gemini south node these people develop a depth of understanding as a result of delving into life's deeper issues.

This nodal aspect involves relinquishing the desire for social standing in favour of understanding. An example of the Sagittarian north node is Eric. Eric was synonymous with sophistication. His parties were legendary and intimate dinners were always a combination of the right people and marvellous conversations.

Eric always seemed to know someone who had inside knowledge about the latest gossip or current scandal. My alarm bells rang one night when I overheard him confidently state an opinion that he had opposed only the day before in different company.

Over the ensuing months I listened carefully to what Eric had to say and often heard him contradict himself. I questioned him about it one day, but he simply laughed with a twinkle in his eye before excusing himself to welcome arriving guests.

Everyone loved Eric and he was much in demand socially, but the price he had to pay was to be a mirror to whoever he was with.

There came a time when Eric developed a certain hunger in his eyes, which I interpreted to mean that his spirit was starving for some nourishment. The parties dwindled and Eric seemed to spend a year or two hiding away from life. When he returned it was immediately obvious that he no longer cared as much about what others thought of him.

At first, for fun, he practised saying aloud the exact opposite of what everyone was arguing. One night as we stood around discussing animal rights, he laughed and excused himself with, 'Well, I'm off to gas some badgers and, while I'm at it, I might steal some eggs from a bird's nest'.

A Gemini friend was quick on the uptake, responding with, 'Fresh eggs? I'm with you. In fact I have a couple of dead pigeons in the back of my car if you fancy a little soup.'

The conversation stopped abruptly and Eric laughed heartily. He was developing the confidence to state what he believed without fear of prejudice.

Capricorn north – Cancer south node

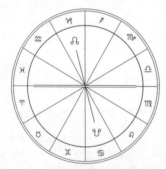

Those with a Capricorn north node are learning about responsibility; responsibility for themselves and responsibility for their spiritual development. Their Cancer south node carries many memories of being nurtured by others and, to some degree, allowing others to take responsibility for them and their development.

This lifetime involves relinquishing the past, resisting the urge to dwell in the safe confines of childhood and learning to face the responsibilities of adulthood.

These people must learn to stand on their own two feet rather than always leaning on other people. The temptation is great for them to slip away into a romantic or safe haven, fuelled by alcohol, drugs, dreaming or carefully structured avoidance.

Family instinct is important for those with a Cancer south node and they tend to see their countries as an extension of their families. This makes them patriotic.

These people find it harder to let go than any of the other nodal types, for they fear that everything may fall apart if they relax. Natural worriers, they need to put their energy into doing something about their problems rather than simply worrying about them.

They can be self-absorbed and they experience great pain at having to leave a person or a situation. They tend to live in the past and there is a tendency to collect old books, photographs and mementos in the hope that, by doing so, they will retain the feelings associated with the event or person.

The Capricorn north node lesson is about the greater community and personal responsibility. These people have a desire to hide away at home and they may spend a lifetime doing so unless life forces them out into the world. When they do venture out into the world they fear that nobody cares for them, and they search for parent-figures to protect them. These parent-figures can be people, organisations or even local governments.

As children, these people felt safe and unable to be judged. As they progress towards their Capricorn north node, they are aware that others judge their efforts by results. When they find a balance between their north and south nodes, they realise the importance of earning respect by acting with honour, while still retaining the south node respect for tradition.

An example of the Capricorn north node is Nadia. Her Cancer south node had encouraged her to hide away from life in the bosom of her family, and she later admitted that she lived through them instead of meeting life head on.

One day her son Michael was shot dead in a shopping centre along with five other people. Nadia was devastated, and her desire to hide from life became even stronger.

After the shock of her son's death, she felt the deep pain, which was followed by anger. She spent the next 12 months screaming at her husband about the injustice of it all until he gave her an ultimatum: 'Do something about it or shut up'. She sulked for a week and then decided to take action.

Nadia ran for the Senate on an anti-gun ticket and was elected. Since then, she has taken a keen interest in the wider world and she is effectively living out her Capricorn north node. This tragedy forced her out into the world, to take responsibility for herself and to make lasting changes that could protect those she cares about.

This is effectively a balance between the Cancerian need for safety and love of family and the Capricorn need for effective management and structure to allow for stability and growth.

Aquarius north – Leo south node

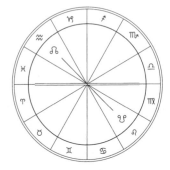

Those with an Aquarius north node are learning about sacrificing personal desires for humanitarian progress.

The Leo south node represents past lives spent focused upon themselves and now they need to ensure that what they have learned benefits others.

In the process of growing into the Aquarius north node, these people must learn to overcome the Leo pride which makes them feel they are better than others. In love relationships and in friendships, the Leo south node tends to make these people want to dominate those around them, making it very difficult to get close to them.

Life often calls those with an Aquarian north node to spend time with people from all walks of life. Any racial prejudice needs to be dissolved until they realise that we are all a part of the human family.

The past-life need for admiration from others is still present in the Leo south node. Fulfilment comes when these people learn to put aside the need for admiration and applause in favour of seeking results that benefit humanity. While they seek applause they find themselves hungry within, and it is only after repeated attempts at personal achievement that they realise there is no fulfilment in such a course.

These people need to feel special and they usually have past-life talents that help them to achieve recognition. An example of the Aquarius north node is Julian, who was much sought after as a violinist at the age of 17.

Julian's ambition was to be the world's greatest living violinist and, having a Leo south node, he was keen to reach for the stars. He travelled to the US, Europe and through parts of Asia establishing a name for himself. By the age of 20, he had recorded a couple of CDs and had toured with several different orchestras. Julian was well on his way to fulfilling his ambition.

During an engagement in an eastern European country, Julian became ill and spent six weeks in a shabby hospital, surrounded by appalling poverty in a country with no funds to help those most in need of medical treatment. At first Julian was adamant that he should receive special attention because he was a foreigner, but his opinion changed when the old woman with whom he was sharing a room died. Unable to afford a bed, she spent the last four days of her life on the floor, alone and wracked with fever.

Julian was shocked to the core. He lapsed into a fever himself for a week and awoke in a safe, clean hospital in his home town. He resolved to do something about the plight of people in poorer countries and has devoted himself to raising funds to sponsor particular hospitals in eastern Europe. He realises that it is sometimes only a drop in the ocean, but as he points out, the ocean consists of millions of tiny drops.

At first, using his south node talents, Julian organised a concert to raise funds. With these funds he visited the hospital he had been admitted to and discussed with the medical staff how extra funds might be used. Still tempted by his Leo south node, he pictured himself as a white knight, saving the lives of those in need. With subsequent payments he simply telephoned and transferred the money anonymously, for as he developed more of his Aquarian north node qualities, he lost the desire for recognition and could focus upon the task at hand — helping others back to health.

Pisces north – Virgo south node

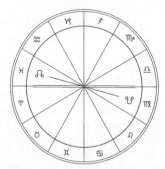

Those with a Pisces north node are learning how to dissolve their rigid beliefs about life. They need to learn to have faith in those things which they cannot understand. They must forgo being sensible, logical and conservative in order to experience life in all its dimensions. Their Virgo south node

carries with it the memories of past lives spent reducing things to their purest form and this routine assessment and analysis is hard to surrender. These people are distrustful of anything they cannot see and touch, as the Virgo south node is sceptical of spirituality and often cynical about emotional fulfilment.

The Virgo south node love of order attempts to put life into some sort of viable structure, however their Pisces north node resists this structure. From time to time, life presents them with unexplainable situations (e.g. psychic experiences) which they will struggle to fit into an acceptable framework.

These people have the ability to solve problems, especially mysteries and puzzles, and although they prefer to examine life's details, they can overlook the big picture. They prefer to have a life which is neat, tidy, routine and rational, yet they are left with an emptiness. This emptiness is the result of having cleared out life's spiritual essence along with the attitudes they sought to eliminate.

While the Pisces north node calls them to appreciate life's abundant garden, the Virgo south node encourages them to dissect each flower, in order to catalogue it and understand it in a scientific form. As they dissect the flowers in life's garden, they lose sight of the fact that the same life force contained within the flowers also propels them and all living things. In their need to separate things into their distinct groups, they forget how we are all interconnected.

Many times throughout life these people start out with a clear plan and a strong focus, only to end up confused and disappointed, wondering why life seems so chaotic or even cruel. These questions can lead them to philosophy or spirituality and, in turn, to life's bigger picture. The Virgo south node past-life doubts appear to pull them back to 'reality' until they can find the faith to trust that life will support them in their search for understanding.

An example of the Virgo south node is Richard. Richard was a surgeon with 15 years' experience and a comfortable life built upon facts and a measurable reality. When he phoned me for a reading, he quizzed me about my qualifications, experience and the level of accuracy he could expect. I was happy to answer his questions as I sensed that he was genuinely sceptical, not cynical about the psychic sciences. Scepticism is healthy in areas where physical evidence is not always immediately forthcoming.

When he came for his reading, Richard was quick to point out that he wasn't 'just another weirdo' and that he was a medical surgeon. He wore the look of a man who seeks an explanation for unbelievable events.

It turned out that 10 days prior to the reading, a woman he was operating on died. He tried to save her life, but it wasn't possible. This, however, was not the cause of his concern. What troubled Richard was that the woman had appeared to him in his dreams at night to reassure him that she was safe and to ask him to pass on a message to her daughter. He rationalised the first dream away as his subconscious need to release the feelings he held about her death, but the first dream was followed by three others, and each time the woman asked why he had not relayed her message to her daughter.

Richard had no explanation for these dreams and he'd begun to suspect that he needed a holiday. In his mind you were either a logical, rational person or you were a 'new-age spoon-bender'.

I suspected that Richard had psychic abilities of which he was unaware, so I asked him some questions.

'Did the woman in question actually have a daughter?'

'Yes, she did.'

'What was the message you were asked to relay?'

'It was that Damian was to seek treatment for allergies, not asthma.'

'And did you tell the daughter this?'

'Er, no. As a doctor I have to be careful, especially about recommending a course of action regarding the health of someone who is not my patient. I mean, imagine how it would appear if people heard about this.'

'I agree, there are legal implications and you are wise not to jump in without thinking things through.'

At my suggestion, Richard contacted the dead woman's daughter and asked if she knew someone named Damian. Damian turned out to be her 12-year-old son who was undergoing treatment for asthma. Richard told the daughter about her mother's dream message on the proviso that she would not treat it as a medical diagnosis.

Richard then commenced studies in psychic development, starting naturally with the results of scientific studies and progressing towards the more obscure areas. What he initially thought might be the end of his career and his life as a rational adult, was in fact the beginning of his exploration of his Pisces north node.

THE ASCENDANT

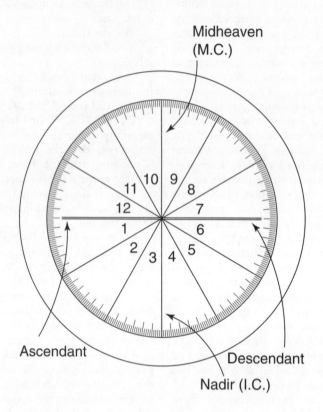

Midheaven
(M.C.)

Ascendant

Descendant

Nadir (I.C.)

The *Ascendant* (or *rising sign*) is the starting point for interpreting a natal chart. It is the sign on the cusp of the first house and it marks the ecliptic rising over the eastern horizon at the moment of birth. The ecliptic is the apparent path of the Sun around the Earth, passing through the 12 zodiac constellations. It is called the ecliptic because eclipses occur on this path.

Since the whole chart hinges on the accuracy of the Ascendant, it is important that the time of birth is accurate. In some cases, being out by 10 or 20 minutes can give an Ascendant in a different sign or place different planets close to the Ascendant.

Many astrologers suggest that the Ascendant or rising sign determines the appearance of the individual and this is

generally true; however, planets found close to the Ascendant in the twelfth or the first house must also be considered.

When the Ascendant is a different sign from the Sun sign, it can alter a person's appearance and/or character traits, making them appear to be another sign. This is why some people do not fit the typical description of their Sun sign. The extent to which the Ascendant affects someone's characteristics varies according to such things as other planets close to the Ascendant.

I was sitting opposite a radio announcer recently and she presented me with a copy of her natal chart. 'I have a Virgo Ascendant,' she stated.

I cast my eyes around the room and found it hard to believe that this was true. She left a trail of mess wherever she went and within five minutes of receiving a copy of the book I was promoting, she had creased the cover in several places. Her behaviour was most unlike the neatness and precision normally found in those with a Virgo Ascendant.

A quick glance at her chart showed that Jupiter was 2 degrees from the Ascendant, lending its influence. The Jupiter influence made her messy and outgoing, almost hiding her Virgo Ascendant.

The Descendant

The *Descendant* is opposite the Ascendant, and marks the degree of the ecliptic which is setting on the western horizon at the moment of birth. It is the sign on the cusp of the seventh house. The seventh house relates to partnerships and the Descendant illuminates the type of people drawn to the person for relationships, partnerships, or friendships.

The Midheaven

The *Midheaven* or *Medium Coeli* (M.C.) marks the degree of the sign which is at the highest point in the sky at the moment of birth. The Midheaven describes what the person identifies with in life. It represents what they admire and endeavour to express, perhaps unconsciously.

The Nadir

Opposite the Midheaven is the *Nadir* or *Imun Coeli* (I.C.). It marks the point immediately beneath the person at the moment of birth. If you were to draw a line down from the Midheaven and then through the peron and through the earth, you would arrive at the Nadir.

The Nadir represents the person's genetic heritage, as it is on the cusp of the fourth house—the house of home and family. This is the person's point of entry to the world.

PROGRESSIONS

The natal chart shows where the planets were at birth. These planets have continued to move through the zodiac. To glimpse where the planets are presently located, consult an ephemeris and draw the planets into the natal chart. This method is called the *physical transits*.

There is another, more commonly used system of progression, called *secondary progressions*. Secondary progressions are measured by the *day-for-a-year method*. This involves allowing one day for each year in the person's life and then adding this number of days to their date of birth to determine where the progressed planets are presently located.

To clarify, here is an example:

1. John asks for a progressed chart and his date of birth was June 16, 1958.

2. The date when he consults you is July 4, 1998. He is currently 40 years of age.

3. To check John's progressed chart add 40 days (one day for each year of his life) to his birth date of June 16, 1958.

4. Forty days onward from his birth date is July 26, 1958.

5. Consult the ephemeris for July 26, 1958: this lists John's secondary progressions.

John's progressed Sun is in Leo according to the date of July 26, 1958, and listed also are all his other progressed planets.

John was born with his Sun in Gemini and although his progressed Sun is in Leo when he consults you, he is still a Gemini. However, there will be a subtle influence of Leo in his nature.

When important aspects are formed between natal planets and progressed planets, or between different progressed planets, you need to spend some time discerning what effect this is having upon the person (see 'Planetary aspects', opposite). For a simple progression, concentrate upon the Sun, Moon, ruling planet (e.g. Venus if the birth sign is Taurus or Libra) and the Midheaven.

PLANETARY ASPECTS

Sun opposition Moon

Aspects are relationships, expressed as angles between planets at various points in the zodiac. As a natal chart is a circle consisting of 360 degrees, most of the aspects are divisions of 360 degrees.

Conjunction: When two planets are in the same degree of longitude, they are considered *conjunct*. It is usual to allow 3 degrees either side, but the closer they are to one another, the stronger the conjunction.

A conjunction means that the energies of the conjunct planets have an effect on one another. For example, Saturn conjunct the Moon causes a more serious outlook emotionally; Mercury conjunct the Sun increases thought patterns and communication abilities.

Square: A *square* is an aspect of 90 degrees between two planets, making them three signs apart. Four planets, each 90 degrees apart, would make up the full circle of the chart, forming the four points of a square.

Squares are formed by planets of different elements; for example, planets in Aries, Cancer, Libra and Capricorn are in the elements of fire, water, air and earth, making them less compatible with one another.

The square is usually considered an *aspect of conflict*, which can be overcome when one masters the lesson contained within the aspect. For example, Mars squared the Moon could manifest as conflict between action (Mars) and feelings (the Moon). When a square occurs between the planets of two charts, there is likely to be conflict between the two parties.

Trine: An aspect of 120 degrees between two planets, making them four signs apart, is known as a *trine*. Three planets, each 120 degrees apart, would make up the full circle of the chart, forming the three points of a triangle.

The trine is considered a *positive aspect*, as it is always formed by planets of the same element. For example, if Jupiter is in Sagittarius and the Sun is in Leo, they are 120 degrees and four signs apart. They are

Angle	Name	Symbol
03 degrees	Conjunction	☌
30 degrees	Semi-sextile	⊻
45 degrees	Semi-square	∠
60 degrees	Sextile	✳
90 degrees	Square	☐
120 degrees	Trine	△
135 degrees	Sesquiquadrate	⊡
150 degrees	Inconjunct	⊼
180 degrees	Opposition	☍

both placed in fire signs, which encourages harmony between them.

Trines tend to bring benefits without direct effort.

Opposition: When two planets are 180 degrees apart, they are considered to be in *opposition* to one another. This placement brings conflict until the opposing planets can be reconciled. For example, if Venus is opposite Mars, it may manifest as an opposition between what the person wants to destroy (Mars) and what they value (Venus).

If planets are in opposition between two charts, the two people concerned are likely to oppose one another according to the planets and houses involved.

Aspects to the Sun

Sun conjunct Moon ☉ ☌ ☽
These people are sensitive and energetic. Impatience can accompany this conjunction, and these people are similar to those born in the New Moon.

Sun squared Moon ☉ ☐ ☽
These people experience conflicts between their emotions and their minds or wills. They can expect emotional upheavals with those around them, especially regarding creative projects. Opposition from the mother or mother figure is indicated in early life.

Sun trine Moon ☉ △ ☽
These people can expect harmony between their emotions and their wills, making them popular and easygoing. They radiate a sense of peace and calm, depending upon the other planetary placements and aspects.

Sun opposition Moon ☉ ☍ ☽
These people swing between high and low energy periods, and they need to adapt their expectations accordingly. They can swing from being wilful to emotional as the Sun and Moon energies within battle for control. They can swing from logic to emotion

without warning, causing confusion to those close to them.

Sun conjunct Mercury ☉ ☌ ☿
This is a common conjunction as the Sun and Mercury are never more than 28 degrees apart from the Earth's perspective. This conjunction increases mental energy and the ability to communicate ideas clearly. It improves teaching ability, but can lead to self-centredness. (Note: Mercury is never more than 28 degrees from the Sun, so this is its only important aspect.)

Sun conjunct Venus ☉ ☌ ♀
These people have artistic abilities, often in music, or at least a strong appreciation of art. Generally positive in outlook, they make friends easily. (Note: Venus is never more than 48 degrees from the Sun, so this is its only important aspect.)

Sun conjunct Mars ☉ ☌ ♂
These people have increased physical vitality and sometimes lack tact in their dealings with others. They can be charismatic, but are aggressive and impatient if opposed. This is a good placement for athletes. It increases the likelihood of success by sheer force of desire and personality.

Sun squared Mars ☉ ☐ ♂
These people experience inner conflict which they tend to project outwards, involving others. Action without forethought can lead to ruin if they do not learn to patience. Their outbursts of anger fuel conflicts around them.

Sun trine Mars ☉ △ ♂
These people are courageous, assertive and open. They have a healthy sense of competition. They can derive as much pleasure from coaching or supporting a team as participating in the competition.

Sun opposition Mars ☉ ☍ ♂
The opposition here is between short-term desire and long-term purpose. When

thwarted, these people can fly into uncontrolled rages, and for this reason they need to find suitable outlets for their energy and inner frustration.

Sun conjunct Jupiter ☉ ☌ ♃
These people have a thirst for knowledge and for travel. They possess leadership ability and usually a strong physical vitality. Others often assist these people to achieve positions of power and responsibility.

Sun squared Jupiter ☉ □ ♃
These people need to remain grounded in reality where ambitions and plans are concerned. They have a tendency to want to be in charge, yet their judgment is often poor where leadership is concerned. This brings them into conflict with those close to them.

Sun trine Jupiter ☉ △ ♃
These people are usually generous and open to others. They can go far in their careers or ambitions, due to their honesty and sincerity. They view problems as challenges and work hard to make their dreams a reality.

Sun opposition Jupiter ☉ ☍ ♃
These people need to remain aware of their own limitations and not become blind to their faults. Their view of themselves prompts them to take wild risks financially or with life, expecting others to have as much faith in them as they have in themselves. Financial losses result from speculation and these people need to weigh up investments carefully before committing themselves.

Sun conjunct Saturn ☉ ☌ ♄
This conjunction indicates someone who is serious, with a well-developed sense of duty and responsibility. As children, they seem like adults inside a child's body, and they take life seriously. These people are usually hardworking. They tend to isolate themselves socially, pursuing hobbies and interests that don't involve others, but in their later years they become more sociable.

Sun squared Saturn ☉ □ ♄
This aspect often indicates a father or father-figure who was demanding and a perfectionist, leaving the child feeling inadequate. As adults, these people tend to strive for unrealistic levels of perfection and can be critical of those who do not measure up to the standard. This is the type of person who achieves 98 per cent in an exam and broods over the lost 2 per cent.

Sun trine Saturn ☉ △ ♄
These people are practical with good powers of concentration. They are usually independent and are prepared to work hard to achieve their goals. They are long-term planners who can quietly go about building a lasting success in life.

Sun opposition Saturn ☉ ☍ ♄
This placement suggests a life of independence, and when others ask or insist that these people participate in group projects, they feel stifled, obligated and perhaps resentful. Stephen, a counselling client of mine, has this placement. He regularly forgets his appointments or arrives late into the hour, dragging his feet and feeling obligated, despite the fact that he's made the appointment. These people only seek help when they are at the end of their tether. Accepting assistance conflicts with their belief that others seek to tear them down.

Sun conjunct Uranus ☉ ☌ ♅
These people often posses original, sometimes eccentric minds. They are independent and resent being controlled by others. They are intuitive, often without realising it. They perceive life from an unusual vantage point, which can make them successful inventors. With a well-placed Mercury, these people have an unusual ability with science and mathematics.

Sun squared Uranus ☉ □ ♅
These people need discipline to keep their impulses in check. Outward displays of

contempt for tradition and conformity can result with this placement, often stemming from the need to shock others out of complacency. Sudden changes in life circumstances are also shown here, and these people need to give others the freedom to live life their own way, as they demand this much from others.

Sun trine Uranus ⊙ △ ♅
Independence and originality are shown with this trine, along with an quick and eccentric mind. These people can solve puzzles rapidly and have an aptitude for mathematics and science.

Sun opposition Uranus ⊙ ☍ ♅
This aspect details an opposition between these people's wills and the wills or needs of others, usually a group. They can reduce their inner stress if they listen to the ideas and opinions of others before insisting upon their own way. Their need to shock others out of their complacency often results in them being excluded from the group.

Sun conjunct Neptune ⊙ ☌ ♆
This conjunction increases sensitivity, especially to the moods and emotions of others. For this reason, these people need to stay away from situations which leave them emotionally and psychically drained. They can find creative outlets a natural expression for their feelings.

Sun squared Neptune ⊙ □ ♆
This placement represents the dissolving of the will, in order to see other ways of living and being. These people may find it difficult to fulfil their goals due to mental confusion and the influence of other people's wishes on their goals. If they allow life to direct them where they need to go, they can release the stress related to this aspect.

Sun trine Neptune ⊙ △ ♆
Natural psychic and healing ability is shown with this aspect. These people achieve their best creatively when they channel their creative energies in one direction. They avoid confrontation, preferring a passive approach to life. They listen carefully to those in need and to life itself, realising that the incidental things in life can be important.

Sun opposition Neptune ⊙ ☍ ♆
This placement describes an opposition between the individual's desire for a more idealistic world and the efforts of those around them to restrain any attempt at change or improvement. These people require strength of will to overcome the degenerative influence of those around them.

Sun conjunct Pluto ⊙ ☌ ♇
This conjunction increases the desire for recognition in the eyes of others. These people do not compromise easily and can be secretive about their hopes and plans. They can expect opposition to their plans from time to time, as they learn to surrender to life and the destiny which awaits them.

Sun squared Pluto ⊙ □ ♇
This placement brings destruction and reconstruction. If these people do not destroy their own efforts, they attract others who will do it for them. The lesson involves transforming their beliefs about themselves and life by destroying those things they create or to which they become attached. When they are able to surrender to the direction life has in store for them, the destruction and the need for it fades from their life, leaving peace and stillness.

Sun trine Pluto ⊙ △ ♇
These people have the ability to see through to the truth of a matter. They have the courage to face themselves honestly and to face others in the same manner.

Sun opposition Pluto ⊙ ☍ ♇
With this placement, the will opposes the need for inner transformation. This can result in power struggles within themselves and with those around them. They may resort to alcohol, drugs or sex to escape this

struggle, but the struggle begins within them and they carry the seed of its creation wherever they go. Consequently, they continually recreate the same struggles until they recognise that those around them are in fact mirroring their own behaviour.

Aspects to the Moon

Moon conjunct Mercury ☽ ☌ ☿
This placement allows for a blending of ideas and emotions. These people are quick-minded and able to utilise their imaginations easily. They resent emotional restrictions in relationships and their moods change rapidly.

Moon squared Mercury ☽ □ ☿
This placement causes conflict between the mind and the emotions. These people feel misunderstood by those around them and they need to take time to sort through their feelings and their thoughts to avoid giving conflicting messages to others.

Moon trine Mercury ☽ △ ☿
The emotions and the mind are wellbalanced in this placement, enabling these people to communicate their thoughts and feelings easily and clearly. They are able to communicate at a level that others can easily understand, for they are intuitive and sensitive to others.

Moon opposition Mercury ☽ ☍ ☿
The mind and emotions oppose one another from time to time, and these people need to be aware of the needs of both aspects of themselves before speaking. They can swing between being completely rational to totally emotional, and this causes tension with those close to them.

Moon conjunct Venus ☽ ☌ ♀
These people are sensitive to the needs of others and enjoy seeing others fulfilled. This makes them popular in social situations. They also find it easy to express their feelings in a harmonious manner, through music, poetry or art, for example.

Moon squared Venus ☽ □ ♀
These people can feel torn between their own needs and the needs of others, often ignoring their own needs in favour of fulfilling those around them. This can cause inner tension. They need to learn to value themselves and their own needs.

Moon trine Venus ☽ △ ♀
This aspect indicates enjoyment of creative and harmonious surroundings. They are often well-liked because they are at ease with their feelings and soon put others at ease also. They are able to fulfil their own needs and the needs of others, benefiting everyone.

Moon opposition Venus ☽ ☍ ♀
People with this opposition feel that they need to be constantly reassured that they are loved by others in order to be happy. They need to develop their sense of self-worth and to find ways to fulfil their own needs, without looking to others to do this for them. They equate self-worth with how much others value them, and this can lead to disappointment when others do not value them.

Moon conjunct Mars ☽ ☌ ♂
These people have a great deal of emotional energy which needs to be channelled carefully, otherwise they tend to seek emotional conflicts for the energetic charge it gives them. They can be self-absorbed emotionally, but can display great emotional courage when required.

Moon squared Mars ☽ □ ♂
People with this aspect need to guard against emotional outbursts when others disagree with their opinions. They experience conflict between their emotions and their need for action. They can be impatient with feelings, preferring instead to act upon impulses.

Moon trine Mars ☽ △ ♂

These people have a strong vitality and they enjoy harmony between emotions and actions. They are enthusiastic and work well within groups towards a common purpose.

Moon opposition Mars ☽ ☍ ♂

This opposition tends to make people quick-tempered and likely to act upon their feelings before they have thought things through. They can be competitive and the Mars energy gives them ability with competitive sports. Sport releases unnecessary tension. Frustration and anger results from mistakes or from not achieving what they desire when they desire it. They need to find acceptable outlets for this anger or they risk alienating family and friends through their aggression.

Moon conjunct Jupiter ☽ ☌ ♃

This conjunction describes people who are generous, sympathetic and popular with others. Social pleasures appeal to them and they are usually positive in outlook, even when life seems bleak.

Moon squared Jupiter ☽ □ ♃

These people fear limitations, especially emotionally. They are proud and need to guard against pointing out the flaws in others in order to shift the focus away from their own feelings and unresolved issues. Acceptance of their limitations and imperfections benefits them immensely.

Moon trine Jupiter ☽ △ ♃

This aspect describes people who are emotionally strong and self-confident. They rarely allow their emotions to cloud their judgment and are generous in their support of those around them. They can laugh at themselves and at life when things don't go according to plan.

Moon opposition Jupiter ☽ ☍ ♃

These people experience opposition between their need to be nurtured and their desire for freedom and space. To compensate for their perceived lack of freedom, they often work frantically or pace about like a caged animal when they feel restricted. Regular walks outdoors and being able to set aside time for their own needs alleviates their inner tension.

Moon conjunct Saturn ☽ ☌ ♄

People with this aspect often feel undeserving of love and affection. They are keenly aware that they must earn emotional support by giving support before they receive it. They need continual reassurance and can appear aloof or shy emotionally. They are natural organisers and often subtly seek control over their friendships and relationships.

Moon squared Saturn ☽ □ ♄

These people regularly feel alone and isolated, and seek constant reassurance from those around them. They sometimes feel that they have to earn love, then become resentful when the love they have 'earned' is not forthcoming.

Moon trine Saturn ☽ △ ♄

Serious and responsible, these people have a low-key approach to emotions. They are dedicated to those close to them and are natural organisers.

Moon opposition Saturn ☽ ☍ ♄

This opposition describes people who often feel alone and isolated emotionally. Their fear of rejection or obligation can paralyse them when they attempt to express their feelings for others. Their aloof exterior hides an inner sensitivity and lack of self-worth. They may have had a parent who was unable to express love for them when they were children, which made them feel unloved.

Moon conjunct Uranus ☽ ☌ ♅

These people are quick-minded and sometimes eccentric in their approach to emotions and feelings. They have a need to understand why they feel what they feel and they may benefit from learning to think before they act. They prefer high levels of excitement and independence, and can be happier conducting a friendship or relationship via the telephone or through correspondance rather than face to face.

Moon squared Uranus ☽ □ ♅
Emotional unpredictability is shown with this placement, and these people need to learn to think before acting. An unusual emotional life appeals to them and they have a strong love of freedom and space. They can be short-tempered and their need to shock others results in conflict from time to time. The conflict here is between the need for nurturing and the need for freedom and space. These people can feel that their need for nurturing and emotional support stifles their ability to be free to pursue their own lives. They can enjoy both when they realise that those who love them do not necessarily want to own them.

Moon trine Uranus ☽ △ ♅
This aspect describes people who are intuitive and quick-minded. They seek out unusual experiences in life and are adaptable when sudden change is required. They are original in their approach to creative solutions and, although they think differently from others, they can work within a team towards a common goal.

Moon opposition Uranus ☽ ☍ ♅
People with this opposition are unpredictable, even to themselves. Alternately friendly and aloof, they swing between the need for emotional closeness and sabotaging closeness through unpredictable behaviour. They perceive that others want to limit their freedom, usually as a consequence of a parent curtailing their freedom throughout childhood. They can experience difficulty in having close live-in relationships as they feel that they are not free. They prefer long-distance relationships, where they can telephone their partners when they need emotional contact and enjoy their freedom at other times.

Moon conjunct Neptune ☽ ☌ ♆
These people are highly intuitive and, because of this, they need to guard against being surrounded by those who might drain them emotionally. They are particularly sensitive to the emotional states of others and periods of time spent alone to replenish their emotional reserves benefits them greatly. Harmony in colours and in music helps them to enjoy an inner harmony, and they are often attracted to the psychic sciences. They need to guard against idealising those around them, for disappointment results when others do not live up to their expectations.

Moon squared Neptune ☽ □ ♆
This aspect describes people who are very sensitive to others and who can be hurt deeply when others disappoint them. When disappointed, they need to guard against retreating into fantasy to avoid pain and loss. Their sensitivity can be channelled into creativity, including acting, painting or clairvoyancy, if they can discipline themselves to remain connected to reality.

Moon trine Neptune ☽ △ ♆
People with this placement are sensitive to energies, both physical and emotional. They are drawn to assisting others to re-balance emotional or psychic energies, but they need to maintain their own balance to remain effective. They show talent for music, writing or painting and can succeed at these things as long as they regularly spend time alone to re-balance their own energies.

Moon opposition Neptune ☽ ☍ ♆
These people are easily confused between feelings and imagination. They can be self-deceiving, especially to avoid emotional loss or pain. This tendency makes it easier for others to deceive them and, when continually deceived emotionally, they often retreat from life and from contact with others. They find it easier to build up a romanticised view of the world in their minds rather than to work on turning their hopes into reality.

Moon conjunct Pluto ☽ ☌ ♇

People with this conjunction are emotionally intense. They have an innate desire to reduce relationships to their essence so they can scrutinise them closely. Power struggles occur in close friendships or relationships when they refuse to surrender or compromise when emotional differences arise. There may have been a dominant mother or power struggles in childhood that are being translated into relationships in adult life.

Moon squared Pluto ☽ □ ♇

Struggle with internal feelings can lead these people to have explosive emotional outbursts from time to time. They continually test the love of those close to them, fearing rejection or betrayal. They have great powers of concentration and creativity which need to be balanced with rest and relaxation. Time spent by the sea or on the water (sailing, swimming, and so on) restores their emotional energy reserves.

Moon trine Pluto ☽ △ ♇

These people, realising their inner strengths, do not need to test the depth of feeling of those close to them. They can trust their intuition to determine the feelings and commitment that others have for them. They are drawn to discovering the hidden depths of those around them.

Moon opposition Pluto ☽ ☍ ♇

This opposition describes an inner conflict between the need to be nurtured and the need to trust their loved ones. Their innate distrust of the motives of others can cause these people to alternate between the struggle for closeness and isolation or rejection. They can be possessive, but they resent possessiveness in others. They need to resolve their jealousies through clear communication with those close to them.

Aspects to Mercury

Mercury conjunct Venus ☿ ☌ ♀

This placement gives a subtle expression to thoughts and feelings, making these people diplomatic and tactful in their approach to others. They often possess refined and uplifting minds, which appreciate music and the arts. (Note: as Mercury and Venus are never more than 78 degrees apart, this is the only important aspect these planets make.)

Mercury conjunct Mars ☿ ☌ ♂

These people have sharp tongues and quick minds. They often enjoy discussions and debates as this allows their quick minds free rein. There is a tendency towards sarcasm and they need to remember that words have the power to hurt others.

Mercury squared Mars ☿ □ ♂

The conflict here is between thoughts and desires. These people can become critical of others as a result of their impatience and their friendships benefit from allowing others to do things at their own pace.

Mercury trine Mars ☿ △ ♂

People with this aspect enjoy a balance between thoughts and desires, and are mentally and physically active. They are quick in thought and effective in action, although not exactly tactful in their handling of others. Their impatience encourages them to find the most expedient way to tell others what they want, which can cause unintended pain. Regular meditation, yoga or tai chi to quiet their busy minds may benefit them.

Mercury opposition Mars ☿ ☍ ♂

These people experience opposition between their thoughts and physical energies. To avoid the likelihood of outbursts of temper, they may benefit from sport or regular exercise as a way of dissipating pent-up energy. In argument, they become confused between their thoughts and their desire to respond immediately to any statement, leaving their argument poorly constructed and more bluster than logic. Time spent thinking things through or writing them down makes them more effective in presenting their case.

Mercury conjunct Jupiter ☿ ☌ ♃
This conjunction signifies people who have versatile minds. They usually enjoy travel, reading and learning. When they have learned all they can in a situation, they become restless to move on to another opportunity for growth. These people can usually communicate complex matters in a simple form, making them good teachers. They are restless, however, making them likely to be the teacher who leaves before the student has completed their studies.

Mercury squared Jupiter ☿ □ ♃
The conflict here is between philosophic and mundane ideas and concepts. Sometimes these people reach a conclusion without thinking things through, and they need to remain disciplined when thinking through complex matters. They find the random-thinking process faster and easier than linear thinking and need to ensure that they do not arrive at conclusions which are inaccurate.

Mercury trine Jupiter ☿ △ ♃
People with this aspect enjoy learning while travelling. They are usually generous and positive with excellent organisational skills, which suits them to positions of leadership. They can switch rapidly from one idea to another and they find it easy to express thoughts or ideas to others.

Mercury opposition Jupiter ☿ ☍ ♃
This opposition describes those who are usually open-minded and optimistic, but they can experience difficulty in choosing a path to follow. They can jump from one school of thought to another, from one course to another and from one belief to another opposing belief without giving any commitment. It is essentially an opposition between knowledge and understanding.

Mercury conjunct Saturn ☿ ☌ ♄
These people are precise in thought, word and deed. They need to guard against mood swings and to improve their ability to express their feelings for others. They are usually direct and to the point when they have something to say and they can be serious in nature.

Mercury squared Saturn ☿ □ ♄
People with this aspect have a strong sense of duty and responsibility, and their powers of concentration are often excellent. Thorough and efficient, they take care of all the details, but need to guard against nervous exhaustion.

Mercury trine Saturn ☿ △ ♄
A well-developed self-control and strong powers of concentration are common characteristics of people with this placement. They plan thoroughly and are good organisers. They are effective teachers and make good problem-solvers when there is a logical process to be followed.

Mercury opposition Saturn ☿ ☍ ♄
This opposition describes people who tend to look on the gloomy side of life and are resistant to new concepts or ideas. They are quickly offended and slow to forgive as their Saturnian tendency to isolate themselves is in opposition to their Mercurian need to communicate and share with others. They need continual assurance that they will be heard if they volunteer their opinion or ideas.

Mercury conjunct Uranus ☿ ☌ ♅
People with this conjunction are usually quick-minded and can leap from one concept to another easily. This type of thinking is well suited to creativity and to certain types of problem-solving. They have well-developed intuitive skills and their thinking can be scattered at times.

Mercury squared Uranus ☿ □ ♅
The important lesson here is to discipline

mental energy. The tendency these people have to conclude a matter or express an idea in haste can lead to half-finished ideas or ideas that require more thought before becoming practical. The effect their ideas have upon others also needs to be considered before being pursued, as this placement can increase curiosity without compassion.

Mercury trine Uranus ☿ △ ♅
This placement encourages creative thinking and intuitive development. Being open to new ideas, these people have the ability to combine ideas or concepts which are not usually related, in order to find new solutions. Self-expression through writing or speaking comes naturally to those with Mercury trine Uranus.

Mercury opposition Uranus ☿ ☍ ♅
This opposition describes people who can be alternately open- and closed-minded to new ideas. Impatience with ideas can lead to valuable concepts being cast aside and these people benefit from regular exercise or meditation to quiet their minds.

Mercury conjunct Neptune ☿ ☌ ♆
People with this conjunction have vivid imaginations and can express their creativity easily, especially through the written or spoken word. They are naturally intuitive, but they can occasionally experience difficulty discerning reality from imagination.

Mercury squared Neptune ☿ □ ♆
This aspect describes people who experience difficulties communicating with others and who base their understanding of others on what they imagine them to be, without checking their ideas against reality. Their imaginations would better serve them if directed towards creative pursuits, ensuring that their relationships with others are based in reality. To assist with this, they need to practise telling others how they feel and asking for feedback in return so they don't confuse what is said with what they imagine was said.

Mercury trine Neptune ☿ △ ♆
These people are able to express themselves creatively, they benefit from learning to channel their ideas and concepts into a tangible form. They prefer harmony in their surroundings as they are sensitive, and time spent outdoors restores their energy when it is depleted.

Mercury opposition Neptune ☿ ☍ ♆
Owing to their reluctance to check what they think with what others feel or believe, these people are often disappointed by those close to them. They imagine how things will turn out and rarely verify whether their friends or partners have the same goal. This lack of communication of ideas and dreams leads to disappointment time and time again. They benefit from keeping dream journals or recording their ideas and inspirations, as it helps them to clarify their goals and creative inspirations.

Mercury conjunct Pluto ☿ ☌ ♇
This conjunction describes people who have keen powers of observation. They can quickly penetrate to the core of a person or a situation to reveal any concealed details. They are attracted to that which is hidden in life and mysteries arouse their curiosity. They are subtle but powerful speakers and can lead others with their words. They need to guard against abusing their verbal power.

Mercury squared Pluto ☿ □ ♇
A natural suspicion accompanies this aspect, and these people seem to anticipate concealed evidence or details. The Pluto need to penetrate to the core of a matter and the Mercury need for facts and details can overrule their natural intuition. Balance needs to be developed between the mind and the intuition with this placement.

Mercury trine Pluto ☿ △ ♇
People with this aspect can quickly understand what motivates others, as they observe them with a combination of logic and intuition. They are quietly powerful

individuals who achieve their goals with a minimum of fuss. This placement helps anyone who needs to listen to and understand others in order to help them.

Mercury opposition Pluto ☿ ☍ ♇
These people often feel that they are misunderstood by those around them and they need to find suitable outlets for their frustration when this occurs. They sometimes experience conflict between their inner desires and their thoughts, and they benefit from some quiet time each day to contemplate what they need on an emotional and spiritual level.

Aspects to Venus

Venus conjunct Mars ♀ ☌ ♂
Friendships, relationships and regular contact with other people are important concerns for those with this placement. The Venusian need for company and the Martian love of conflict can make for a passionate life, especially in relationships. These people can be alternately peaceful and then restless.

Venus squared Mars ♀ □ ♂
This aspect describes people who alternate between loving and hating those close to them, which can confuse and upset their loved ones. Physical exercise to release the Martian anger or aggression which surfaces from time to time benefits them.

Venus trine Mars ♀ △ ♂
This aspect brings harmony between the Venusian love of peace and affection and the Martian courage and love of excitement to make these people both courageous and loving. They are usually loyal to their partners and are often creative.

Venus opposition Mars ♀ ☍ ♂
These people can switch from love to hostility quite rapidly, especially when opposed in their plans. Regular exercise can relieve pent-up emotions when disappointments occur and prevent them venting their frustration upon those close to them.

Venus conjunct Jupiter ♀ ☌ ♃
People with this conjunction are usually generous, faithful and affectionate. They enjoy learning and prefer to learn or travel with partners than alone. They are often favoured by others, who help them in fulfilling their plans and achieving their goals.

Venus squared Jupiter ♀ □ ♃
This aspect indicates a conflict between the desire for material things and the desire for philosophical ideals. If these people pursue material things they are likely to put on weight in their later years and accumulate possessions, which may hold them back in their spiritual development. If they pursue philosophical ideals, they gain a depth of understanding about life that will benefit them, although they may find themselves struggling financially on occasion.

Venus trine Jupiter ♀ △ ♃
People with this aspect enjoy a balance between what they value in themselves and what they value in life. They are usually loyal and act with integrity in their dealings with others. To keep learning, they continually expand their circle of friends or make friends from all walks of life.

Venus opposition Jupiter ♀ ☍ ♃
Although positive in outlook, these people need to develop a sense of appropriate limits where socialising, food and drink are concerned. They tend to indulge themselves beyond what they can afford. Sometimes their love of sensual fulfilment overrides their need for spiritual fulfilment.

Venus conjunct Saturn ♀ ☌ ♄
These people are usually restrained and serious, and find it difficult to express their feelings. Friendship is very valuable to them, and they are loyal and careful to maintain their friendships. They don't like

to spend money, preferring instead to save all they can.

Venus squared Saturn ♀ □ ♄

The conflict here is between the need for love and the belief that love must be earned. These people tend to delay receiving emotional fulfilment until they have done all the work necessary to feel as though they deserve it. Meanwhile, those close to them feel unappreciated. Instead of earning lasting fulfilment, they can benefit from accepting love and support from others as and when it is offered.

Venus trine Saturn ♀ △ ♄

People with this aspect work hard to establish and maintain long-lasting friendships based on loyalty. They steadfastly support their friends in times of need. This aspect combines the seriousness and responsibility of Saturn with the desire for beauty, friendships and love of Venus, resulting in people who feel responsible for those they love. They often act to assist those around them before tending to their own needs.

Venus opposition Saturn ♀ ☍ ♄

These people are unable to enjoy life when there are responsibilities to be met. Their need to be responsible stops them from participating when those around them are enjoying themselves, and the lesson here is that there is a time to work and a time to play. They often feel unloved and unworthy of love, and, in order to receive the love they seek, they must first learn to love themselves.

Venus conjunct Uranus ♀ ☌ ♅

This conjunction describes people who have magnetic personalities which hover between independance and intimacy. The Venusian need for company is opposed to the Uranian need for space and freedom. Those close to them can find their behaviour confusing as they are affectionate one minute and aloof the next. These people are attracted to the unusual in their surroundings, preferring irregular or even bizarre furnishings and friends. They are usually not possessive of friends or material things, and they avoid being possessed by others.

Venus squared Uranus ♀ □ ♅

People with this aspect are in the process of changing those things which they value. The Uranian energy periodically forces them to relinquish their hold over their material possessions and their friends, in order to re-evaluate their lives. Their friendships, relationships and work environments change abruptly and they need to be able to adapt rapidly to new circumstances.

Venus trine Uranus ♀ △ ♅

These people have achieved a balance between those things they value and their need for independence, as they do not cling to their possessions or their friends. They are able to release old friendships and relationships gracefully and remain confident that new opportunities abound.

Venus opposition Uranus ♀ ☍ ♅

This aspect describes people who feel an opposition between their need for love and their desire for freedom. Their fear of being possessed can lead them to prefer long-distance relationships. They need to guard against becoming obligated in their love relationships, as these feelings lead to inner resentment or the desire to escape the confines of stifling situations.

Venus conjunct Neptune ♀ ☌ ♆

Beauty and harmonious surroundings are extremely important to these people. They are naturally intuitive, especially with those close to them. They seek perfect love and tend to idolise their partners, which leads to disappointments. Seeking spiritually what they cannot find in the physical world can benefit them. They are usually gentle in nature and romantic in their outlook.

Venus squared Neptune ♀ □ ♆

The conflict here is between personal desires and group desires. The desire for personal fulfilment needs to be dissolved before these people can contribute to the fulfilment of a group or of humanity. To this end, they need to undergo periods of self-sacrifice.

Venus trine Neptune ♀ △ ♆

This aspect increases creative expression, generosity and idealism. These people are content to ensure the happiness of others and they attract people who return their generosity.

Venus opposition Neptune ♀ ☍ ♆

Those with this opposition are periodically torn between things of material and spiritual importance. The lesson here is for these people to truly value themselves, which enables them to take a long-term view of their happiness and fulfilment. This usually encourages them to pursue spiritual fulfilment. This aspect can describe opposition from those close to them regarding the things they value in life.

Venus conjunct Pluto ♀ ☌ ♇

These people can be both idealistic and possessive in relationships. They need to guard against jealousy. They can learn a great deal through relationships by transforming their own or their partners' attitudes to love and sharing. They are usually loyal and intense in relationships.

Venus squared Pluto ♀ □ ♇

This aspect signifies the destruction of old beliefs about relationships and value systems. This transformation occasionally manifests itself as betrayal by friends or partners. These people are repeatedly disappointed by the actions of those around them, which forces them to fall back on their own emotional reserves. When they forgive the hurt others have caused, they can see how the problems arose from the differences between what they value and what others value. In simple terms, others assist these people to transform their attitudes to relationships, often painfully.

Venus trine Pluto ♀ △ ♇

These people can assist others to transform their lives and their value systems, as Pluto gives them a clear memory of their own struggles in the past. They are sensitive to the needs of others and capable of assisting them in subtle ways.

Venus opposition Pluto ♀ ☍ ♇

This aspect tends to increase possessive traits and these people need to understand that jealousy can be destructive. Because they repel others, they in turn feel abandoned. Struggle for control in relationships is common for people with this placement, and they need to learn to surrender to love. When they surrender, the power struggles dissolve and their emotional needs can be met.

Aspects to Mars

Mars conjunct Jupiter ♂ ☍ ♃

People with this aspect are straightforward in their manner, even tactless at times. Their enthusiasm appears boundless and they accept the cuts and bruises life gives them as part of the price of achievement. They are keen to learn and to try new things, but resent being told what to do. They exude a confidence which makes others want to trust them and they can count upon this to assist them in life.

Mars squared Jupiter ♂ □ ♃

The conflict here is between the Martian need for conflict and action and the Jupiterian need for expansion. This makes these people high achievers, but they need to guard against alienating those around them with their need for speedy results and disregard for quality.

Mars trine Jupiter ♂ △ ♃

People with this aspect enjoy freedom, space and the great outdoors. Sports and competition appeals to them, and they display a positive and confident outlook on life, despite temporary setbacks. This aspect increases the discipline given to their abundant energy, resulting in solid achievements.

Mars opposition Jupiter ♂ ☍ ♃
These people seek competition where there is none and have a tendency to disrupt peaceful situations. They need to understand that their innate competitiveness keeps others at a distance. They benefit from taking up a sport, as it provides an outlet for their competitive natures as well as their abundant energy.

Mars conjunct Saturn ♂ ☌ ♄
This conjunction indicates great powers of concentration and tenacity. These people finish what they start, as they possess remarkable self-discipline and attention to detail. They usually have a good control of their tempers and are suited to sports such as long-distance running and endurance events.

Mars squared Saturn ♂ □ ♄
These people feel restricted by time, gravity and their physical bodies, and they need to find an outlet for their frustration. As they tend to suppress their anger, they can suffer from skin complaints as their bodies express what their mouths will not. They enjoy nature, which calms them, and prefer time alone to relax.

Mars trine Saturn ♂ △ ♄
Serious in nature, these people are dedicated and attentive to detail. They derive satisfaction from seeing a job done well and can display discipline over their enthusiasm, which allows them to pace themselves and enables them to achieve what they set out to achieve.

Mars opposition Saturn ♂ ☍ ♄
This aspect describes those who are often torn between their desires and their responsibilities. They are alternately hard-working and then resentful for feeling obligated to complete tasks. Setting up strong boundaries around work and play could benefit them. They need to guard against clashes with authority, as they act out their inner conflicts.

Mars conjunct Uranus ♂ ☌ ♅
People with this aspect treasure their freedom and resent others telling them what to do. Although they are individual in their thinking, they can be closed-minded to the ideas of others from time to time. Confined spaces and emotional confinement can trigger outbursts of temper or actions which are eccentric and sometimes destructive. They have great courage and honesty.

Mars squared Uranus ♂ □ ♅
These people tend to be impulsive and unpredictable. They have short attention spans and constantly crave things that are new or different. They usually resent authority and their need for freedom could bring problems until they learn self-discipline. Careers or lifestyles involving plenty of freedom suit them, and they need to grant others the same freedom they seek for themselves.

Mars trine Uranus ♂ △ ♅
This aspect describes those who are restless and hardworking. They enjoy their freedom and can display unusual views about life. Although impulsive, they are more tolerant than most people of different approaches when shown other ways to do things. They are adaptable and enthusiastic about implementing change.

Mars opposition Uranus ♂ ☍ ♅
These people can feel the need to tear down the old way of doing things in favour of a new approach. Unfortunately, they usually want to tear down the old *before* they have a viable plan with which to replace it. As they mature, they develop patience which assists them to harness the Martian energy to pursue some of their Uranian ideas.

Mars conjunct Neptune ♂ ☌ ♆
People with this conjunction need to be cautious when pursuing their dreams, in

order to ensure they are attainable. This aspect can give energy and enthusiasm for pursuit of dreams, but it can also lead to a confusion of purpose, as Neptune dissolves the Martian sense of purpose.

Mars squared Neptune ♂ □ ♆
Setbacks tend to dampen the enthusiasm of these people, as they feel that they should be able to get it right the first time, just as they imagined they could. Clarity of mind and patience need to be developed as these people can be persuaded by others into pursuits for which they are unsuited.

Mars trine Neptune ♂ △ ♆
This aspect combines the enthusiasm of Mars with the inspiration of Neptune, and is indicative of people who can turn their dreams into reality with a minimum of fuss. Keenly sensitive to artistic things and harmonious surroundings, they are patient and compassionate with others. They are often found supporting causes such as animal shelters or working in support of the underprivileged.

Mars opposition Neptune ♂ ☍ ♆
People with this aspect can find themselves torn between the need to dream and the desire for action. Without patience and discipline, they are likely to want to give up on their plans at the first sign of a setback or look for a short cut. After many failed short cuts, they learn the value of discipline and of the need to believe in themselves despite setbacks.

Mars conjunct Pluto ♂ ☌ ♇
These people are courageous and rarely give up on a desired goal. They are pragmatic in their approach to life, accepting what they cannot change and changing what they can. They are suited to positions of power and responsibility, and this aspect increases the resilience when health problems arise. They are strong-willed and may need to develop tolerance for the opinions of others.

Mars squared Pluto ♂ □ ♇
People with this aspect are intense in their approach to life and this can exhaust those close to them. They can become overly focused upon their goals and need to develop a sense of perspective to avoid seeing only their goals and ignoring life itself. They are often successful because they work hard, and they can be ruthless enemies.

Mars trine Pluto ♂ △ ♇
Inner strength and courage are increased with this placement. These are independent people with strong tempers, which they rarely display due to their self-discipline. Their true strengths shine through in times of crisis, when they display courage and nerves of steel against all odds.

Mars opposition Pluto ♂ ☍ ♇
The intensity of these people can be off-putting to others, who find them too single-minded. They can find themselves torn between the Martian desire for conquest and action and the Plutonian desire for transformation. Until they find a balance between the two, they are likely to tear down those things they build up or achieve.

Aspects to Jupiter

Jupiter conjunct Saturn ♃ ☌ ♄
People with this conjunction are attentive to detail and disciplined in their approach to tasks. They are capable of focusing upon the small things without losing sight of the bigger picture. They are goal-oriented and usually achieve what they set out to achieve.

Jupiter squared Saturn ♃ □ ♄
The conflict here is between the Jupiterian need for travel and adventure and the Saturnian need for structure and results. These people are restless and tend to start on a new project before they have completed the present one. Few goals are achieved or projects completed until they can find a balance between their need for high

achievement and their constant need for new horizons.

Jupiter trine Saturn ♃ △ ♄
These people are natural decision-makers and leaders, capable of planning and delegating to ensure completion of goals. Success is likely with their combination of hard work and foresight.

Jupiter opposition Saturn ♃ ☍ ♄
Often strict with themselves, these people set high goals and expect perfect results at the first attempt. When expected results are not forthcoming, they want to move on to another job, place or relationship. When they do make a change in the interests of starting afresh, usually the new situation soon replicates the one they left behind. They benefit from keeping several projects going at once, because they can then switch from one to another when delays occur or results are not immediately forthcoming.

Jupiter conjunct Uranus ♃ ☌ ♅
Those with this conjunction are quick-minded and possess clear judgment along with a thirst for knowledge, are open to new ideas and are tolerant of other's viewpoints. They desire freedom to learn and to explore life, and may avoid commitment in relationships as they feel it curbs their freedom.

Jupiter squared Uranus ♃ □ ♅
These people are quick-minded and can become impatient with those who prefer to reflect upon alternatives before deciding. They can also become impatient to see their ideas accepted by others and made real. Physical exercise, including walking, helps them to release some of their impatience and allows them to sort their ideas into those that are workable and those that are not.

Jupiter trine Uranus ♃ △ ♅
New ideas, concepts and philosophies appeal to people with this aspect, and they are usually tolerant of other people's ideas. They are capable of seeing new approaches to old problems and they arrive at solutions rapidly. They are often keen to pursue unusual paths of learning and to push the frontiers of acceptable knowledge. They thrive on new ideas and fresh experiences, and usually display clear judgment.

Jupiter opposition Uranus ♃ ☍ ♅
People with this placement can experience opposition between the need to question what they believe and the need to convince others of the importance of a particular idea or philosophy. They are independent and need plenty of freedom to pursue their own path in life. They need to guard against becoming too fixed in their beliefs about life. They can embrace radical beliefs as a reaction to their upbringing and need to question their philosophies from time to time.

Jupiter conjunct Neptune ♃ ☌ ♆
These people tend to be idealistic and even unrealistic on occasion. They are suited to religious or philosophic pursuits, and to the psychic sciences, but they need to guard against always expecting others to act from good motives. These people pursue ideas that can be unworkable in the real world. They are usually generous and sympathetic with their time and energies to those in need.

Jupiter squared Neptune ♃ □ ♆
This aspect describes people who need to be more realistic in their approach to life. They can expect others to be perfect and become bitterly disappointed when others let them down. They remain childlike in their attitudes and suffer great distress when others fail them. By utilising the Jupiterian straightforwardness to renegotiate with others when they fail to achieve their goals, these people can avoid becoming dis-illusioned altogether.

Jupiter trine Neptune ♃ △ ♆
People with this aspect are philosophical and possess a combination of realism and

idealism. They are often inspired by people and situations around them, and they can inspire others to achieve their potential. They are generous and compassionate with those who need their help.

Jupiter opposition Neptune ♃ ☍ ♆

These people tend to feel torn between the need to change the world and the desire to escape from it. The Jupiterian need to learn and to understand one's environment is confused by the Neptunian need to have a perfect world, even if this means living in dreams. The study of religion or philosophy and history could enable these people to understand humankind's continual struggle with the duality of humanity and spirituality. This might lead to a more realistic appraisal of the world and enable them to live in the present.

Jupiter conjunct Pluto ♃ ☌ ♇

People with this conjunction have deep intuitions and strong desires. They have an innate urge to make their mark in the world, and their combination of clear vision and tenacity enables them to achieve their goals. They can experience inner resistance to being directed by others and they need to appreciate those things that others can teach them. They usually have magnetic personalities and make good leaders. They find it difficult to forgive those who hurt them, although in later life this becomes a little easier.

Jupiter squared Pluto ♃ □ ♇

This aspect often indicates a desire for power and an impatience to lead others. These people need to remain open-minded to the ideas and opinions of others, or they could find that others retreat from them, finding them too fanatical about an idea or concept. If they can develop patience and humility, they usually achieve positions of power later in life. If they push hard to achieve a position of power early in life, they are likely to encounter obstacles and dissent.

Jupiter trine Pluto ♃ △ ♇

These people possess an insight into others and a far-reaching vision of life. This combination suits them to leadership positions and in times of crisis they can keep calm and seek viable solutions. They are continually reassessing themselves in order to improve and they expect high standards of themselves. They can encourage and inspire others, and, in positions of leadership, they are apt to transform that which is in their command, although in a gentle and subtle manner.

Jupiter opposition Pluto ♃ ☍ ♇

People with this aspect can be torn between the Jupiterian need to learn and discover and the Plutonian need to transform. This can lead them to destroying the beliefs and ideas of others before they determine whether these ideas have any merit. They have a desire to learn which they sometimes undermine by not completing the study undertaken. Developing an open mind for the opinions and ideas of others could open the way for growth and fulfilment, if they can accept that they are equal to others.

Aspects to Saturn

Saturn conjunct Uranus ♄ ☌ ♅

This conjunction details a need for stability along with a restlessness for change. People with this aspect take their responsibilities seriously, yet they also seek freedom to do as they please. They are likely to surprise those around them by changing homes, jobs or relationship partners unexpectedly due to their inner need for change and freedom from responsibilities. Learning to place less emphasis upon obligations and responsibilities could help them to reduce their inner tension.

Saturn squared Uranus ♄ □ ♅

These people sometimes allow tensions to build within them to an alarming point, resulting in outbursts of anger. Beneath the outburst is a cry for help for release from restrictions or obligations. They are usually keen to take on new responsibilities, but later they feel resentful that they are not free to do as they please. They need to learn to set boundaries around what they are prepared to do for others, in order to give them time for their own pursuits.

Saturn trine Uranus ♄ △ ♅
There is a balance between personal desires and responsibilities with this aspect. These people are good organisers, and patient and thorough in completing tasks. They need to learn when to stop working and start relaxing, as they tend to overwork and deplete their energies. Engineering, physics and the sciences may appeal to them as they possess a logical turn of mind.

Saturn opposition Uranus ♄ ☍ ♅
People with this opposition can feel torn between responsibilities and the desire to be free. When receiving direction from others, they can feel restricted or obligated, which builds resentment within them. They need to set aside some time every day, or at least once a week, to do exactly what they want to do. This allows them to endure those periods when they have responsibilities. It could benefit them to remember that they are often in such situations by choice; for example, they might feel that their job restricts them, but they are in the job by choice.

Saturn conjunct Neptune ♄ ☌ ♆
These people tend to be melancholy. They take setbacks to heart and need to learn to shrug off disappointments. They need to ensure that they don't retreat from life after disappointments, but instead learn from experience. This position can encourage a sense of martyrdom.

Saturn squared Neptune ♄ □ ♆
This placement indicates those who are often divided between the pursuit of material things and spiritual learning. Maintaining a balance between the two is important, for if

they pursue a material life, they will suffer loss materially from time to time as a reminder of spiritual values.

Saturn trine Neptune ♄ △ ♆
People with this aspect are hardworking, especially when it comes to turning their dreams into reality. The Neptunian ability to dream and the Saturnian capacity for hard work and careful planning make for a powerful combination when it comes to success in career or in fulfilling their plans. They are capable of helping others to achieve their plans and have compassion for those who do not work hard in pursuit of goals.

Saturn opposition Neptune ♄ ☍ ♆
Those with this opposition feel torn between the Saturnian need for material possessions and for structure, and the Neptunian need for spiritual development. If they pursue material success, they usually feel insecure about their wealth and worry that others want to take it away from them. If they pursue spiritual development, they feel the lack of material support and fear they will end their lives in discomfort and material poverty. Maintaining a balance between these needs can bring a deep sense of fulfilment and inner peace.

Saturn conjunct Pluto ♄ ☌ ♇
These people are hardworking and determined. They need to guard against depression by resting periodically and balancing their work with play. They are tenacious, but the combination of the Saturnian need for structure and continuity and the Plutonian need for transformation can cause inner conflict. They may transform people and situations around them, yet resist transformation within. They make disciplined leaders and good organisers.

Saturn squared Pluto ♄ □ ♇
People with this aspect can expect periods of disruption to their routines, despite their attempts to avoid change. They experience setbacks in the pursuit of their career goals

as they need to transform their attitudes to life in order to achieve and maintain success. This may take the form of being separated from their work environment (e.g. retrenchment) when they have learned the lesson the job offered. They seek power and positions where they have control over others, and until they learn humility they can expect obstacles and opposition from those they govern. When they accept that effective leaders serve those they lead, these people find those around them appreciate their organisational abilities. After such realisations, opposition to their plans diminishes.

Saturn trine Pluto ♄ △ ♇

People with this placement are natural leaders and organisers. They are tenacious and unruffled in times of crisis. Endowed with self-discipline, commonsense and the ability to apply themselves to their goals in a practical way, they are at home with structure and equally successful when structure falls apart around them.

Saturn opposition Pluto ♄ ☍ ♇

These people often feel torn between the Saturnian need for structure and the Plutonian need for transformation. They tend to avoid transformation themselves, preferring instead to transform those around them. This can lead to conflicts with friends, coworkers and family members until they learn to compromise with others. They also need to allow others freedom to experiment, without imposing structures upon them.

Aspects to Uranus

Uranus conjunct Neptune ♅ ☌ ♆

This conjunction increases the psychic abilities and allows for the pursuit of new approaches to learning. These people are humanitarian in their approach to life and prefer a rational, level-headed approach to spirituality. They seek to benefit humanity in a practical manner.

Uranus squared Neptune ♅ □ ♆

Although people with this aspect have psychic abilities, they tend to be erratic in their approach to things psychic, spiritual and religious. They have a desire for creative expression and for freedom, and if these desires are thwarted they seek escape through drugs and alcohol, or through daydreaming or schemes which have little foundation in reality. They experience conflicts with those in their social groups from time to time.

Uranus trine Neptune ♅ △ ♆

These people have a balance between the Uranian need for human equality and the Neptunian need for spiritual development. This enables them to see beyond their own needs in favour of the needs of others, especially the impoverished or underprivileged. They are open-minded to the beliefs of others and have natural psychic abilities which are easily developed.

Uranus opposition Neptune ♅ ☍ ♆

People with this placement feel pulled between the Uranian need to understand humanity and life, and the Neptunian need for spiritual development. They can swing between religious fanaticism and philosophic uncertainty. Life brings abrupt changes in their business or social lives, so these people can learn new approaches to life rather than retreating from life into dreams. They release inner tensions through creative expression and they have ability to develop themselves psychically.

Uranus conjunct Pluto ♅ ☌ ♇

People with this conjunction transform themselves and those around them suddenly, and they need to guard against misuse of their powers. They have an innate need to change the way society operates. With patience, they can be influential in improving the lives of those around them. They have strong powers of concentration and adapt to new approaches rapidly.

Uranus squared Pluto ⛢ □ ♇

These people need to accept that they do not necesarily belong to groups who share their beliefs. This aspect transforms the need to belong to communities, and these people need to be independent without feeling resentful. They are powerful in transforming the lives of others, yet they resist inner transformation.

Uranus trine Pluto ⛢ △ ♇

People with this aspect have strong psychic abilities and they are tolerant of others' approaches to life. When problems arise they often find an unconventional or unexpected solution. They are intense and unconventional in their thinking, and often seek to join groups who share their beliefs about life.

Uranus opposition Pluto ⛢ ☍ ♇

This opposition indicates conflict between the Plutonian need for transformation and the Uranian need for understanding of humanity. These people need to tread carefully when attempting to scrutinise the motives of those around them. They experience conflicts with those in their social group and with coworkers until they appreciate that others have the right to believe what they like about life, no matter how absurd their beliefs appear to be. Their interest in the psychic sciences and in psychology develops later in life and they have talents in these areas.

Aspects to Neptune

All aspects to Neptune have been covered except for Neptune's relationship to Pluto. There are no conjunctions, squares, trines or oppositions between Neptune and Pluto in the 20th century.

Aspects to Pluto

All aspects to Pluto have been covered earlier in this section.

Aspects to the Ascendant

Any planet or Moon's node found close to the Ascendant (within 5 degrees) will affect the appearance and the outward nature of the person. When a planet appears upon the Ascendant, its effects are immediately apparent when meeting the person; for example, Mars on the Ascendant gives the person more courage and confidence, while Saturn on the Ascendant makes them appear aloof at first meeting as these people take time to warm to others.

A north node on the Ascendant increases the individual's desire to fulfil their destiny . The south node in this position encourages them to remain in their south nodal past-life experiences and to resist their destiny.

Planets conjunct the Ascendant

Sun: These people display a need to express themselves and they often give a positive and confident first impression.

Moon: These people are sensitive to the moods and emotions of others. They can be shy at first meeting and usually have vivid imaginations.

Mercury: Quick-minded and comfortable expressing themselves, these people enjoy conversing with others. They can be indecisive at times.

Venus: The first impression these people usually give to others is one of beauty and harmony. They often have dimples in their cheeks when they smile.

Mars: These people appear impatient and forthright at first meeting. They enjoy challenges and adventures.

Jupiter: The first impression these people usually give to others is one of enthusiasm and directness. They appear to be easygoing and confident.

Saturn: These people can appear aloof at first. They can seem suspicious and will scrutinise others the first few times they meet before they let their guards down. They appear serious and thoughtful.

Uranus: Those with Uranus in this position often appear unselfconscious and eccentric. They are usually sociable and others feel at ease with them.

Neptune: These people can appear dreamy and somewhat fragile at first meeting. They are often shy in the company of people they do not know.

Pluto: These people can appear intense at first meeting. Their magnetic intensity belies hidden depths and often inner turmoil. There is usually a strong sexual or emotional presence about these people.

CHART-READING PROCEDURE

There are many different methods for interpreting a natal chart, and astrologers each have their own preferences. The one included here is the procedure I prefer. It doesn't matter which method you use, as long as you follow a system. Beginners can be erratic in their approach to chart reading, but mistakes are a natural part of learning and practice improves performance.

When you first start giving readings, it is best to draw up the wheel before you meet with the subject, to give you time to scrutinise the chart and research unusual or unfamiliar planetary aspects.

As you can see, the chart is a wheel or circle consisting of 360 degrees. Each of the 12 zodiac signs occupies 30 degrees of the chart. The Sun moves through the zodiac at the rate of about 1 degree a day.

If a person is born on April 15, then you know that they are born in the sign of Aries. You can also ascertain the degree of the sign of Aries by remembering that the Sun usually enters Aries on March 21. March 21 to April 15 are 24 days apart, which means that the Sun is around 24 degrees of Aries when the person was born.

Reading procedure

1. Check the Ascendant. This is the face the person projects to the world, so it makes sense to start here.

2. Notice what *sign* and what *degree* of the sign the Ascendant falls in and explain this to your subject. The purpose of noting the degree of the Ascendant is that any other planet at that degree in another sign could make an aspect to the Ascendant (e.g. 11 degrees Gemini Ascendant and Sun 11 degrees Libra would mean that the Sun is trine the Ascendant).

    In the sample chart, the Ascendant is Gemini and the degree is 11.07 (11 degrees and 07 minutes of a degree). This Ascendant describes Joanna as someone who enjoys communicating

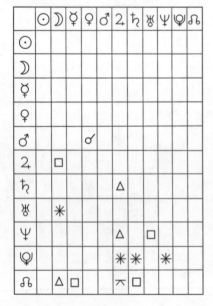

Joanna
10/06/1953
22:30
Sid. time:
23:44

Lunar phase

with others and who is rarely lost for words.

3. Check which planet rules the sign the Ascendant falls in. Joanna's chart has a Gemini Ascendant, which means the ruling planet is Mercury. This gives Joanna some of the Mercury qualities, such as a quick mind and manual dexterity.

4. Check which element rules the Ascendant. For example, a Gemini Ascendant has the element of air. This means that Joanna's has an 'airy' energy; she is quick-thinking and focused on ideas and concepts.

5. Note the Descendant. This is opposite the Ascendant and divides the sixth and seventh houses. It represents the type of people the subject will attract in friendships or in love relationships.

   In the sample chart, the Descendant is Sagittarius. This means that Joanna is likely to attract Sagittarian types; people who are usually forthright, philosophical and who probably enjoy travel and learning.

6. Make a mental note of the Ascendant's ruling planet and where it falls in the chart.

   In the sample chart, Mercury falls in the fifth house in the sign of Scorpio. This gives Joanna the ability to penetrate the defenses of others or to reveal hidden parts of a situation. Scorpio ruling the fifth house suggests that she can maintain a focused concentration on creative endeavours and that she can be strict with her children.

7. Check whether there are any conjunctions to the Ascendant's ruling planet. For example, if the Sun is conjunct Mercury in the chart, explain this to your subject. (Note: there are no conjunctions in the sample chart.)

8. Observe the sign the Midheaven falls in and the degree of that sign. Take a few minutes to explain these. In the sample chart, the Midheaven is 25.38 degrees Pisces. This means that Joanna wants to be seen as developing and displaying the Piscean qualities of compassion for others and patience with animals. She also identifies with the Piscean tendency to put the needs of others before her own needs.

10. Note whether the sign the Midheaven falls in is a fixed, cardinal or mutable sign. In Joanna's chart it is Pisces and Pisces is a mutable water sign. This makes her adaptable to circumstances and sometimes changeable emotionally.

11. Note which planet rules the sign of the Midheaven. In the sample chart, the Midheaven ruling planet is Neptune.

12. Note the sign and the house in which the Midheaven ruling planet falls and explain its significance to your subject.

   In the sample chart Neptune is 23.13 degrees Libra. This means that Joanna has an innate need to help those around her achieve inner peace and harmony.

13. Check which sign the Nadir falls in. In the sample chart, it falls in Virgo. Explain to the subject how the Nadir relates to their home or early home life. Joanna's Nadir in Virgo suggests a need for order in the home and a desire to analyse what is important in the home environment (emotionally, materially and so on).

14. Ensure the subject understands what you have said so far and clarify the points covered if necessary.

15. Note which house the Midheaven's ruling planet falls in. In the sample chart, Neptune falls in the fourth house. This suggests that Joanna is dissolving her attitudes to home and to her emotional roots. It is possible that a parent or sibling is assisting Joanna to dissolve these attitudes.

16. Note whether the Nadir is in a cardinal,

fixed or mutable sign. In the sample chart, it is a mutable sign. This means that in her early home life, Joanna had to adapt periodically to changing circumstances.

17. Observe which sign the ruling planet of the Nadir is found in. In the sample chart, it is Mercury and Mercury can be found in Scorpio. As mentioned previously, this describes Joanna's tendency to delve beyond the surface presented by people or situations to reveal what lies beneath.

18. Note which house the Nadir's ruling planet falls in. In the sample chart, Mercury is found in the fifth house. This suggests that Joanna communicates easily with children. She has the ability to teach or inspire children, and as Scorpio rules the fifth house, she may have great success teaching children with learning disabilities.

19. Note the subject's Sun sign. In the sample chart, the Sun is in Libra. Explain some of the qualities of the Sun sign to your subject. They will probably relate easily to this part as most people know their Sun sign and their sign's basic qualities.

    In Joanna's chart, the Sun in Libra suggests that she has a sense of fairness, diplomacy and tact, and that she is mentally active. She is inclined to initiate action, is generous and needs to guard against periods of laziness.

20. Note the opposite sign to the Sun sign, as this represents the opposition the subject can expect in life. In the sample chart, it indicates that Joanna probably experienced opposition from her Aries eleventh house in the form of over-confident or pushy family members in her formative years, which may have made her want to throw all Libran tact out the window and fight back.

21. Establish whether the Sun is in a cardinal, fixed or mutable sign. What is the element of that sign? What house does the Sun fall in? What degree of that house? In Joanna's chart, the Sun is in a cardinal air sign and it falls in the fourth house. Her Sun is 12.59 degrees Libra. This means that she is likely to lead or initiate action (cardinal sign), that she is mentally active and likely to plan things (air sign). Her home is important to her (Sun in the fourth house) and she is likely to be at ease verbally as her Sun is trine the Ascendant. This is because her Ascendant is 11 degrees Gemini and her Sun is 13 degrees Libra, making them almost 120 degrees apart or *trine* one another (see page 165).

22. Take a few moments to notice any prominent aspects to the Sun. In Joanna's chart, apart from the trine aspect previously mentioned, there are no conjunctions, squares or obvious aspects to the Sun.

23. Note the sign in which the Moon is located. In Joanna's chart the Moon is in Virgo. This suggests that she prefers a low-key approach to her emotions and needs to guard against being self-critical or worrying unneccessarily, as stress may effect her digestive system.

24. Note the phase of the Moon. In Joanna's chart the Moon is one sign behind the Sun, so it must be a Balsamic Moon. (Remember that when the Moon is in the same sign as the Sun it is a New Moon and when it falls in the opposite sign to the Sun it is a Full Moon. As Joanna's Moon is in Virgo, one sign before Libra, her Moon is one phase before the New Moon, which is the Balsamic Moon.)

25. Check which house the Moon is in. In the sample chart, the Moon is in the fourth house. This means that Joanna experiences strong dreams periodically, which offer her insight into her life. It is important to her that her home is

peaceful and harmonious, and she has a tendency to collect family memorabilia.

26. Note which element the Moon sign is. In Joanna's chart the Moon is in an earth sign, meaning that Joanna has a practical approach to emotions.

27. Note what degree the Moon is in the sign. In the sample chart, the Moon is 27.03 degrees Virgo. In itself this has no great significance, but it is important to notice the degree of each planet because you may notice another planet at the same degree of another sign, forming an aspect.

28. Check whether any planets are conjunct the Moon. Explain to the subject how this affects their emotional approach to life. In the sample chart, there are no conjunct planets.

29. Note which planets, if any, have aspects to the Moon. In Joanna's chart the Moon is squared Jupiter. This suggests that she was not encouraged to grow and develop through loving support by her parents or guardians in her formative years, possibly leaving her feeling that she needs more love in order to fulfil her potential. Remember that squares signify conflict, and in this case it is an inner conflict between reaching for goals and receiving emotional nurturing.

30. Note whether the Moon has any aspects to the Sun. In the sample chart, there are no aspects between the Moon and the Sun.

31. Observe the planetary placements. Notice whether they are clustered together, evenly spaced around the chart or opposing one another. In Joanna's chart, all the planets are below the horizon (in houses one to six). This suggests that she will be more at home away from the public eye and content to live a quiet life.

32. Now proceed through each of the planets, noting the sign in which they fall, their house position, whether they are retrograde and any aspects they make to other planets, to the Ascendant or to the Moon's nodes in the following order:

> Mercury
> Venus
> Mars
> Jupiter
> Saturn
> Uranus
> Neptune
> Pluto

The reading procedure may appear complicated at first, but in time you will find that it flows in a seamless format. Your readings will be like conversations, and you will give your subject information that will help them with their current circumstances and with their spiritual lessons.

CHART INTERPRETATION CHECKLIST

Ascendant

Descendant

Ascendant's ruling planet

Midheaven

Nadir

Sun

Moon

Planetary placement

Mercury

Venus

Mars

Jupiter

Saturn

Uranus

Neptune

Pluto

Summary

RELATIONSHIPS

Some people limit their understanding of astrology to Sun sign astrology, and this can be limiting where relationships are concerned. In simple terms, any sign can enjoy a relationship with any other sign. It is the Ascendant, Moon placement and other planetary placements which make two people more or less compatible. A person's particular planetary placements mean it is likely that there are one or two signs with whom they rarely come in contact with socially, but this doesn't mean they would never enjoy a relationship with any one of those signs.

When I hear someone state that 'I don't like Scorpios', for example, I am left wondering if they have had one or more bad experiences in a relationship with a Scorpio. I usually point out that although all Scorpios share the same basic lesson, they are not all the same — each of us is unique.

Relationships involve many aspects, including initial attraction, sexual compatibility, emotional and mental compatibility, and the ability to get along with one another in day-to-day life. As Mark and Alicia are both Virgoans, for example, you might expect that they would perceive life from a similar viewpoint, enhancing their chances for a compatible relationship. The Virgoan love of orderliness became a contentious issue in their relationship, however, because Mark is a complete slob around the house. With his Sagittarius Ascendant and a Libra Moon he doesn't appear to be a Virgoan at all. Alicia has a Virgo Sun *and* Ascendant, making her very precise indeed.

Alicia found Mark too noisy, messy and clumsy to bear, and, six months after moving in together, she moved out. Mark breathed a sigh of relief and talked positively about being able to see a ring of grime around the bath and not give it a second thought.

When looking at a natal chart you can see what type of relationship patterns and contradictions are contained within the person. To give a more accurate relationship reading, it is best to look at both partners charts. This is called a *synastry* reading. The object is to determine the couple's suitability and relationship potential.

What to look for in a synastry reading

Start the reading at the *seventh house cusp*. The sign which rules the seventh house cusp indicates what the person needs emotionally which might be supplied by a partner.

Notice whether the seventh house signs are compatible. If one partner has Aquarius on the seventh house cusp, they seek freedom and space in relationships. If the other partner has Taurus on the seventh house cusp, they prefer to have their partner close by and enjoy plenty of physical contact and closeness. Of course, you should take into account the compatibility indicated elsewhere in the chart, for humans are filled with contradictions.

Observe which planets have marked aspects to the partners' planets, and what sign each planet is in. The outer planets will probably be found in the same sign if the partners are in the same age group, as some planets spend years in each sign.

The fifth house rules love affairs and emotional risks are shown here. Your task as an astrologer is to determine whether the relationship (if it is new or about to commence) will make the transition from the fifth house to the seventh house. Will it make it from an affair to a deeper relationship?

The second house details what each partner values within themselves and with their possessions. Are they selfish, co-operative or sharing by nature?

The eighth house indicates how each person deals with their partner's finances and

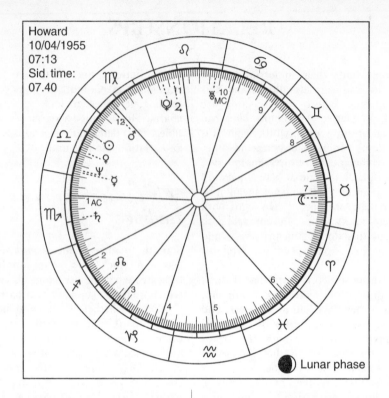

Howard
10/04/1955
07:13
Sid. time:
07.40

Lunar phase

those things their partner values. How selfish or how committed to fulfilling their partner sexually is shown here, too. Scorpio on the eighth house cusp, for example, is likely to increase the person's depth of passion, yet they are likely to be keen to ensure their partner is satisfied.

Marc and Marlene came to me for a synastry reading and Marc's eighth house cusp was ruled by Capricorn. People with this placement take the needs of their partners very seriously. They risk becoming responsible for their partners' happiness, which is unrealistic.

I asked Marc if he took seriously his responsibility for pleasing Marlene sexually and she laughed. 'Yes, he does indeed,' she replied.

Business partnerships are also affected by the second and eighth house cusps.

The fourth house deals with the home and how the couple expects the home to be, according to how it was when they were

growing up. Tensions can rise in day-to-day life if there are conflicts with the fourth house cusps.

The outer planets, although often in the same sign in both charts, are important according to the house they fall in and the aspects they make to the partner's chart.

In the example opposite, the corresponding position of Howard's Jupiter in Joanna's chart indicates where Howard can benefit her. His Jupiter is conjunct her Pluto in the third house in Leo. This suggests that Howard can benefit Joanna through communication with those close to her, including siblings, neighbours and those around the family home. As his Jupiter is conjunct her Pluto, she is likely to transform his attitude to third house affairs.

If you were to transpose Howard's planets in their current positions into Joanna's chart, the position of Howard's Uranus indicates where he will be a catalyst for change within Joanna. This change often occurs suddenly or without Howard's knowledge. His Uranus is found in Cancer in Joanna's second house, suggesting that Howard will be a catalyst for change regarding Joanna's finances and those things she values within herself and around her.

If you were to transpose Joanna's planets in their current positions into Howard's chart, the position of Joanna's Neptune indicates where Joanna is assisting Howard to dissolve the issues of the house and sign where it is located. This effect is subtle and more evident upon reflection. Her Neptune is found in Libra in Howard's twelfth house. This suggests that Joanna is assisting Howard to dissolve his karma and to weigh up his future life direction carefully.

Where Joanna's *Pluto* is found in Howard's chart is where she is transforming Howard's attitudes to the affairs of the house and the sign where it is found. This effect could arouse some resistance from Howard, resulting in a power struggle between them. Joanna's Pluto is in Leo in Howard's eleventh house, suggesting that she is transforming his attitudes to friendships, to people from other cultures, or to those who hold alternative beliefs about life.

In general terms, the sign containing Venus in a woman's chart describes the qualities she is seeking within herself and the sign containing Mars indicates what she is seeking in a man. In Joanna's chart Venus is in Virgo, so within herself she is seeking a more discerning approach to life. Mars is also in Virgo, indicating that she seeks a man who is discerning and practical in his approach to life.

Broadly speaking, the sign containing Mars in a man's chart indicates the qualities he is seeking within himself and the sign containing Venus indicates what he is seeking in a woman. Howard's chart shows that his Mars is in Virgo, suggesting that the qualities Joanna is seeking within a man Howard is also seeking within himself. This strengthens their relationship, for they seek the same direction for Howard. Howard's

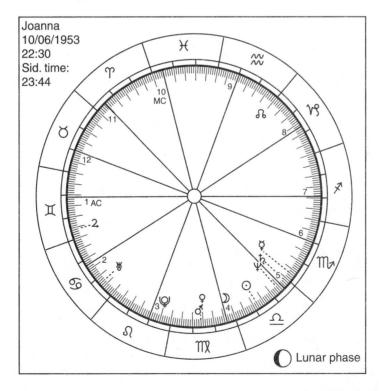

Joanna
10/06/1953
22:30
Sid. time:
23:44

Lunar phase

Venus is in Libra, which is where Joanna's Sun is found, so once again there is accord.

If there are any south node aspects (conjunctions), they indicate past-life ties. This is sometimes the case if there are any planets in the twelfth house. Howard's Mars is conjunct Joanna's south node, suggesting a past-life connection which could have been competitive (Mars seeks competition), or Howard could have been a male sibling of

HEALTH AND THE SUN SIGNS

Sign	Health area	To re-balance
Aries	Head. Headaches and accidents to the head area. Burns and cuts due to recklessness. Head colds, fevers and nosebleeds.	Regular walks and outdoor activities. Avoid excessive spicy foods and alcohol.
Taurus	Neck and throat tension. Stiff neck and tension held in shoulders. Excess weight. Under-active thyroid gland.	Regular massage of neck and shoulders. Melodious music. Avoid eating sweet rich foods or eating when stressed or depressed.
Gemini	Nervous strain and exhaustion resulting from restlessness of mind. Chest and lungs, asthma, pleurisy. Insomnia. Arms and hands.	Increased physical activity to match the mental activity. Meditation.
Cancer	Worry affecting stomach and digestive areas. Slow lymphatic system affecting removal of waste from the body. The breasts.	Increase physical exercise such as swimming to improve lymphatic system and to decrease tendency to worry.
Leo	Heart and spine areas. Backache and problems with the blood system. Heart disease. Hardening of the arteries. High/low blood pressure.	Regular physical exercise to maintain heart and to keep the spine supple. Ensuring a period of play each day to keep the heart buoyant.
Virgo	Nervous tension and worry. Digestive system and the bowels. The small intestine and the abdomen.	Meditation and time spent examining the mental attitude to health and wellbeing. Best to avoid hot, spicy foods as they upset the digestive system. Unhurried eating.

Joanna's (Mars can represent brothers).

Conjunctions often produce harmony between the partners. Squares describe challenges that require energy in order to be resolved. Trines pave the way for communication between the partners, and oppositions can produce tension until those concerned find a pattern of compromise. (These aspects are explained on page 165.)

Sign	Health area	To re-balance
Libra	Kidneys and weight gain. Vestibular sense which controls physical balance. Lack of muscle and nerve tone.	Regular exercise with someone to accompany them to make it more enjoyable. Harmonious surrounds. Music. Periods spent consuming only juices to cleanse the kidneys.
Scorpio	Hormones. Reproductive organs. Bowel, bladder, urethra and sweat glands.	Periods of fasting and eliminating foods from the diet. Encourage moderation in foods, alcohol and in sexual behaviour.
Sagittarius	Hips, thighs and the sciatic nerve. The liver and the pancreas for insulin levels. Overactivity weakening the system. Increased weight on the hips and thighs. Accidents, cuts and burns.	Moderation in use of energies. Regular exercise such as walking as best thinking occurs when walking or outdoors. Open spaces ensure a sense of freedom and confidence.
Capricorn	Arthritis. Problems with knees and teeth. The skin and the skeletal system. The hair and the nails. Poor circulation. Constipation.	A positive attitude will make all the difference here, along with physical exercise and a diet high in fibre.
Aquarius	Ankles and wrists. Body electricity and circulation of body energy, including the blood. Nervous tension and anxiety.	Exercise which re-balances body energies such as tai chi or aikido. Fresh air and nature to restore energies. Eccentric approaches to health preferred but unnecessary.
Pisces	The immune system, the thymus gland and the feet. The cerebrospinal fluid and the spinal canal. Aura weakness. Fluid retention and sometimes hormone imbalances.	Mental focus to be directed away from illness and toward inner and outer peace and harmony. Time spent by the sea heals Pisceans and they need an environment free of psychic or emotional upheaval. A high protein diet can assist in building the blood.

PRACTICE CHARTS

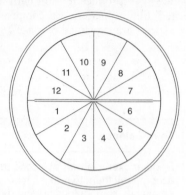

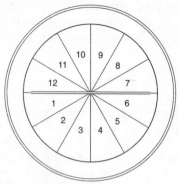

Name._____

Date of Birth:_____

Time:_____

Location:_____

Longitude:_____ east/west

Latitude:_____ north/south

Name:_____

Date of Birth:_____

Time:_____

Location:_____

Longitude:_____ east/west

Latitude:_____ north/south

PLANET	ASPECTS	☉	☽	☿	♀	♂	♃	♄	♅	♆	♇
SUN	☉										
MOON	☽										
MERCURY	☿										
VENUS	♀										
MARS	♂										
JUPITER	♃										
SATURN	♄										
URANUS	♅										
NEPTUNE	♆										
PLUTO	♇										
AC	AC										
MC	MC										

PLANET	ASPECTS	☉	☽	☿	♀	♂	♃	♄	♅	♆	♇
SUN	☉										
MOON	☽										
MERCURY	☿										
VENUS	♀										
MARS	♂										
JUPITER	♃										
SATURN	♄										
URANUS	♅										
NEPTUNE	♆										
PLUTO	♇										
AC	AC										
MC	MC										

Notes: _____
_____
_____
_____
_____
_____
_____

Notes: _____
_____
_____
_____
_____
_____
_____

GAINING PRACTICAL EXPERIENCE

Starting with your own chart and then drawing up the charts of family and friends is the way most budding astrologers expand their knowledge.

After you have studied a dozen charts, you may feel confident enough to move on to the charts of relatives and acquaintances, or to friends of friends. Self-confidence comes from experience, so you need to ensure that you are keeping up your skills with regular readings. Sandra, a past student of mine, set out to interpret two charts each week for six months — within four months, word had spread and she was giving five chart readings a week.

Two years later, she has a part-time position in a book store giving chart readings, and she loves it. She is able to brush up on astrology by reading books and studying charts between clients, so that even quiet days are not wasted.

Being such a deep study, astrology requires regular effort and application if you aim to develop a thorough understanding. Observing people can help you to keep in practice.

Astrology is not just about reading books and interpreting charts. Astrology is a system of classification that can be applied to people, businesses, major projects and political directions. Everywhere about us are examples of astrology at work, if we are able to notice the subtle signs and details.

Be aware that, although the planets were in a particular sign or house when we were born, we each have free will to determine how we will apply the influence of the planet or aspect.

Most people consult an astrologer when things are grim or the stress becomes to much and they cannot find a cause for their present circumstances or current frustration. As an astrologer, you are in a position to offer them insight into themselves and into their lives.

If you listen carefully to your client, they will tell you in what area of life they seek the most clarity. If they talk of responsibilities, look for aspects to Saturn. If they speak of loss or inner transformation, look for aspects to Pluto. If they seek life direction, look for Jupiter. If they feel misunderstood by those close to them, look for Mercury and the third house. Astrology is a powerful tool for offering insight to enable others to fulfil their life's purpose. Use it wisely, for with power comes responsibility.

Chart wheel offer

For readers who do not have access to an astrology computer program, chart wheels (without interpretation) are available by post. You can then consult this book for interpretation of the chart.

Paul Fenton-Smith offers a single wheel for A$5 or three wheels for A$10, posted within Australia or New Zealand.

The following details are required for a natal chart wheel:

- Name
- Date of birth
- Location of birth (nearest large town or city if born in a village or small town)
- Time of birth (am/pm)
- Name and contact telephone number of purchaser in case of queries

For those who do not know their time of birth, a solar chart is available for the same fee. The wheels supplied will be similar to Howard and Joanna's sample charts (pages 192 and 193), and they include a chart listing all the aspects.

Send your cheque or money order to:

The Academy of Psychic Sciences
59 Centennial Avenue
Lane Cove NSW 2066
Australia

Please allow three weeks for delivery.

Bibliography

Avery, Jean 1982, *The Rising Sign: Your Astrological Mask*, Doubleday, New York, New York.

Chambers, Howard V. 1966, *An Occult Dictionary for the Millions*, Sherborne Press, Los Angeles, California.

Cole, Robert 1980, *The Book of Houses*, Entwhistle Books, Glen Ellen, California.

Fenton, Sasha 1989, *Rising Signs*, The Antiquarian Press, London.

Fenton-Smith, Paul 1995, *The Tarot Revealed*, Simon & Schuster Australia, Sydney.

Green, Jeff 1987, *Pluto and the Evolutionary Journey of the Soul*, Llewellyn Publications, St Paul, Minnesota.

Heindel, Max 1973, *The Message of the Stars*, L.N. Fowler & Co., London.

Kurrels, Jan 1990, *Astrology for the Age of Aquarius*, Anaya Publishers Ltd, London.

Leo, Alan 1978, *The Complete Dictionary of Astrology*, Astrologer's Library, New York. Distributed by Samuel Weiser Inc., New York.

Lofthus, Myrna 1983, *A Spiritual Approach to Astrology*, CRCS Publications, Sebastapol, California.

Para Research 1983, *World Ephemeris for the 20th Century*, Whitford Press, Pennsylvania.

Parker, Julia and Derek 1991, *Parker's Astrology*, Angus & Robertson, Sydney.

Schulman, Martin 1984, *Karmic Astrology Volume I*, Samuel Weiser Inc., New York.

Index

A
air signs, 12
Allen, W.F. (Alan Leo), 9
Aquarius, 45–8, 65, 79, 88,
    96, 104, 112, 120–1,
    129, 195
  Moon's north node, 148–9,
    159–60
  Moon's south node, 153
Aries, 13–14, 59, 76, 85, 93,
    101, 109, 117, 126, 194
  Moon's north node, 148–9,
    150
  Moon's south node, 155–6
Ascendant, 55, 162–3
  aspects to, 184
  planets conjunct, 184–5
aspects, planetary, 165–85
astrology
  defined, 8
  history, 8–9

B
Balsamic Moon, 71, 72
birth charts, 54

C
Caesar, Julius, 9
Cancer, 21–4, 60–1, 77, 86,
    94, 102, 110, 118,
    126–7, 135–6, 194
  Moon's north node, 148–9,
    152–3
  Moon's south node, 158–9
Capricorn, 42–4, 64–5, 79,
    88, 95–6, 104, 111–12,
    120, 128–9, 195
  Moon's north node, 148–9,
    158–9
  Moon's south node, 152–3
cardinal signs, 12
chart interpretation, 54
chart-reading procedure,
    186–90
charts, 54
  solar, 58
Chiron, 9
Christmas, 9
conflict, aspect of, 165
conjunction, 165
Copernicus, Nicholas, 9
Crescent Moon, 71, 72
cusp (doorway), 55
cusp (meeting of two signs),
    12

D
day-for-a-year progressions,
    164
Descendant, 162, 163
detriment, planetary, 74–5
Disseminating Moon, 71, 72

E
earth signs, 12
Easter, 8
ecliptic, 162
eighth house, 56–7, 68–9, 82,
    91, 98, 107, 115, 123,
    132, 140–1
elements, 12
eleventh house, 57, 69, 83,
    92, 99, 108, 116, 124,
    133, 142
ephemeris, 12, 54–5, 58
exaltation, planetary, 74–5

F
fall, planetary, 74–5
fifth house, 56, 67, 81, 90,
    97–8, 106, 114, 122,
    130–1, 139–40
fire signs, 12
first house, 55, 66, 80, 89, 96,
    105, 112–13, 121, 129,
    137–8
First Quarter Moon, 71, 72
fixed signs, 12
fourth house, 56, 67, 81,
    89–90, 97, 106,
    113–14, 122, 130, 139
Full Moon, 71, 72

G
Galileo, 9
Gemini, 18–20, 60, 76–7,
    85–6, 93–4, 101–2,
    109–10, 118, 126, 135,
    194
  Moon's north node, 148–9,
    151–2
  Moon's south node, 157–8
Gibbous Moon, 71, 72
glyphs of signs and planets,
    53
  see also symbols

H
health, 194–5
  Aquarius, 47
  Aries, 14

Cancer, 23
Capricorn, 43–4
Gemini, 19
Leo, 26
Libra, 32
Pisces, 50–1
Sagittarius, 40
Scorpio, 36
Taurus, 16
Virgo, 29–30
houses, 54–70
  Jupiter in, 105–8
  Mars in, 96–100
  Mercury in, 80–4
  moon in, 66–70
  Neptune in, 129–34
  Pluto in, 137–43
  Saturn in, 112–16
  Uranus in, 121–5
  Venus in, 89–92

I
Imun Coeli (I.C.), 162, 163
inner planets, 74
intercepted houses, 55

J
Jupiter, 101–8, 167, 170, 173,
    175, 177–8, 184–5
  aspects to, 179–81
  returns, 146

L
Last Quarter Moon, 71
  see also Third Quarter
    Moon
Leo, 25–7, 61, 77, 86, 94, 102,
    110, 118, 127, 136, 194
  Moon's north node, 148–9,
    153
  Moon's south node,
    159–60
Libra, 31–3, 62–3, 78, 87,
    94–5, 103, 111, 119,
    127–8, 136–7, 195
  Moon's north node, 148–9,
    155–6
  Moon's south node, 150
lunar returns and opposition,
    146

M
Mars, 93–100, 166–7, 169–70,
    172–3, 175, 184
  aspects to, 177–9

Medium Coeli (M.C.), 162,
163
Mercury, 76–84, 166, 169,
184
aspects to, 172–5
Midheaven, 162, 163
Moon, 59–72, 166, 184
aspects to, 169–72
in houses, 66–70
nodes, 147–61
orbit, 74
phases, 71–2
in signs, 59–66
mutable signs, 12

N
Nadir, 162, 163
natal charts, 54
Neptune, 126–34, 168, 171,
174, 176–7, 178–9,
180–1, 182, 183, 185
aspects to, 184
discovery, 9
returns, oppositions and
squares, 146
New Moon, 71, 72
ninth house, 57, 69, 82–3, 91,
98–9, 107, 115, 123–4,
132–3, 141
nodes, Moon's, 147–61
north node, 147, 148–9

O
Old, W.R. ('Seraphial'), 9
opposition, 166
orbits, planetary, 74
outer planets, 74

P
physical transits, 164
Pisces, 49–51, 65–6, 79–80,
88–9, 96, 104–5, 112,
121, 195
Moon's north node, 148–9,
160–1
Moon's south node, 154–5
Placidus De Tito, 54
Placidus system, 54
planetary aspects, 165–85
planetary influence, 74–5
planetary returns, 74, 146
planetary strengths, 75
planets, 73–143
Pluto, 135–43, 168–9, 172,
174–5, 177, 179, 181,
182–3, 183–4, 185
aspects to, 184
discovery, 9
returns, oppositions and
squares, 146

positive aspect, 165–6
practical experience, 197
progressions, 164

Q
quadruplicities, 12

R
relationships, 191–5
retrograde motion
(planetary), 126
retrograde planets, 74
returns, planetary, 74, 146
rulership, planetary, 74–5

S
Sagittarius, 38–41, 63–4,
78–9, 87–8, 95, 103–4,
111, 120, 128, 137, 195
Moon's north node, 148–9,
157–8
Moon's south node, 151–2
Saturn, 109–16, 167, 170,
173, 175–6, 178,
179–80, 185
aspects to, 181–3
returns and oppositions,
146
Scorpio, 34–7, 63, 78, 87, 95,
103, 111, 119–20, 128,
137, 195
Moon's north node, 148–9,
156–7
Moon's south node, 150–1
secondary progressions, 164
second house, 55, 66–7, 80,
89, 96–7, 105, 113,
121, 129–30, 138
seventh house, 56, 68, 82,
90–1, 98, 106–7,
114–15, 123, 131–2,
140
signs of zodiac, 12–53
health and, 194–5
Jupiter in, 101–5
Mars in, 93–6
Mercury in, 76–80
Moon in, 59–66
Neptune in, 126–9
Pluto in, 135–7
Saturn in, 109–12
Uranus in, 117–21
Venus in, 85–9
sixth house, 56, 68, 81–2, 90,
98, 106, 114, 122–3,
131, 140
solar charts, 55, 58
solar returns, 146
south node, 147
squares, 165

Sun, aspects to, 166–98
Sun signs see signs of zodiac
symbols of aspects, 165
see also glyphs
synastry reading, 191–5

T
Taurus, 15–17, 59–60, 76, 85,
93, 101, 109, 117–18,
126, 194
Moon's north node, 148–9,
150–1
Moon's south node, 156–7
tenth house, 57, 69, 83, 91–2,
99, 107, 115–16, 124,
133, 141–2
third house, 56, 67, 80–1, 89,
97, 105–6, 113, 121–2,
130, 138–9
Third Quarter Moon, 72
see also Last Quarter Moon
trine, 165–6
triplicities, 12
twelfth house, 57–8, 70, 83–4,
92, 99–100, 108, 116,
124–5, 133–4, 142–3

U
unequal house system, 54
Uranus, 117–25, 167–8,
170–1, 173–4, 176,
178, 180, 181–2, 185
aspects to, 183–4
returns, oppositions and
squares, 146

V
Venus, 85–92, 166, 169, 172,
184
aspects to, 175–7
Virgo, 28–30, 61–2, 77–8,
86–7, 94, 102–3,
110–11, 119, 127, 136,
194
Moon's north node, 148–9,
154–5
Moon's south node, 160–1

W
water signs, 12
wheels, 58, 196
Moon phase, 71–2

Z
zodiac signs see signs of zodiac